The Middle East *in* Transition

An Instructional Guide

2nd edition

By M. E. Ahrari, Glen Blankenship, Richard J. Brow,
Christopher L. Brown, Craig Kauffman, Louisa Moffitt,
Daniel S. Papp, and Julia Johnson White

To be used in conjunction with the Southern Center for International Studies'
five-part videotape, *The Middle East in Transition*, featuring excerpts
from the Southern Center's Annual Meetings of the Former U.S. Secretaries
of State and Defense.

For updates to the essays and timelines of the Middle East visit
www.southerncenter.org.

Published by

© 1994, 2004 The Southern Center for International Studies
Atlanta, Georgia

Support for this publication was provided
by the Joseph B. Whitehead Foundation
and the State of Georgia.

SCIS

The Southern Center for International Studies (SCIS) is an independent center for thought and opinion on international affairs and U.S. foreign policy. SCIS is a 40-year-old nonprofit educational institution based in Atlanta, Georgia. SCIS seeks to inform. It does not take political positions or attempt to influence policy.

Since its inception, SCIS has played a leading role in developing the international infrastructure that exists today in the southeastern region of the United States. Through its Peabody Award-winning annual conferences with former Secretaries of State and Defense, and its conferences with former Secretaries of the Treasury, U.S. Ambassadors to the United Nations, and world leaders, SCIS promotes global awareness and understanding by placing important international issues on the national public agenda.

The primary mission of SCIS is to internationalize the thinking of the American public. In keeping with its mission, SCIS is currently producing an innovative, ten-part multimedia educational series. The seven units published to date are:

- *The End of the Soviet Union*
- *The Middle East in Transition*
- *Latin America in Transition*
- *East Asia in Transition*
- *Russia and the Other Former Soviet Republics in Transition*
- *Africa in Transition*
- *Europe in Transition*

Additional packages will focus on North America, South Asia, and the World. Updates on each of the published packages are available on the SCIS Web site (www.southerncenter.org). New editions of the videotapes and instructional guides will be produced as needed.

Requests for copies should be addressed to:
The Southern Center for International Studies
320 West Paces Ferry Road, N.W.
Atlanta, Georgia 30305
tel: 800-261-5763   fax: 404-261-0849
E-mail: info@scis.org
www.southerncenter.org

SPONSORS

The Southern Center for International Studies wishes to thank the Joseph B. White-head Foundation and the State of Georgia for their funding of this educational package. We also wish to thank the following contributors for their assistance in the production of the videotapes:

Alabama Power
AmSouth
AT&T
BellSouth
BellSouth International
Coordination Council
    for North American Affairs
Daimler-Benz AG
Exxon Education Foundation
Ford Foundation
General Dynamics
General Electric Foundation

Grumman Corporation
Lockheed Aeronautical Systems
Medical Information
    Management Systems
REN Corporation USA
South Central Bell
Southtrust Corporation
State of Alabama
State of Georgia
University of Georgia
Volvo
Vulcan Materials Company

Hundreds of thousands of Muslim pilgrims circle the Kaaba in a final visit to the Grand Mosque in Mecca, Saudi Arabia, February 3, 2004.

The Middle East *in* Transition

TABLE OF CONTENTS

List of Maps

List of Photographs

PREFACE

In 1991, the Southern Center for International Studies (SCIS), together with a number of outstanding academic experts and teachers, began to develop *The World in Transition*, a series of multimedia educational materials focusing on different regions of the world. The series provides a broad global perspective on historical, political, economic, social and cultural, and foreign-policy issues. This project was undertaken because academic institutions needed high-quality, up-to-date educational materials that reflect the rapid and important changes taking place in today's world. A unique feature of the series is the use of excerpts from annual SCIS conferences with former world leaders, former U.S. Secretaries of State and Defense, former Ambassadors to the United Nations, and excerpts from interviews with international and regional experts in the video component.

In 1992, SCIS published its first unit, *The End of the Soviet Union*. Throughout the 1990s five additional packages were added to the series: *Europe After the Cold War* (1994); *The Middle East in Transition* (1994); *Latin America in Transition* (1995); *East Asia in Transition* (1996); and *Russia and the Other Former Soviet Republics in Transition* (1998). In 2000, SCIS published its seventh unit, *Africa in Transition*, and in 2002 replaced the 1994 publication *Europe after the Cold War* with *Europe in Transition*. These materials have received widespread critical acclaim and are now being used in schools in all 50 states.

This second edition of *The Middle East in Transition* follows the outline of the original unit, but contains updated essays and additional activities. Like the other units in the series, there is an instructional guide and video, which together provide a unique multimedia approach to learning about the Middle East and how it relates to the rest of the world.

The **instructional guide** is comprised of *essays* that provide critical background information needed to understand the issues and events under discussion; *lesson plans*, including worksheets and handouts that enable teachers to present their students with a rich and diversified educational experience; *transcripts* of the video; *maps*; *charts*; *graphs*; *photographs*; *bibliography*; and *statistical grids*.

The **video** is divided into five segments, each corresponding to lesson plans in the instructional guide. All of the video segments begin with brief newsreel and historical footage documentaries followed by excerpts from SCIS's conferences with former Secretaries of State and Defense.

In addition to the instructional guide and video, SCIS also publishes a **correlation chart** and a **workshop leader's guide** for each unit in the series. The correlation chart provides teachers with information on how the lessons in the instructional guide best fit into the traditional middle school and high school social studies curricula. The workshop leader's guide is designed for teacher trainers who conduct workshops for other teachers on the best way to use the materials in the classroom.

The World in Transition educational units offer teachers four significant advantages: quality, context, comprehensiveness, and timeliness.

Quality. The educational materials have been assembled by outstanding scholars and teachers. They are well-organized and offer a wealth of information and analysis needed by teachers.

Context. Each set of materials is designed to provide educators and students with a broad base of knowledge on a particular region of the world. Therefore, the information includes not only current issues and events, but also geographic and historic information, providing the context necessary to clearly understand future events in the region. The series as a whole provides a broad global perspective.

Comprehensiveness. Each package examines current issues and events from different perspectives, giving educators a broad-based approach essential for fully understanding a region of the world.

Timeliness. The educational guides address the important issues of yesterday and today, so that students can understand the unfolding events of the world. As important issues and events occur, the packages are updated on the Center's Web site, www.southerncenter.org, through essays and international timelines.

These educational materials are designed for maximum flexibility. They can be used at various educational levels and in a number of disciplines. They can be used as supplemental or primary course materials. Using the entire package will provide students with an excellent in-depth understanding of the region under study. Using the complete series will give students a global perspective. Regardless of the option chosen, teachers and students will develop a much fuller understanding of contemporary international affairs and the forces that drive them.

Given the rapid changes in today's world and the difficulty in keeping up with those changes, these unique educational materials provide teachers and students with the means to not only stay informed, but also to understand how international issues and events affect their lives. In addition to high schools, these materials are currently found in middle schools as well as in university graduate classrooms, in executive training courses for business professionals, and in the Air Force senior ROTC programs.

AUTHORS, EDITORS, AND PROJECT TEAM

AHRARI, M.E. Coauthor of the background readings (1st edition). Professor of National Security and Strategy, Joint Forces Staff College. Author of five books and over 40 articles concentrating on Middle Eastern affairs and U.S. foreign policy. B.A., Southern Illinois University. M.A. and Ph.D., Eastern Illinois University.

BLANKENSHIP, Glen. Coauthor of the lesson plans (1st edition). Program Director, Georgia Council on Economic Education, Atlanta, Georgia. B.A. and M.Ed., Georgia State University, Atlanta, Georgia. D.A.S.T. and Ph.D., Emory University, Atlanta, Georgia.

BROW, Richard J. Coauthor of the background readings (1st edition). Research and Development Officer with the School of Oriental and African Studies in London, England. Organized numerous Middle East Outreach programs. Author of several Middle East curriculum packages for teachers. Received B.A. from Concordia University in Montreal and M.A. in Middle East Area Studies from University of London.

BROWN, Christopher L. Coauthor of the background readings and Coauthor of selected lesson plans. Research Director and Internship Coordinator, the Southern Center for International Studies, Atlanta, Georgia. Adjunct Professor, Georgia State University, Atlanta, Georgia. B.A., The University of the South, Sewanee, Tennessee. M.A. and Ph.D., University of Georgia, Athens, Georgia.

HIGGINS, Clare. Project Editor. Publications Manager, the Southern Center for International Studies, Atlanta, Georgia. B.A., University of North Carolina at Greensboro. M.A., University of Sussex, Brighton, United Kingdom.

KAUFFMAN, Craig. Coauthor of the background readings. Library Director, the Southern Center for International Studies, Atlanta, Georgia. B.A., The College of Wooster, Wooster, Ohio. M.S., George Mason University, Fairfax, Virginia.

MOFFITT, Louisa. Coauthor of the lesson plans. Teacher, Marist School, Atlanta, Georgia. Recipient of a Joseph Malone Fellowship for study in Syria and Kuwait, and a Fulbright Grant for study in Israel and Egypt. B.A. and Ed.S., Emory University, Atlanta, Georgia. M.A.T., M.Ed., Ph.D., Georgia State University, Atlanta, Georgia.

PAPP, Daniel S. Coauthor of the Study Guide and Project Codirector (1st edition). Senior Vice President for Academics and Fiscal Affairs, Board of Regents of the University System of Georgia. Professor of International Affairs at the Georgia Institute of Technology (former). Author of seven books and over 60 articles on foreign and defense policy. B.A., Dartmouth College. Ph.D., University of Miami (Coral Gables).

WHITE, Julia Johnson. Project Director and Producer of the videotapes in *The World in Transition* educational series. Vice President, Legal Counsel, and Cofounder of the Southern Center for International Studies. Executive Producer and Producer of the Southern Center's Peabody Award-winning television programs. M.B.A., Emory University, Atlanta, Georgia. J.D., Emory School of Law, Atlanta, Georgia.

REVIEWERS

Background Essays

AHRARI, M.E. Ph.D. Professor of National Security and Strategy, Joint Forces Staff College.

SAFI, Omid. Ph.D. Assistant Professor of Philosophy and Religion, Colgate University, Hamilton, New York.

STEIN, Kenneth. Ph.D. William E. Schatten Professor of Contemporary Middle Eastern History and Israeli Studies; Director, Middle East Research Program of Emory University; Director, Institute for the Study of Modern Israel; and Middle East Fellow of the Carter Center, Emory University, Atlanta, Georgia.

MACKEY, Sandra. Veteran journalist, award-winning author, and commentator. Recent publications include *The Reckoning: Iraq and the Legacy of Saddam Hussein* (2002), *The Iranians: Persia, Islam, and the Soul of a Nation* (1996), and *Politics: The Turbulent World of the Arabs* (1995).

Lesson Plans

RYCKELEY, Rebecca H. Social Studies Teacher. Social Studies Department Chairman, Starr's Mill High School, Fayetteville, Georgia.

SPRADLIN, Cindy. Social Studies Teacher. Talented and Gifted Program Department Chair, Roswell High School, Roswell, Georgia.

TYREE, Dale. Social Studies Teacher. North Springs High School, Atlanta, Georgia.

ACKNOWLEDGMENTS

The World in Transition educational series is the culmination of efforts by many talented people including scholars, educators, and SCIS staff and friends. It is only through the untiring efforts of these many individuals working collectively that the Southern Center for International Studies has been able to consistently achieve the highest degree of excellence in these educational materials.

This second edition of *The Middle East in Transition* updates the 1994 Instructional Guide, which would not have been possible without support from the Joseph B. Whitehead Foundation. I would like to thank Clare Higgins, Publications Manager; Craig Kauffman, Library Director; Christopher L. Brown, Research Director, and the SCIS research staff for their dedication in updating this publication, so that it reflects the post 9/11 world we now inhabit. You will see that while much has changed in the Middle East since we initially published this guide, much has also stayed the same.

My deepest gratitude goes to SCIS's Education Advisory Board, which each year evaluates, supports, and offers ideas that strengthen these educational materials. Special recognition goes to both the original authors of the excellent background readings and activities as well as the authors of the revised portions of the study guide: M.E. Ahrari, Glen Blankenship, Richard J. Brow, Christopher L. Brown, Craig Kauffmann, Louisa Moffit, and Daniel S. Papp.

In terms of the videotape, I wish to thank Tom Johnson and Kathy Christensen of CNN; the MacNeil/Lehrer NewsHour; and ARD Network in Germany for allowing us to use news footage for the videotape; and Peter White III and his colleagues, Elizabeth Callan, Patricia Ellis, Frank Fitzmaurice, and Karen Watson for making the videotapes more student-friendly and interesting by incorporating this footage into excerpts from conferences with the Secretaries. Additionally, I would like to thank Crawford Post Productions for their work on this project.

I also wish to thank Felicia Breedlove for assisting me in the editing of the conference videotapes; Dale Tyree for his critique and editing of the instructional manual; Marcia Hoinville, Kelli Fisher, Cassady Craft, and Tom Scollard for their assistance in researching the Center's conference tapes and transcripts for needed subject matter; Linda Helms for her independent evaluation of the educational materials; Richard Gentry and Vance Mason for their technical assistance on finalizing the instructional manual; Gloria Reálin for her administrative support; and Diane Sloan for assisting the authors and producers in coordinating the project and for preparing the transcripts.

There are two other individuals whose contributions have been felt in many ways: Dr. Cedric Suzman, who gave advice and council every step of the way, and most importantly Peter White, SCIS president, to whom I am forever grateful not only for his tireless efforts in acquiring the funding for this project, but also for his encouragement, support, and much-needed advice.

The videotape portion of this project is dedicated to Peter Christopher White III, who remains my inspiration.

Julia Johnson White

Julia Johnson White
Project Director and Producer

BACKGROUND LESSON

AN OVERVIEW OF THE MIDDLE EAST

Background Lesson of 5 Lessons for the
Southern Center for International Studies'
Multimedia Educational Package
THE MIDDLE EAST IN TRANSITION

Reuters/Yannis Behrakis

*The Middle East is the birthplace of three of the world's most important monotheistic religions,
Christianity, Islam, and Judaism. All three religions consider Jerusalem, shown here in a view
from the Mount of Olives, a holy city.*

THE BACKGROUND LESSON

of the SCIS Educational Package
THE MIDDLE EAST IN TRANSITION

AN OVERVIEW OF THE MIDDLE EAST

The Middle East is a region of immense global importance. Commonly regarded as the "cradle of civilization," the Middle East is strategically located, sitting astride major trading lanes and lines of communications that form a land bridge between Africa, Asia, and Europe. It is also the site of the world's largest oil reserves.

In addition, the Middle East is the birthplace of three of the world's most important religions: Christianity, Islam, and Judaism, each of which in turn is subdivided by ethnic, regional, denominational, and cultural differences.

The Middle East has also at times been torn by conflict and warfare. The reasons for this include, but are not limited to: historical animosity, disputes over land and water, control of oil reserves, ethnic and religious differences, foreign intervention, and disparities in wealth.

Clearly, the Middle East is a complex, diverse, and important region of the world. The purpose of this lesson will be to provide an overview to the region's geography and resources, religions, and history.

GEOGRAPHY AND RESOURCES

Stretching from Morocco in the West to Iran in the East, the Middle East covers a large amount of land. It is important to note that the name "Middle East" is a recent one, first coined in 1902 by a U.S. naval officer, and reflecting a bias that places Europe at the center of the world. While there is no universal definition of which countries are included in the Middle East, for the purposes of *The Middle East in Transition*, the region is defined to include four geographical subregions:

1) North Africa (Morocco, Algeria, Tunisia, Libya, and Egypt);
2) the Arabian Peninsula (Saudi Arabia, Bahrain, Qatar, United Arab Emirates, Oman, and Yemen);
3) the Eastern Mediterranean area of Turkey, Syria, Lebanon, Israel, the West Bank and Gaza Strip, Jordan, and Iraq; and
4) Iran.

Several major rivers run through the region, including the Nile, the Tigris, and the Euphrates. Nevertheless, much of the region is extremely dry. The Sahara Desert covers much of North Africa, and much of the Arabian Peninsula is desert as well. Water is thus a valuable resource in the Middle East, and a frequent source of conflict.

While poor in water, the Middle East is rich in oil. The region holds the world's largest oil reserves, and much of the Middle East's economy is built around oil wealth. Some 70 percent of the world's oil reserves are in the Middle East,[1] and in 2001, 36 percent of the world's oil production came from the region.[2]

This does not mean that every country in the Middle East is rich. Nor does it mean that everyone within oil-rich countries is wealthy. In many Middle Eastern states, poverty is a fact of life. Countries such as Egypt, Jordan, Morocco, Syria, and Tunisia have little or no oil. Even in oil-rich countries, wealth is unevenly distributed and there are large numbers of poor people.

RELIGION

As noted earlier, three of the world's most important religions, Christianity, Islam, and Judaism, were founded in the Middle East. Not surprisingly, then, religion has long played a major role in the region, as it does today.

In some ways, Christianity, Islam, and Judaism are similar. All three stem from a common ancestor, Abraham. All are monotheistic. All are based on divinely revealed scriptures. All accept the concept of Judgement Day, the existence of human free will and human sin, and the necessity for repentance.

Even so, the religions are also very different. Judaism teaches that God will send a Savior to redeem humankind, but that this Savior has not yet come. Christianity teaches that Jesus is the Savior that Judaism still awaits. Islam teaches that Jewish and Christian prophets were divinely inspired, that Jesus was a great prophet but not a Savior, and that Muhammad was the last and greatest prophet.

Most of the people of the Middle East are Muslims, that is, believers in the religion of Islam. Most are also Arabs, although there are numerous other groups, including Jews, Persians (Iranians), Kurds, Berbers, and Armenians.

It is important to note that "Muslim" and "Arab" are not the same thing. Muslims are followers of Islam, a religion founded in the seventh century A.D. by Muhammad, while Arabs are an ethnic group subdivided into many different tribes, clans, and families. While all Arab states profess Islam as their primary religion, not all Arabs are Muslims. Several Arab countries, such as Lebanon, Egypt, and Jordan, have significant Arab Christian minorities. Also, not all states that have large Islamic populations are Arab, or even located in the Middle East. Non-Arab states with significant Islamic populations include Afghanistan, Bangladesh, Bosnia, Indonesia, Iran, Malaysia, Niger, Nigeria, Pakistan, Somalia, and Turkey. Even though Islam is truly a global religion, and the majority of Muslims in the world live outside the Middle East, Islam remains a strong force within the region.

HISTORY

Although Christians, Jews, and Muslims all regard the Middle East as the birthplace of their religions, much of the Middle East's history revolves around the expansion of Islam as the predominant religion in the region. Islam was founded by Muhammad in 610 A.D. in Mecca, a city in modern-day Saudi Arabia, after he claimed he received revelations from God (Allah in Arabic) via the angel Gabriel. Within only a few decades, Islamic followers spread Muhammad's teachings throughout the Arabian Peninsula and into neighboring lands, creating an Islamic empire.

After Muhammad died, conflict soon developed over who would succeed him as leader, or caliph. Hopes for Islamic unity disappeared, and Islam developed several sects. The most significant split occurred around 661 and led to the Shia and Sunni branches of Islam. Shias believed that only descendants of Ali, the fourth caliph and brother-in-law of Muhammad, should be caliph, while Sunnis believed that Muhammad intended for the Muslim community to choose a caliph by consensus.

Despite the split, the Arab Empire remained powerful. By the eighth century, the Arab Empire ruled northern Africa. In 710, Islamic forces crossed into Spain and advanced northward. However, in 732, they were defeated by Charles Martel in the Battle of Tours. Islam's northward advance stopped, but Islam remained the dominant religion in Spain for many centuries. Other Islamic armies extended Islam's influence eastward through Iran to modern-day Afghanistan, Pakistan, and the borders of China.

The Arab realm nurtured a sophisticated and advanced culture. Science, learning, law, medicine, and the arts flourished. Arab traders journeyed to sub-Saharan Africa and Asia, spreading Islam as they went. For several centuries, the Arab Empire prospered. Islam had truly become one of the world's most important religions, and the future looked bright for the Arab people.

Eventually, however, the Arab Empire went into decline. Internally, succession struggles, worldly pleasures, policy debates, and religious disagreements eroded the strength that had helped the Arabs establish their empire. The Arab Empire also faced severe external challenges. Christian Crusaders began probing the Middle East in the 11th century, eventually launching a major assault that captured Jerusalem, sacred to all three of the Middle East's religions, in 1099. The Christians held the city until 1187, when Saladin recaptured it for Islam and the Arabs.

By 1231, the Mongols had descended on the Middle East. They withdrew in the late 1200s, but at the end of the 14th century, they returned, ravaging Iraq, Persia, and Syria. After this, although Islam remained a powerful force in the Middle East, the Arab Empire never recovered.

Other empires based on Islam grew and prospered. One of the most important was run by the Ottoman Turks, a non-Arabic people living in what is today Turkey. By the 15th century, the Ottoman Empire had grown strong enough to challenge, and, in 1453, defeat the Christian Byzantine Empire in Constantinople. Over the next two centuries, the Ottoman Turks expanded their empire into the Eastern Mediterranean area and Egypt.

However, by the 19th century, the Ottoman Empire was challenged by four separate forces. The first was in Egypt, where Muhammad Ali fought against Ottoman control, eventually attaining Egypt's semi-independence. Second, in Syria, Lebanon, and Iraq, Arab national movements opposed Ottoman rule. Third, in Arabia, the puritanical Wahhabis fought for control. Finally, in several locations in the Middle East and North Africa, Western European states acquired influence and colonies at the expense of the Ottoman Empire.

Indeed, at the beginning of World War I, the Ottoman Empire was regarded as "the sick man of Europe and Asia." At the war's end, the Ottoman Empire collapsed, and the Arab portions were severed from what emerged as Turkey.

THE DEVELOPMENT OF
CURRENT POLITICAL AND SOCIAL FORCES

After World War I, Arab nationalism, a political movement seeking the creation of one giant Arab state, became a potent force. However, the European colonial powers believed that most Arabs were not ready to rule themselves. Thus, the League of Nations gave Palestine and Iraq to Great Britain as mandates and gave Syria to France as a mandate. Meanwhile, Egypt moved toward quasi-independence, although it remained essentially a British protectorate. In Saudi Arabia, Wahhabi Muslims established their own state.

With the great Islamic empires in decline and most Arabs frustrated in their efforts to establish independent states, the stage was set for many Muslims and Arabs to formulate new solutions to the problems that confronted them. Many people proposed different solutions to the challenges, but four groups moved to the forefront.

The first was the modernizers. They generally believed that the problems confronting Islamic and Arab societies were caused by an inability to adapt to the scientific and technical revolutions that had swept the West. While they did not necessarily advocate abandoning religious teachings, they wanted to reform Islamic institutions to make their societies less bound by tradition and more open to change. Often, modernizers reinterpreted Islam so it was not in conflict with reform. The most successful proponent of modernization was Kemal Ataturk in Turkey, who instituted Western-style political and economic reforms in his country. Shah Riza Pahlavi in Iran was also a modernizer in economics, but he insisted on maintaining political power in his own hands.

Conservative traditionalists were the second group who proposed solutions to the problems of Islam and Arabs. They believed that Muhammad's teachings remained valid, that Muslims had become too worldly and had to return to Muhammad's way of doing things, and that non-Islamic influences had to be rejected.

The leading conservative traditionalist sect was the Wahhabi movement, centered on the Arabian Peninsula. By the early 20th century, Wahhabis under Ibn Saud had extended their control to much of the peninsula. After the Ottoman Empire collapsed, Ibn Saud consolidated his control in Arabia except for Yemen, Oman, the Persian Gulf coastal emirates, and Kuwait. Even so, the Saud realm was poor. The Saud family's major revenue sources were from Muslim pilgrims to Mecca and a small annual subsidy that Great Britain provided for strategic reasons.

Then, in 1932, oil was discovered in nearby Bahrain. Ibn Saud had reservations about allowing Westerners into his kingdom to explore for oil, but given his country's poverty, he soon signed an agreement with Standard Oil of California. Oil wealth poured in, both to Saud's kingdom and to other fortunate states on the Arabian peninsula.

With this new source of wealth, many traditionalist regimes adopted new views about how Islamic societies should be shaped. Ibn Saud and other rulers in Kuwait, the United Arab Emirates, and Oman concluded that traditional Islamic teachings should be followed, but oil wealth could be used to improve living conditions and the quality of life. Usually, those in control benefited the most. Nevertheless, many citizens in the oil-rich states enjoyed an improved standard of living.

Revolutionary Arab nationalists provided a third view about what had gone wrong in Islamic Arab societies and what should be done. Many argued that Islamic societies had to modernize, and that Arab nationalism could eliminate Western imperialism and restore the Arab people to their rightful place in the world. Most revolutionary nationalists emphasized nationalism and development more than Islam, but few rejected Islam. Algeria's Ahmed Ben Bella, Egypt's Gamal Abdel Nasser, Syria's Hafez Assad, Libya's Muammar Khadaffi, and Iraq's Saddam Hussein all fit into this category.

Finally, radical Muslims, sometimes called fundamentalists, called on Muslims everywhere to return to traditional Islamic institutions and teachings, to reject everything Western or non-Islamic, and to struggle against non-Islamic influence and presence wherever it was found. To radical Muslims, violence against those who were not true believers in Allah was acceptable, and sometimes necessary. Large, radical Islamic movements developed in Algeria, Egypt, Iran, Lebanon, Sudan, and Tunisia.

Radical Muslims strongly opposed the other three leading directions of change in the Islamic world. They rejected reformers and modernizers as anti-Islamic, condemned conservative traditionalists as hypocrites, and considered revolutionary nationalists self-serving opportunists who cared more for their relationship with the imperialists than for unity based on Islam. Thus, radical Muslims opposed both non-Islamic societies and governments and Islamic governments that they defined as outside the realm of "true Islam."

CONCLUSIONS

Obviously, the Middle East contains a complex mix of outlooks, attitudes, and cultures. Muslims, Christians, and Jews, Arabs and non-Arabs, all contribute to the region's diversity. Moreover, as we have seen, the Middle East has also been impacted by external influences and interests. It is a complex region where history, religion, oil, and water all set the stage for potent conflict.

THE BACKGROUND LESSON

AN OVERVIEW OF THE MIDDLE EAST

Activity 1

*What countries are in the Middle East,
and where are they?*

ACTIVITY OBJECTIVE

The student will develop an understanding of the geographical importance of the Middle East, learn the names of the countries in the Middle East, and know where they are.

MATERIALS AND RESOURCES

❑ SCIS Videotape, *The Middle East in Transition*, Background Lesson,
  "An Overview of the Middle East"
❑ Teacher Resource 0.1, "Political Map of the Middle East"
❑ Handout 0.1, "Outline Map of the Middle East"
❑ Teacher Resource 0.2, "Remembering Middle Eastern Countries—A Script"
❑ Worksheet 0.1, "The Five Pillars of Islam"

STRATEGIES

Begin this activity by showing students the SCIS videotape, *The Middle East in Transition*, Background Lesson, "An Overview of the Middle East." The purposes of this videotape lesson are to show students that the Middle East is a complex region and to raise several issues that students will confront in their study of the region.

Next, explain to your class that establishing a sense of place is an important factor in understanding people of other cultures. The region known as the Middle East received its name from Europeans, who referred to countries that were not too distant from the east of Europe as the "Middle East" and countries that were a long distance from the east of Europe as the "Far East." Geographically and strategically, the Middle East is an extremely important location, sitting astride trade and communication routes that connect three continents (Africa, Asia, and Europe).

Some students might enjoy creating their own mnemonic devices to help them remember the countries of the Middle East. They should take the first letter of each country in the Middle East, grouped by sub-regions, and develop a sentence based on those first letters. By remembering the sentences, they should be able to find the location of each of the countries in the Middle East.

Before class begins, make a transparency of Teacher Resource 0.1, "Political Map of the Middle East." On the chalkboard, write the following list of countries: Algeria, Bahrain, Egypt, Iran, Iraq, Israel, Jordan, Kuwait, Lebanon, Libya, Morocco, Oman,

Qatar, Saudi Arabia, Syria, Tunisia, Turkey, United Arab Emirates, and Yemen. When class begins, distribute one copy of Handout 0.1, "Outline Map of the Middle East" to each student. Instruct students NOT to write on these maps, but to use these maps as references.

Point out that students need to be familiar with the absolute and relative locations of countries in the Middle East. Then, say to students, "Today at the end of class I am going to ask you to fill in the names of nineteen Middle Eastern countries on an outline map. Let's see how many of them you need to learn. Everyone point to the location of Kuwait on your map." [*Scan the room looking at fingers to show you are checking.*] "It seems that several of you don't know. See if you can point to the location of Syria." [*Check again quickly.*]

Then tell the class, "Today, I am going to show you some tricks that will help you learn and remember the names and locations of each of the countries in the Middle East." Teacher Resource 0.2, "Remembering Middle Eastern Countries—A Script," provides one method for helping students learn the place-name geography of the Middle East.

Most Middle Eastern states are predominantly Muslim. All Muslims share five essential beliefs that are known collectively as the "Five Pillars of Islam." As an extension activity, distribute to the students Worksheet 0.1, "The Five Pillars of Islam," which offers a more complete explanation of these basic beliefs. By completing the worksheet, the students will be able to compare similar practices among Islam, Christianity, and Judaism.

The key to Worksheet 0.1, "The Five Pillars of Islam" is below:

	Shahada	*Salat*	*Zakat*	*Sawm*	*Hajj*
Tradition in Islam	there is only one God; Muhammad is his prophet	prayers are performed five times daily	charity amounting to 2½% of one's income is offered	fasting during the month of Ramadan	making a pilgrimage to Mecca at least once in a lifetime
Similar Tradition in Christianity	belief in one God; Jesus Christ is the son of God; the Trinity	prayer on an individual basis; no prescribed times	followers are urged to tithe 10% of their income	some followers "give up" items or practices during Lent	no ritual pilgrimage required although many religious sites recognized
Similar Tradition in Judaism	belief in one God	three sets of prayers recited each day: sunrise, noon, and sundown	Biblical tithing is followed; followers also give of their time to charity [Tzadakeh]	fasting is observed during Yom Kippur	reverence for the Western Wall; "Next year in Jerusalem" is a greeting, but no pilgrmage required

POLITICAL MAP OF THE MIDDLE EAST

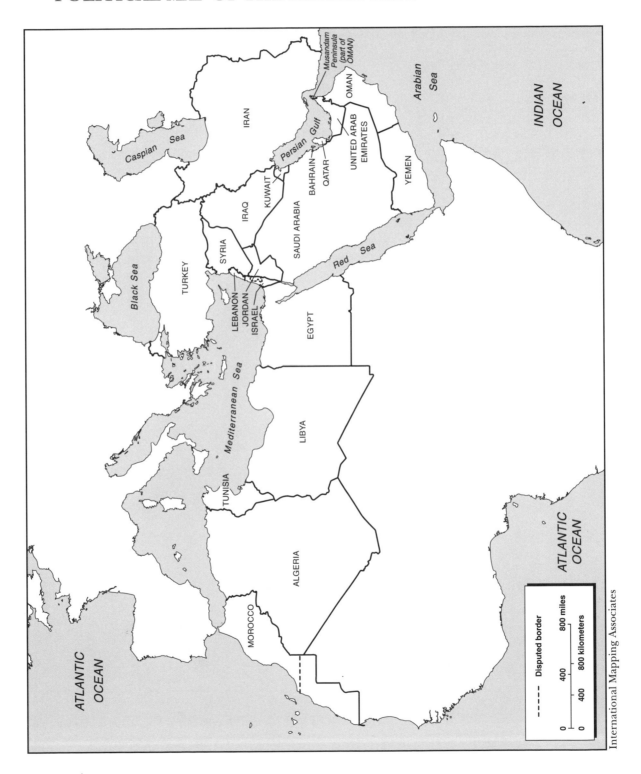

International Mapping Associates

OUTLINE MAP OF THE MIDDLE EAST

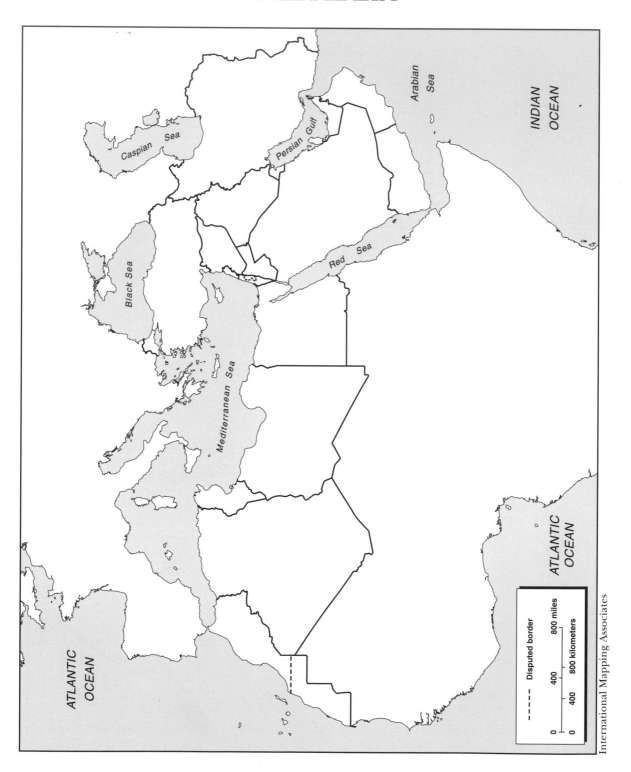

REMEMBERING MIDDLE EASTERN COUNTRIES
A Script

The following is a script that can be used to help students learn and remember the names and locations of countries in the Middle East. It can be adapted as appropriate for your class.

"Today, I am going to show you some tricks that will help you learn and remember the names and locations of the countries in the Middle East. As I point to the countries on the transparency, please follow along on your map.

a. **United Arab Emirates** [*point to the name on the transparency*] starts with the letter "U" and the country is shaped like a "U." Now point to the United Arab Emirates on your map. . . [*checking*]. Remember, the United Arab Emirates is U-shaped.

b. **Oman** is over the ocean and is the only country separated into two parts, by the United Arab Emirates. Remember, Oman is over the ocean [*point to the two parts of Oman on the transparency*]. Now, point to Oman on your map.

c. Now review. Everyone point to the location of the United Arab Emirates . . . United Arab Emirates is U-shaped. . . [*Check.*] How many pointed here? [*Show correct location on the transparency.*] Good. Now point to Oman. Remember, Oman is over the ocean and the only country that is separated . . . [*Show.*] How many got both correct?

d. Oman forms one tip of the United Arab Emirates "U." The other tip is the state of **Qatar**. [*Point to the location of Qatar on the transparency.*] Remember, the Q-tip is Qatar. Find Qatar on your map. [*Check.*]

e. The next six countries follow the alphabet . . . I, J, I, K, I, L . . . get the point? **Israel** (the first "I" in the series) comes to a point. [*Show Israel's location on the transparency.*] The other countries follow in alphabetical order from left to right, west to east. Point to Israel on your map. [*Check.*] The next letter is "J" and the next country is **Jordan**. Remember the alphabet pattern (I, J, I, K, I, L)? Next is "I" again, **Iraq**. [*Point to Iraq on the transparency.*] **Kuwait** comes next. [*Point to Kuwait on the transparency.*] The final "I" is **Iran**. Let's review. Remember the point of the pattern? Israel contains the point. Point to Israel on your map. [*Check.*] Now, Jordan, Iraq, Kuwait, Iran. How many of you got all these countries correct? Good. Now we need to find the "L" country, **Lebanon**. To get from Iran to Lebanon, a person would run from Iran back toward Israel. Lebanon is north of Israel. [*Point to the location of Lebanon on the transparency.*] Find Lebanon on your map.

f. **Saudi Arabia** is the country that is immediately *south* of the alphabetical states. [*Point to Saudi Arabia on the transparency.*] Find Saudi Arabia on your map. How many of you found Saudi Arabia? See the island in the Persian Gulf *between* Saudi Arabia and Qatar? It is **Bahrain**, between Saudi Arabia and Qatar. Point to Bahrain on your map. Let's review. Put your finger on Oman . . . United Arab Emirates . . . Qatar . . . Saudi Arabia . . . Bahrain.

g. Saudi Arabia is *east* of **Egypt**, and Egypt is shaped like a square. Find Egypt on your map. [*Point to Egypt on the transparency.*] Good. **Syria** is shaped like a triangle. [*Point to the location of Syria on the transparency.*] Now, point to Syria on your map.

h. **Yemen** forms the shape of the top part of the letter "Y." [*Point to Yemen on the transparency.*] Find Yemen on your map. [*Check.*] How many got it correct?

i. The final four countries are located in North Africa. They are **Morocco**, **Algeria**, **Tunisia**, and **Libya**. Find these countries on your map. The first letter of each country, from west to east, is also the first letter in the phrase "Most Arabs teach location." [*Point to the countries on the transparency.*] Now you know the locations of countries in the Middle East almost as well as Middle Easterners do! Congratulations!"

When most errors have been eliminated, have students put their names on their papers and fill in the names of the countries on the map. When they finish, collect the papers and check for accuracy.

Adapted from: Glen Blankenship, "Place-Name Geography: Facts We Can Teach." *Georgia Social Studies Journal*, Vol. 20, No. 2, Fall 1989, pages 18–22.

THE FIVE PILLARS OF ISLAM

The five pillars of Islam are the framework of the Muslim life: faith, prayer, concern for the needy, self-purification, and the pilgrimage to Mecca for those who are able.

I. Faith

There is no god worthy of worship except God and Muhammad is His messenger. This declaration of faith is called the *Shahada*, a simple formula which all the faithful pronounce. In Arabic, the first part is *la ilaha illa' Liah*—'there is no god except God;' *ilaha* (god) can refer to anything which we may be tempted to put in place of God—wealth, power, and the like. Then comes *illa' Liah*, 'except God', the source of all Creation. The second part of the Shahada is *Muhammadun rasulu' liah*; 'Muhammad is the messenger of God.' A message of guidance has come through a man like ourselves.

II. Prayer

Salat is the name for the obligatory prayers which are performed five times a day, and are a direct link between the worshipper and God. Theoretically, there is no hierarchical authority in Islam, and no priests, so the prayers may be led by a learned person who knows the Koran, chosen by the congregation. These five prayers contain verses from the Koran, and are said in Arabic, the language of the Revelation, but personal supplication can be offered in one's own language. Prayers are said at dawn, noon, mid-afternoon, sunset, and nightfall, and thus determine the rhythm of the entire day. Although it is preferable to worship together in a mosque, a Muslim may pray almost anywhere, such as in fields, offices, factories, and universities. Visitors to the Muslim world are often struck by the centrality of prayers in daily life.

III. Charity

One of the most important principles of Islam is that all things belong to God, and that wealth is therefore held by human beings in trust. The word *zakat* means both 'purification' and 'growth.' Our possessions are purified by setting aside a portion for those in need, and, like the pruning of plants, this cutting back balances and encourages new growth. Each Muslim calculates his or her own *zakat* individually. For most purposes this involves the payment each year of 2.5 percent of one's capital. A pious person may also give as much as he or she pleases as *sadaqa*, and does so preferably in secret. Although this word can be translated as 'voluntary charity' it has a wider meaning. Muhammad said, "Even meeting your brother with a cheerful face is charity."

IV. The Fast

Every year in the month of Ramadan, all Muslims fast from first light until sundown, abstaining from food, drink, and sexual relations. The word *sawm* refers to these practices. Those who are sick, elderly, or on a journey, and women who are pregnant or nursing are permitted to break the fast and make up an equal number of days later in the year. If they are physically able to do this, they must feed a needy person for every day missed. Children begin to fast (and to observe the prayer) from puberty, although many start earlier. Although the fast is most beneficial to the health, it is

13

regarded principally as a method of self-purification. By cutting oneself off from worldly comforts, even for a short time, a fasting person gains true sympathy with those who go hungry as well as growth in one's spiritual life.

V. Pilgrimage

The pilgrimage to Mecca—the *Hajj*—is an obligation only for those who are physically and financially able to perform it. Nevertheless, about two million people go to Mecca each year from every corner of the globe, providing a unique opportunity for those of different nations to meet one another. Although Mecca is always filled with visitors, the annual *Hajj* begins in the twelfth month of the Islamic year (which is lunar, not solar, so that the *Hajj* and Ramadan fall at various seasons of the year). Pilgrims wear special clothes: simple garments which strip away distinctions of class and culture, so that all stand equal before God.

The close of the *Hajj* is marked by a festival, the *Eid al-Adha*, which is celebrated with prayers and the exchange of gifts in Muslim communities everywhere. This, and the *Edi al-Fitr*, a feast day commemorating the end of Ramadan, are the main festivals of the Muslim calendar.

———

Adapted from *Understanding Islam and the Muslims*. The Islamic Affairs Department, Embassy of Saudi Arabia, Washington, D.C., 1989. [*Reprinted with permission.*]

Directions: Use information in the reading to identify the basic traditions and beliefs of Islam. Next, use media center resources to identify similar traditions in Christianity and Judaism.

	Shahada	*Salat*	*Zakat*	*Sawm*	*Hajj*
Tradition in Islam					
Similar Tradition in Christianity					
Similar Tradition in Judaism					

THE BACKGROUND LESSON

AN OVERVIEW OF THE MIDDLE EAST

Activity 2

What are some similarities and differences between Islam, Judaism, Christianity and how do these religions view terrorist violence?

ACTIVITY OBJECTIVE

The students will examine some of the similarities and differences between the world's major monotheistic religions and assess how they view terrorist violence.

MATERIALS AND RESOURCES

❏ Worksheet 0.2, "Introduction to Christianity, Islam, and Judaism"
❏ Teacher Resource 0.3, "Introduction to Christianity, Islam, and Judaism: KEY"
❏ Worksheet 0.3, "Quotations from Holy Books"
❏ Handout 0.2, "Three Faiths Form One Feuding Family"

STRATEGIES

Islam is the religion practiced by the majority of the people living in the Middle East. However, the region is the birthplace of all three of the world's major monotheistic religions: Christianity, Judaism, and Islam. The vast majority of the followers of each of these religions reject religious violence, though there are also examples of violent acts perpetrated in the name of all three. This activity allows students to explore similarities and differences between these religions and discuss how they address religious violence.

Begin this activity by dividing the class into groups of three to four students. Distribute to each group Worksheet 0.2, "Introduction to Christianity, Islam, and Judaism." After the groups have had a chance to fill in their worksheets, use Teacher Resource 0.3, "Introduction to Christianity, Islam, and Judaism: KEY," to discuss similarities and differences between the three religions with the class.

Although some students may be familiar with the Old Testament and New Testament, many will probably be less familiar with the Koran. Continue this activity by distributing Worksheet 0.3, "Quotations from Holy Books" to the groups. After the groups have completed their worksheets, raise the following questions with the class:

- Which of the quotations do you think come from the Old Testament? [*none*]
- Which of the quotations do you think come from the New Testament? [*none*]
- Which of the quotations do you think come from the Koran? [*all ten passages are from the Koran*]

15

- Do you think most people recognize the connections between these three religions?

Conclude this activity by distributing Handout 0.2, "Three Faiths Form One Feuding Family." After the students have had a chance to read the article, raise the following questions with the class:

- How do many Americans view Muslims? [*The article points out stereotypes, such as people living in desert areas, American athletes such as Muhammad Ali and Kareem Abdul-Jabbar, and terrorists.*]
- What is the world's most populous Islamic country? [*Indonesia*]
- Why are struggles between Jews, Christians, and Muslims "family feuds"? [*because of common geographic roots and religious frameworks*]
- How do Judaism, Christianity, and Islam compare when it comes to accepting or rejecting violent attacks like the terrorist attacks on the World Trade Center and Pentagon? [*Though there are exceptions, the overwhelming majority of Christians, Muslims, and Jews reject such heinous attacks.*]
- Does the Taliban represent the views of the majority of Muslims? [*No*]
- Why do some Muslims feel threatened by Western culture? [*because they feel that they are exploited by Western capitalism and that their cultural values are compromised by expanding Western influences*]
- What is a jihad? [*"a struggle in the path of God" against aggression or for justice; a jihad has strict rules against the harming of innocent people*]

INTRODUCTION TO CHRISTIANITY, ISLAM, AND JUDAISM

Directions: For each statement below, determine whether the question applies to Christianity, Islam, or Judaism. Each statement may apply to more than one religion. Write the appropriate letter (C, I, or J) in the blanks.

_____ 1. Their Holy Book is called the Koran.

_____ 2. Jesus is considered the Son of God.

_____ 3. This religion accepts both the Old and New Testaments as Holy Books.

_____ 4. Followers participate in a pilgrimage to Mecca.

_____ 5. This religion is the oldest of the three.

_____ 6. Abraham is regarded as the father of their people.

_____ 7. This religion believes in one Supreme Being.

_____ 8. This religion accepts the Old Testament as its only Holy Book.

_____ 9. Abraham and Moses are considered prophets.

_____ 10. Jerusalem is considered a holy city.

_____ 11. Followers of this religion call themselves Muslims.

_____ 12. The Ten Commandments are accepted as guidelines for ethical behavior.

_____ 13. Jesus is recognized as an important prophet.

_____ 14. This religion has a number of denominations or sects.

_____ 15. This religion believes in the divine creation of the universe.

_____ 16. This religion is the second-oldest of the three religions.

_____ 17. Their Holy Book includes the story of the birth of Jesus at Bethlehem.

_____ 18. Their place of worship is a church.

_____ 19. Their place of worship is a mosque.

_____ 20. Their place of worship is a synagogue.

Adapted from materials developed by the Center for Middle Eastern Studies, University of California, Berkeley.

INTRODUCTION TO
CHRISTIANITY, ISLAM, AND JUDAISM: KEY

Directions: For each statement below, determine whether the question applies to Christianity, Islam, or Judaism. Each statement may apply to more than one religion. Write the appropriate letter (C, I, or J) in the blanks.

I   1. Their Holy Book is called the Koran.

C   2. Jesus is considered the Son of God.

C, I   3. This religion accepts both the Old and New Testaments as Holy Books.

I   4. Followers participate in a pilgrimage to Mecca.

J   5. This religion is the oldest of the three.

I, J   6. Abraham is regarded as the father of their people.

C, I, J   7. This religion believes in one Supreme Being.

J   8. This religion accepts the Old Testament as its only Holy Book.

C, I, J   9. Abraham and Moses are considered prophets.

C, I, J   10. Jerusalem is considered a holy city.

I   11. Followers of this religion call themselves Muslims.

C, I, J   12. The Ten Commandments are accepted as guidelines for ethical behavior.

I   13. Jesus is recognized as an important prophet.

C, I, J   14. This religion has a number of denominations or sects.

C, I, J   15. This religion believes in the divine creation of the universe.

C   16. This religion is the second-oldest of the three religions.

C, I   17. Their Holy Book includes the story of the birth of Jesus at Bethlehem.

C   18. Their place of worship is a church.

I   19. Their place of worship is a mosque.

J   20. Their place of worship is a synagogue.

Adapted from materials developed by the Center for Middle Eastern Studies, University of California, Berkeley.

QUOTATIONS FROM HOLY BOOKS

Directions: Each statement below comes from a Holy Book. Indicate whether you think the source of each statement is: (A) the Old Testament or Torah; (B) the New Testament; or (C) the Koran.

_____ 1. And We said: O Adam! Dwell thou and thy wife in the Garden, and eat ye freely of the fruits thereof where ye will; but come not near this tree lest ye become wrongdoers.

_____ 2. O Children of Israel! Remember My favor wherewith I favored you and how I preferred you to all creatures.

_____ 3. And remember when We deliver you from Pharaoh's folk, who were afflicting you with dreadful torment slaying your sons and sparing your women.

_____ 4. We believe in God and that which is revealed unto us and that which was revealed unto Abraham, and Ishmael, and Isaac, and Jacob, and the tribes, and that which Moses and Jesus received, and that which the prophets received from their Lord.

_____ 5. And when the angels said: O Mary! Lo! God hath chosen thee and made thee pure, and hath preferred thee above all the women of creation.

_____ 6. And when We did appoint for Moses forty nights of solitude, and then ye chose the calf, when he had gone from you, and were wrongdoers.

_____ 7. And I come confirming that which was before me of the Torah, and to make lawful some of that which was forbidden unto you. I come unto you with a sign from your Lord, so keep your duty to God and obey me.

_____ 8. She said: My Lord! How can I have a child when no mortal has touched me? He said: So it will be! God createth what He will.

_____ 9. And remember when the angel said: O Mary! Lo! God giveth thee glad tidings of a word from Him, whose name is the Messiah, Jesus, son of Mary, illustrious in the world and the hereafter, and one of those brought near unto God.

_____ 10. One among them said: Kill not Joseph, but if ye must be doing, fling him into the depth of the pit. Some caravan will find him.

Prepared by Mounir Farrah, reprinted with permission.

19

THREE FAITHS FORM ONE FEUDING FAMILY

By Gayle White

For many Americans who hear the word Muslim, one of three images comes to mind: a Bedouin on a camel, an American athlete in silk shorts, or an international terrorist.

Each is correct to a limited extent.

Many of the world's Muslims do live in desert areas. Some prominent American athletes—Muhammad Ali and Kareem Abdul-Jabbar, for instance—are Muslim. And a few Muslims have attempted to justify terrorism through their religion.

But Islam is much broader and deeper than any of those snapshots. More than a billion people are Muslims, and Islam is the majority religion in more than 50 countries from Indonesia to sub-Saharan Africa, from Central Asia to Eastern Europe.

To label Islam a "Middle Eastern religion" is as misleading as to classify Christianity or Judaism in those terms, said Abdullahi An-Na'im, professor of law and a fellow of the Law and Religion Program at Emory University.

Although all three faiths were founded in the region, they spread beyond it. Today, more Muslims live in sub-Saharan Africa than in the Middle East, he said, and Indonesia has more Muslims than any other country.

In the United States, many African-Americans have converted to Islam. Most are Sunni, or orthodox Muslims, although a small percentage are affiliated with the more separatist Nation of Islam.

Besides their common geographic roots, Judaism, Christianity, and Islam claim a common father in Abraham and share a moral code in the Ten Commandments, said An-Na'im, an internationally recognized scholar on Islam and human rights. Struggles between Jews, Christians, and Muslims, therefore, are actually family feuds.

Islam is the youngest of the world's three great monotheistic religions. Its founder was Hadhrat Muhammad, a merchant's son born in Saudi Arabia about 570.

Muhammad said that when he was about 40, he was visited by a figure identified as the angel Gabriel. Some two years later, he again claimed to receive messages from God, which continued through his life.

Many of these messages coincided with the teachings of Judaism and Christianity.

"The framework for this new religion was decidedly biblical," said Devin Stewart, chairman of the Department of Middle Eastern Studies at Emory University. "This is seen in many aspects of the new faith, not least in its insistence on monotheism . . . the idea that there is one and only one God, who created and sustains life and, therefore, should be worshipped and thanked. The concepts of sin, the soul, the afterlife, heaven and hell, the Day of Judgment, are all familiar."

And, just as some Jews and Christians sometimes cite their religion to justify their political positions, so do some Muslims.

"People tend to think of what's happening now—the Taliban and bin Laden

—in terms that are purely religious," said John Iskander, assistant professor in religious studies at Georgia State University. "They depoliticize what's happening and focus entirely on Islam. They ask, 'Is Islam a violent religion?'"

The answer is yes and no, he said. "Islam is practiced in all kinds of different ways, but the history has been more tolerant than intolerant."

Many Muslims have opposed the Taliban because they believe it is not representative of true Islam, he said, just as most Christians denounce the bombing of abortion clinics by people who claim their authority is based in Christianity.

Other Muslims who reject the indiscriminate violence of the terrorist attacks on the World Trade Center and the Pentagon may have some sense of satisfaction that America has been humbled, said Fred Denny, an Islamic specialist at the University of Colorado in Boulder. They feel threatened by the spreading of Western culture and values, and exploited by Western capitalism.

Even though Arab Muslims own the land over much of the world's oil supply, many do not feel they control the oil, said An-Na'im of Emory.

"It is physically controlled by Muslim countries, but it is economically controlled by Western interests."

"There is a sense that Muslim values are compromised increasingly as Western power has extended influence throughout the world," said Denny. "There is also a very great sense of grievance on the part of some Muslim peoples—Afghanistan is one place—that have been subjected to modern totalitarian regimes.. . . So, we've got extremist groups, mostly fairly small, that will commit extreme acts."

Those acts are frequently couched in religious terms, especially jihad.

The word is often equated with a holy war, but actually means "struggle in the path of God."

"Jihad may include armed conflict, but it has strict rules—one of which is not to harm innocent people," Denny said.

Add to that the fact that suicide is condemned in Islam, and hijacking airplanes into buildings occupied by office workers is "sincerely and formally rejected as utterly inauthentic by the highest Muslim authorities," Denny said.

The vast majority of Muslims in the world want to be participants in the larger world "and not left behind," he said.

"I think one of the hopes for Muslims is in the large Muslim diaspora in Europe and the Americas—not just North America but Brazil, Chile, Mexico, and Argentina," Denny said. "I think the future hope may lie in mediation between Western Muslims in those countries and their nations and regions of origin—and a lot of hard work, patience, and diplomacy."

As someone who has spent his life studying Islam and has visited and lived in Islamic countries, Denny feels grief both over the situation in the United States and over those in some of the world's Muslim nations.

He has hope that they can live in peace. "I'm not optimistic in a foolish sense," he said, "but I'm not giving up."

Source: *The Atlanta Journal*, September 19, 2001.

Countries with Largest Muslim Population

Country	Muslims	Total population
1. Indonesia	170 million	212 million
2. Pakistan	136 million	157 million
3. Bangladesh	106 million	129 million
4. India	103 million	1 billion
5. Turkey	62 million	67 million
6. Iran	61 million	68 million
7. Egypt	54 million	69 million
8. Nigeria	48 million	112 million
9. China	37 million	1 billion

Sources: Adherents.com; *World Christian Encyclopedia, 2001*; *CIA World Factbook*; *The Top 10 of Everything*; *Knight Ridder Tribune.*

Glossary

Allah: "The God." Muslims believe that he is the Supreme Being, the one and only God. Allah is the same God worshipped by Jews and Christians.

Islam: Religion preached by the Prophet Muhammad. It means "surrender" or "submission to the will of God."

Jihad: A Quranic [or Koranic] term for the legitimate struggle against aggression or striving for justice.

Mosque: House of worship for Muslims.

Muhammad: Islam's final prophet; Muslims believe he received revelations from Allah that were transmitted by the angel Gabriel.

Muslim: A person who submits to Allah and follows the teaching of Islam. Muslims accept some Old Testament books, including the story of Moses receiving the Ten Commandments.

Quran (or Koran): The holy book of Islam.

Shi'ite [Shia]: A branch of Islam found primarily in Iran and parts of Iraq that split from the Sunni in a disagreement over Muhammad's successor.

Sufism: Islamic mysticism, based on renunciation of wealth and devotion to religious study and meditation.

Sunni: The major branch of Islam, representing about 90 percent of the world's Muslims. Its name is derived from the word sunnah, or path.

Sources: Michael D. Coogan, "Illustrated Guide to World Religions"; *Encyclopaedia Britannica; World Book Encyclopedia Copyright*

THE BACKGROUND LESSON

AN OVERVIEW OF THE MIDDLE EAST

Activity 3

What approaches have different Middle Eastern countries taken to modernization?

ACTIVITY OBJECTIVE

The student will examine approaches to reform and modernization that different Middle Eastern states have used.

MATERIALS AND RESOURCES

❑ SCIS Background Reading, Background Lesson, "An Overview of the Middle East," section entitled, "The Development of Current Political and Social Forces"
❑ Worksheet 0.4, "Reform and Modernization"

STRATEGIES

Since the beginning of the twentieth century, one of the primary sources of tension in the Middle East has been the issue of modernization. Leaders of Middle Eastern states had to formulate new solutions to the problems that confronted them.

Although many different types of leaders came forward, four types stood out: modernizers, conservative traditionalists, nationalists, and radical Muslims (also often called "Fundamentalists" or "Islamists").

Begin the activity by distributing to the class SCIS Background Reading, Background Lesson, "An Overview of the Middle East," section entitled, "The Development of Current Political and Social Forces." After the students have read the material, they should be able to identify these four approaches to modernization.

Distribute Worksheet 0.4, "Reform and Modernization." Have students analyze these four reform efforts. Students should be prepared to participate in a discussion of the success of each approach in terms of the political, social, and economic situations in the Middle East, and in individual countries in the Middle East, today.

Next, ask students to write a concise one-sentence definition of each of the four categories identified on the worksheet: modernizers, conservative traditionalists, nationalists, and radical Muslims. Ask, "What are the difficulties of trying to place a country into a particular category?"

Conclude this activity by dividing the class into groups of 4-5 students and giving each group the following assignment:

Imagine that you are the head of a newly-emerging state in the Middle East. You face all of the problems that were discussed in the essay and in the previous activities: the need to industrialize, a lingering legacy of imperialism, the need to establish an independent government, the necessity of preserving social stability, the task of defining the role of Islam in the new country, and the relationship of your country to the Arab world in general. Choose one of the four approaches described in the background reading and create an outline explaining the ways in which your new state will address these issues.

When the groups finish, have students explain their choices. Then lead a class discussion asking students to consider the following questions:

1) What are the main factors that should be taken into consideration to bring about successful reform?
2) What are the difficulties of imposing reforms on traditional societies?
3) Why have efforts at reform been more successful in some countries than others?
4) In what ways have some of the countries of the Middle East limited the extent of Western influence? Is this a wise policy? Why or why not?
5) What would be your response to a group of Radicals (Islamists) in your country? In what ways could you address their concerns without losing power?
6) Is modernization positive? Why or why not?

REFORM AND MODERNIZATION

Approach to Reform	Type of Government Sought	Type of Leadership Promoted	Role of Islam	Relations with West	Example Countries/ Leaders
Modernizers					
Conservative Traditionalists					
Revolutionary Nationalists					
Radical Islamists					

Egyptian President Anwar Sadat, left, U.S. President Jimmy Carter, center, and Israeli Prime Minister Menachem Begin clasp hands on the north lawn of the White House after signing the peace treaty between Egypt and Israel on March 26, 1979. President Carter was pivotal in bringing the two leaders together for negotiations at Camp David. Sadat and Begin were awarded the 1978 Nobel Peace Prize for their work towards the agreement. The rest of the Arab world shunned Sadat for making peace with the Israelis. He was assassinated in 1981.

LESSON 1

U.S. Interests in the Middle East

Lesson 1 of 5 Lessons for the
Southern Center for International Studies'
Multimedia Educational Package
THE MIDDLE EAST IN TRANSITION

Reuters/Arko Datta

A U.S. soldier patrols in front of an oil refinery in Baiji, 19 miles north of Tikrit, Iraq, September 22, 2003. U.S. forces stepped up security around Iraq's oil infrastructure to prevent sabotage that would cut off exports from the north of Iraq.

LESSON 1

of the SCIS Educational Package
The Middle East in Transition

U.S. INTERESTS IN THE MIDDLE EAST

Even though it is several thousand miles from the Middle East, the United States often finds itself directly involved in Middle Eastern affairs. For example, the United States has twice sent troops into Lebanon, once in the 1950s and once in the 1980s. It has frequently taken the lead in trying to negotiate a settlement to the Arab-Israeli conflict. The two largest recipients of U.S. foreign aid are Israel and Egypt.

In 1990, the U.S. sent nearly half a million men and women to the Persian Gulf region to liberate Kuwait, and it kept thousands of troops in the area for over a decade in an attempt to contain Saddam Hussein's regime. Following the September 11, 2001, terrorist attacks in the U.S., the region became a primary battleground in the "war on terrorism." In 2003, the U.S. once again went to war against Iraq, this time overthrowing Saddam Hussein and stationing more than 100,000 troops in the country.

Why is the U.S. so interested and involved in this region? Is it because the Middle East has oil? Is it because the United States is so committed to Israel? Is it because of the various terrorist groups based in the region? Are there other reasons that American diplomats, military personnel, and other public officials concentrate so much on the Middle East? In this lesson, we will explore five reasons behind U.S. interests and activities in the Middle East.

REGIONAL STABILITY AND GEOSTRATEGIC CONCERNS

Because the Middle East is strategically located across vital trade, communications, and transportation lanes between Europe, Asia, and Africa, the United States has long sought to prevent the region from falling under the control or influence of countries hostile to U.S. interests.

The history of U.S. involvement in Middle Eastern affairs began with the U.S. naval campaign against Tripoli in 1803 and 1804. More recently, from the end of World War II until 1971, the United States was content to allow Britain to "police" the Middle East. The presence of British forces in the Middle East was a holdover from Britain's colonial era, but the British presence did maintain a degree of stability in the region. For example, when Iraq tried to acquire territory from Kuwait in 1961, Britain sent 45 ships to Kuwait's coast. Iraq backed down.

Nevertheless, even in this period the United States sometimes acted to defend regional stability and its own Middle Eastern geostrategic interests. In 1946, the U.S. sent a naval force to the eastern Mediterranean to counter Soviet pressure on Turkey. The same year, the U.S. complained to the UN Security Council that the U.S.S.R. had not withdrawn its troops from Iran at the end of World War II as Moscow had agreed to do. The Soviets then withdrew. In 1954, the United States took an active behind-the-scenes role in restoring the Shah of Iran to power. In 1957, the U.S. again sent warships to the eastern Mediterranean, this time to keep Jordan's government in power. Then, in 1958, the U.S. sent marines to Lebanon to prevent the outbreak of a civil war and a potential takeover by forces perceived as hostile to the United States.

In addition, in 1955, the U.S. helped create the Baghdad Pact, which included Iran, Iraq, Pakistan, Turkey, and the United Kingdom. Since Iraq was technically still at war with Israel, the U.S. did not join. However, when Iraq withdrew from the Pact in 1959, the U.S. formed the Central Treaty Organization (CENTO), which included Iran, Pakistan, Turkey, and the United States. The U.S. also kept military forces in the Middle East during this period to maintain its presence and to counter possible Soviet expansion. The U.S. Sixth Fleet has operated in the Mediterranean Sea since the end of World War II, and a naval group of two to four destroyers and one command ship has been based in Bahrain since 1948.

This was a relatively small military presence. Thus, when Britain withdrew its military forces from "east of Suez" in 1971, the United States had to rethink its regional strategy.

To cope with the new situation, the U.S. government formulated the "Twin Pillar" strategy, in which the United States based the promotion of regional stability and the defense of its geostrategic interests on close relationships with two friendly governments in the area, Saudi Arabia and Iran. Throughout the 1970s, the U.S. collaborated closely with these two states.

The "Twin Pillar" strategy came undone in 1979 when Ayatollah Khomeini's Islamic revolution overthrew the Shah of Iran and when the Soviet Union invaded Afghanistan. Khomeini's revolution brought an extremely anti-American government to power, effectively destroying the Twin Pillar strategy, while the December 1979 Soviet invasion of Afghanistan underscored the limits of American military power around the Persian Gulf.

The U.S. began immediately to redress its weaknesses in the area. First, in January 1980, President Jimmy Carter proclaimed the Carter Doctrine, declaring that "an attempt by any outside force to gain control of the Persian Gulf region will be regarded as an assault on the vital interests of the United States." Carter also warned that such an assault would "be repelled by any means necessary, including military force."

Next, the United States developed military force structures, airlift and sealift capabilities, and regional relationships that allowed it to better project military force into the area. The U.S. created the Rapid Deployment Joint Task Force, which became the Central Command, whose task was the defense of U.S. interests stretching from Pakistan to Kenya to Egypt. Other U.S. military units were restructured to permit fast movement over long distances, and also received extensive desert warfare training. In addition, the U.S. helped friendly regional states improve their own defense capabilities, and acquired access to facilities in Egypt, Kenya, Oman, Saudi Arabia, Somalia, and in the Indian Ocean. At some of these locations, the U.S. stored military equipment for ground warfare, should it be needed at some future time. All these activities began during the last year of the Carter presidency, and were accelerated under President Ronald Reagan.

In addition to these activities, when warfare broke out between Iraq and Iran in 1980, the U.S. "tilted" toward Iraq during the eight-year war, providing it with arms and military information. There were two reasons for this. First, Iran was extremely anti-American. Not only had Iran held U.S. Embassy personnel in Tehran hostage for over a year, but the Iranian government was actively participating in terrorist activities directed against the United States and other Western interests. Second, as had been the case in U.S. policy toward the Middle East in general and the Persian Gulf region in particular throughout the Cold War, the United States did not want the region to come under the control or influence of the Soviet Union or any other country hostile to the United States.

By the early 1990s, however, several of the conditions shaping U.S. policy in the Middle East had changed. With the collapse of the Soviet Union, the region was no longer viewed as a Cold War battleground. After the 1991 Persian Gulf War, the U.S. was no longer willing to support Iraq as a counterbalance to Iran. Indeed, the long-time U.S. policy of supporting one country against the other—Iran until the revolution in 1979, Iraq until its invasion of Kuwait in 1990—had not produced a desirable result. So in 1993, the Clinton administration announced a new policy, termed "dual containment," which aimed to weaken both Iran and Iraq through strict economic sanctions and diplomatic isolation. This policy continued throughout the 1990s.

Another turning point came on September 11, 2001. The devastating terrorist attacks in the United States, which destroyed the World Trade Center complex, left part of the Pentagon in shambles, and killed 2,752 people,[1] greatly altered both the substance and gravity of U.S. interests in the Middle East. As a result, U.S. geostrategic interests in the region are now largely defined by the U.S.-led "war on terrorism." Key concerns include the U.S. occupation and nation-building efforts in Iraq, containment of Iran, and the establishment of a lasting peace between Israel and its Arab adversaries. To support these interests, roughly 200,000 American troops are stationed in the Middle East.[2]

The War on Terrorism. In a speech to the joint session of Congress on September 20, 2001, President George W. Bush committed the U.S. to a lengthy campaign against terrorism that will be "unlike any other we have seen." He put on notice terrorists—and the countries that harbor them—throughout the world, especially those associated with Saudi militant Osama bin Laden. Bin Laden had long been accused of supporting terrorist activities from his hideout in Afghanistan, and is blamed for the September 11 attacks on the U.S.

Many of the world's terrorist groups are based in the Middle East, where anti-Americanism runs deep. Key factors fueling this anti-Americanism include: the presence of U.S. troops in several of the region's countries; U.S. support for Middle Eastern regimes seen as corrupt and authoritarian; U.S. support for Israel; the continuing plight of the Palestinians; the ongoing military confrontation in Iraq; seeming American unilateralism and arrogance on the world scene; enduring economic despair; and, broadly, perceptions of cultural subversion and capitalist exploitation within the U.S.-led global economy. Importantly, the vast majority of Arabs and Muslims condemn acts such as the attacks on the World Trade Center and the Pentagon. Unfortunately, legitimate Arab criticisms of the U.S. and its policies have often been twisted by fanatical rhetoric, such as that frequently used in Middle Eastern schools and employed by Middle Eastern media outlets. This has allowed terrorist organizations to exploit the above factors to stir resentment of the United States and build support for their cause.

Clearly the "war on terrorism" is one of the most complex wars ever undertaken, if not the most complex. A dilemma for the U.S. is that its success is dependent, to a certain degree, on cooperation from Middle Eastern governments. Frequently these governments have a difficult balancing act to maintain, cooperating to varying degrees in the war on terrorism to avoid being seen as an enemy of the U.S., while at the same time managing populations deeply opposed to U.S. policies and often sympathetic to the views espoused by Islamic militants. Most Middle Eastern governments have provided some support to the U.S., such as freezing the financial assets of bin Laden's al Qaeda movement and sharing intelligence. Some countries, such as Egypt, Jordan, and Yemen, have gone further by cooperating with U.S. law-enforcement agencies and pursuing suspected terrorists. Other countries have seemingly played both sides, lending some assistance to the U.S. while either turning a blind eye to certain terrorist activity, as in the case of Saudi Arabia, or actively supporting terrorism, as in the case of Syria.

While terrorism and the fight against it will likely be with us for the foreseeable future, the hope is that enlightened leadership in the U.S., the Arab world, Europe, and elsewhere will reduce the number of terrorist activities by addressing their root causes. As UN Secretary-General Kófi Annan has put it:

> Terrorism threatens every society. As the world takes action against it, we . . . [should] address the conditions that permit the growth of such hatred and depravity. We must confront violence, bigotry, and hatred even more resolutely. The United Nations' work must continue as we address the ills of conflict, ignorance, poverty, and disease.[3]

Regime Change in Iraq. In 2002, after invading Afghanistan to destroy al Qaeda bases and remove the Taliban regime from power, the U.S. turned its attention toward Iraq as the next target in the "war on terrorism." The Bush administration accused Iraq of continuing to develop weapons of mass destruction (WMD) in violation of the cease-fire treaty Iraq signed after losing the 1991 Persian Gulf War. Further, the U.S. government argued that UN weapons inspections were incapable of dismantling Iraq's weapons program and that, if left in place, Saddam Hussein's dictatorial regime could become a dangerous ally of international terrorist organizations. As a result, the U.S. abandoned its traditional policy of containing Iraq and pursued a new policy of regime change.

In March 2003, the U.S. invaded Iraq, overthrew the government of Saddam Hussein, and established a U.S.-led provisional government. As a result, the long and difficult task of rebuilding Iraq into a stable, secure, and democratic society will remain central to U.S. interests in the region for many years to come (see Lesson 2, "The Persian Gulf War and Its Continuing Aftermath").

Containing Iran. The May 1997 election of a liberal Muslim cleric, Muhammad Khatami, to the presidency in Iran has led to some conciliatory steps by the country towards its neighbors and the West. Khatami has also pressed for greater openness in Iranian society. However, his efforts to implement reform have regularly been blocked by the more powerful, conservative Muslim clerics, who want to maintain a rigid society based on the tenets of Islam. The conservative Guardian Council has used its power to annul laws passed by the parliament, close pro-reform newspapers, imprison journalists, and block reformist politicians from running for office. Frustration with the slow pace of reform has led to increasingly bold protests and growing disillusionment among Iranian youth, who comprise a majority of the population (see Lesson 4, "Other Middle Eastern Issues").

Some analysts have argued that the U.S. should do more to engage Iran and support Khatami as he tries to make Iran a more responsible player in the international community. They argue that isolating the Islamic regime only limits the U.S.'s ability to promote change. European governments have sought to strengthen Iranian moderates by engaging in dialogue and increasing economic contacts. Proponents of this strategy point to the success of France, Britain, and Germany in persuading Iran to open its nuclear facilities to International Atomic Energy Agency (IAEA) inspectors in 2003 as an example of the benefits of engagement.

Those who favor containing Iran, however, argue that the government sponsors terrorist organizations and that isolating the regime is more important than establishing business contacts. Furthermore, it is difficult for the U.S. to directly support Iran's reformers. Opposition to U.S. influence is a centerpiece of the country's Islamic regime. As a result, strong U.S. support for specific reformers, such as Khatami, can reduce their credibility in Iran by breeding suspicion that they are too beholden to U.S. interests.

In the fall of 2001, U.S.-Iranian relations improved somewhat as Iran became an unlikely but important ally in the U.S. effort to overthrow the Taliban regime in Afghanistan. Iran had long opposed the Taliban and actively supported the Northern Alliance, an interethnic band of rebels in northern Afghanistan working to oust the Taliban. Iranian diplomacy proved helpful in organizing the Northern Alliance forces before and during the war, as well as in forming an interim Afghan government in the war's aftermath.

Nonetheless, relations deteriorated markedly in January 2002 when President Bush, in his first State of the Union Address, labeled Iran as part of an "axis of evil," accusing the country of pursuing nuclear weapons and exporting terrorism. Iran fiercely denied the charges, arguing that its nuclear program was designed only for developing nuclear power. While Iranian officials acknowledged aiding Palestinian groups, they argued that a distinction should be made between international terrorist organizations like al Qaeda and Palestinian groups like Hamas and Islamic Jihad, which they view as national liberation movements. Following the speech, reformers and conservatives in Iran suspended their infighting to join in opposing the U.S. characterization, which they regarded as bullying, ignorant, and counterproductive.

In 2003, tensions further increased as U.S. officials accused Iran of meddling in Iraqi politics after the fall of Saddam Hussein. The U.S. is particularly wary of Iran's influence with Iraq's majority Shia population, some of whom have expressed a desire to establish in Iraq an Islamic regime similar to Iran's. Allegations that Iran was supporting anti-U.S. groups in the region as well as intensifying its nuclear program led to increasing calls by conservative U.S. legislators and government officials for the Bush administration to adopt a policy of regime change in Iran.[4] In early 2004, the administration remained split on the issue of how best to deal with Iran, with some members advocating a policy of destabilization and others advocating non-interference in Iranian affairs. Whichever strategy the U.S. government chooses to pursue, relations with Iran will clearly remain at the forefront of U.S. interests in the coming years.

ISRAEL

The United States has also been deeply involved in Middle Eastern affairs because of Israel. Since Israel's creation in 1948, the U.S. has been an ardent supporter of the Jewish state, providing large quantities of economic and military assistance and extensive diplomatic and political support. Even today, Israel remains the largest recipient of U.S. foreign aid. There are several reasons why the United States has been so closely identified with Israel.

First, because of the atrocities visited upon the Jewish people by the Nazis during World War II, there has been widespread sympathy in the United States to the need for a Jewish state, a homeland where Jewish people can live without fear of domestic persecution by the government.

Second, U.S. sympathy for Israel has been strengthened over the years by four major Arab-Israeli wars, in 1948, 1956, 1967, and 1973. During the last three of these wars, Arab forces were supplied by the Soviet Union. Therefore, Israel was often seen in the United States as an American ally in the Cold War.

Third, despite disagreements and Israel's frequent willingness to pursue its own policies independent of U.S. preferences, Israel has often been a U.S. ally in the Middle East. Israel frequently points out that it is the only democracy in the Middle East. The U.S.-Israeli relationship is strengthened because of such shared values.

Fourth, the American Jewish community, as well as the fundamentalist Christian movement in the U.S., have often been extremely vocal supporters of Israel. This, of course, adds to the already-strong support within the United States for Israel.

This does not mean that the United States and Israel see eye to eye on all issues. They do not. For example, ever since Israel occupied the Gaza Strip and the West Bank during the 1967 Arab-Israeli War, the United States has refused to recognize Israel's occupation as legitimate. Similarly, the United States and Israel have had major disagreements over Israel's policy of encouraging Israeli citizens and new Jewish immigrants to Israel to move to and settle in the occupied West Bank. The United States has also on occasion objected to Israel's treatment of the Palestinian and Arab peoples living in the West Bank and Gaza Strip, who are not considered full citizens by Israel.

Despite these disagreements, the maintenance of a free and independent Israel remains a primary U.S. interest in the Middle East. Virtually everyone agrees that the United States and Israel are close friends, if not formal allies. This special relationship frequently leads the United States to become involved in Middle East peace processes (see Lesson 3: "The Arab-Israeli Conflict"). In some ways, the close U.S.-Israeli relationship makes the U.S. uniquely suited to helping broker peace agreements between Arabs and Israelis. The Israelis see the U.S. as one of the only countries they can trust not to compromise their vital interests. The Arabs often see the U.S. as the only country that can pressure Israel to make painful concessions. And the U.S. is one of the few countries capable of supporting a peace agreement with economic aid, security guarantees, and other incentives.

OIL

The United States also considers the Middle East vitally important because it produces much of the world's oil (36% in 2001)[5] and has 70 percent of the world's known oil reserves (see Chart 1). The Middle East is also the cheapest place in the world to extract the product. Within the Middle East, the most critical subregions for oil production and oil reserves are the Arabian Peninsula, as well as Iraq and Iran, both bordering the Persian Gulf. Thirty percent of the world's total oil production in

2001 and 66 percent of the world's oil reserves the same year were situated in these subregions.[6]

Chart 1
World crude oil reserves

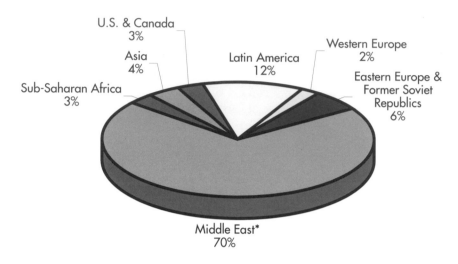

Source: Energy Information Administration, "World Crude Oil and Natural Gas Reserves" (Washington, D.C.: Department of Energy, January 2003).

*Note that the definition of the Middle East used in *The Middle East in Transition* includes the countries of North Africa.

The United States is by far the world's largest single consumer of oil, accounting for one quarter of total consumption (see Chart 2). In 2002, 24 percent of U.S. crude oil imports came from the volatile Persian Gulf area.[7] As a result, the political, social, and economic dynamics of the Gulf region remain critical to U.S. energy and economic security concerns.

Chart 2
World oil consumption

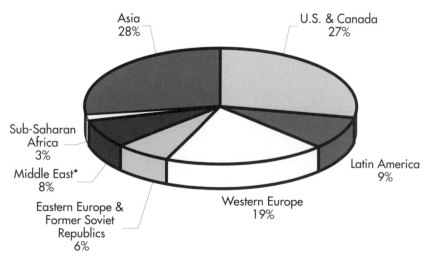

Source: Energy Information Administration, "World Petroleum Consumption, 1992-2001" (Washington, D.C.: U.S. Department of Energy, March 14, 2003).

Middle Eastern oil is even more important to the economies of other industrialized countries. In 2001, the European Union imported about 31 percent of all the oil it used from the Middle East, the vast majority of it coming from the Persian Gulf area.[8] In the same year, Japan imported 76 percent of the oil it used from the Persian Gulf region.[9] Given that world oil demand is expected to double over the next 30 years as the use of automobiles proliferates throughout the developing world, Middle Eastern oil will be central not only to American economic growth, but also to global stability.

For decades, the U.S.'s heavy reliance on Middle Eastern oil has been a source of concern for U.S. administrations. When Iraq invaded Kuwait in 1990, the oil reserves under Iraq's control increased from about 10 percent of the world's known oil reserves to about 20 percent. This caused considerable concern in the United States and elsewhere. However, of even greater concern was the fear that Saddam Hussein, Iraq's leader, intended to order his armed forces to continue down Saudi Arabia's Persian Gulf coast and establish control over Saudi and United Arab Emirate oil reserves as well. Had Iraq done that, Saddam would have controlled about 54 percent of the world's oil reserves.

This was a major reason that the United States responded so forcefully to the Iraqi invasion of Kuwait. Some people even concluded that the primary reason for the U.S. response was because of oil. The U.S. denied that this was the case, arguing that other issues, such as international law, morality, and the future of the post-Cold War international order were at stake as well. But no one denied that oil played a major role in the U.S. decision to oppose Iraq's invasion of Kuwait.

When the U.S. went to war against Iraq a second time in 2003, some critics again saw oil as a motivating factor. Iraq still contains the world's second-largest known oil reserves, after Saudi Arabia, and the country has significant unexplored reserves. After the war, the UN, which previously oversaw Iraqi oil sales under its oil-for-food program, gave the U.S. and Britain the authority to administer and develop Iraq's oil industry. Some Iraqis, as well as members of other oil-producing states in the region, fear that the U.S. is seeking to control Iraq's oil to satisfy its own narrow self-interest. U.S. officials have tried to allay these concerns by allowing the Iraqi Governing Council's Oil Ministry, headed by Ibrahim Bahr Al Uloum, to handle the day-to-day affairs of the country's oil industry. However, authority ultimately rests with the U.S.-led Coalition Provisional Authority. The Iraqi Oil Ministry is subject to an oversight board headed by former ConocoPhillips executive Robert E. McKee, leading to concerns that Iraqis may not have a free hand in running the industry. As Iraqis and Americans negotiate control over the country's oil, the U.S. is clearly seeking to avoid the appearance of running roughshod over Iraqi decision-making. The manner in which the U.S. handles Iraq's oil industry will be critical to defusing resentment over Operation Iraqi Freedom.

PREVENTING THE SPREAD OF WEAPONS OF MASS DESTRUCTION

The United States has long been concerned about the spread of weapons of mass destruction (WMD)—nuclear, chemical, and biological weapons—to the Middle East, and elsewhere around the world as well. Given the hostilities that exist in the Middle East, preventing the proliferation of these weapons in this region is an extremely high U.S. priority.

Unfortunately, this is a difficult objective to achieve. It is generally known that Israel already has weapons of mass destruction in its arsenal, even though it has not formally admitted to possessing them. Among other Middle Eastern states, Iran, Iraq, and Libya either have the ability or have tried to develop the ability to make nuclear, chemical, and biological weapons.

Over the last decade, the U.S. has focused its attention in this regard on Iraq, both because of the Persian Gulf War and because of Saddam Hussein's use of chemical weapons in the Iran-Iraq War. Saddam also used chemical weapons against the Kurds, an ethnic group living in Iraq, Iran, and Turkey that has been fighting to establish its own independent state. Although the United States had long been aware of Iraq's efforts to develop WMD, the U.S. and the rest of the international community were amazed to discover after the Persian Gulf War how advanced the Iraqi nuclear, chemical, and biological weapons programs were.

In April 1991, as part of the terms for ending the Persian Gulf War, Iraq accepted UN resolution 687, requiring it to end production of WMD and to allow monitoring by a team of UN inspectors, known as UNSCOM. However, throughout the 1990s, Iraq's relations with the UN, and particularly the U.S., were tumultuous, with recurrent crises only sporadically being offset by periods of cooperation (see Lesson 2: "The Persian Gulf War and Its Continuing Aftermath"). In December 1998, tensions once again escalated when the Iraqi government announced it was ending all cooperation with UN inspectors and refused to allow inspectors access to its facilities. After UN personnel were evacuated, the U.S. and Britain launched massive air strikes to punish the Iraqi regime.

In 2003, the issue of WMD in the Middle East became the center of world attention as the ongoing battle with Iraq over weapons inspections came to a head. Convinced that Saddam Hussein possessed WMD, was developing ties with al Qaeda, and was subverting the inspections process, the U.S. and Britain invaded Iraq in an attempt to overthrow the regime. The allies justified the action by saying the prospect of an Iraqi government that might share WMD with terrorists posed an imminent threat to the U.S. and the world, and therefore warranted preventive military action.

By early 2004, allied forces had yet to find evidence of Iraqi WMD or cooperation between the Iraqi government and al Qaeda. While proof may yet be found, the difficulty in discovering any conclusive evidence has undermined the American and British argument that Saddam's regime constituted the type of imminent threat that justified preventive military action.

Criticism of the American and British governments intensified in June 2003 after it was revealed that some of the allegations made regarding Iraq's pursuit of WMD proved to be incorrect. In addition, some U.S. intelligence officials have said they were pressured by the Bush administration to find evidence justifying the case for war. Others claim that administration officials simply ignored intelligence that did not fit their agenda.[10] When pressed on the issue, Deputy Defense Secretary Paul Wolfowitz acknowledged that the issue of WMD was used to justify war against Iraq "for bureaucratic reasons . . . because it was the one reason everyone could agree on."[11] Nevertheless, President Bush and Prime Minister Blair have strongly denied the charges, saying that while some intelligence was misinterpreted, on balance the intelligence suggested that Saddam Hussein was in possession of WMD.

The U.S. has also expressed concern that Iran may be pursuing WMD. With assistance from Russia, Iran is close to completing several nuclear reactors, which it says are designed only for generating power. In June 2003, Mohamed El Baradei, head of the International Atomic Energy Agency, issued a report accusing Iran of violating some of the "nuclear safeguards agreements" that were intended to prevent civilian energy programs from being used as a cover for weapons programs. The report raised international pressure for inspections of the country's nuclear program to be enhanced. The IAEA set a deadline of October 31, 2003 for Iran to divulge all information regarding its nuclear program and made clear that failure to do so would result in sanctions by the UN Security Council.

While Iran initially refused to comply, in October the foreign ministers of Britain, France, and Germany met with Iranian leaders and convinced them to cooperate. Iran subsequently issued a report in which it admitted to hiding many of the details of its 18-year-old nuclear program and violating its IAEA agreements by producing enriched uranium. Iran agreed to temporarily suspend all uranium-enrichment and plutonium-processing activity, accept intrusive, surprise inspections of its nuclear sites, and adopt an additional inspection protocol that would turn the new rules into law. In November, the IAEA passed a resolution condemning Iran's 18-year cover-up of its nuclear activities, but applauded its newfound cooperation and elected not to refer the matter to the UN Security Council.

However, several countries, particularly the U.S., question Iran's willingness to cooperate and doubt that Iran has given up its nuclear ambitions. Rather, they fear that Iran has simply decided to pursue its nuclear activities narrowly within the limits of international regulations for the time being. The danger is that once Iran is able to enrich uranium and extract plutonium from spent reactor fuel rods, it will have all the skills and materials necessary to eventually withdraw from the Nuclear Nonproliferation Treaty (NPT) with the required 90 days notice and quickly develop nuclear weapons.

Iranian and Arab leaders dismiss the U.S. allegations as politically motivated. They fear that U.S. officials are attempting to create international concern about WMD in order to justify more military action in the region. Furthermore, they argue that the U.S. focus on the proliferation of WMD among Persian and Arab states is hypocritical since Israel is the only Middle Eastern state known to possess nuclear weapons. Concern about Israel's possession of WMD has prompted the 22-nation Arab Group to push for a UN resolution to eliminate all WMD in the region. Leaders from non-nuclear states in the Middle East and other parts of the world also point out that the U.S. is actively developing new generations of nuclear weapons in violation of the NPT. In their eyes, the U.S.'s expansion of its nuclear weapons program and its support for Israeli WMD undermines its moral authority to prevent other states in the region from developing their own programs.

HUMAN RIGHTS AND JUSTICE ISSUES

Human rights and justice issues abound in Middle Eastern affairs. Here, as elsewhere, the United States has long maintained that it is vitally concerned with promoting human rights and justice. And here, again as elsewhere, the United States has two central difficulties with promoting human rights and justice.

The first difficulty is defining human rights and justice in the appropriate regional context. If a government denies rights to its people because of their religious or ethnic background, and that government is based on a culture or religion that approves of such discrimination, should its actions be ignored, or should they be criticized and condemned? If a religion teaches that women should be subservient to men, are women's rights being violated? If two groups have competing claims to a specific piece of land, and both groups' claims go back decades and even centuries, whose land is it? Why?

The second difficulty for the United States is deciding what policies to implement to promote human rights and justice once they are defined. Should the U.S. apply political or economic pressure to influence a country to change practices that the U.S. believes violate human rights or are unjust? If so, what kind of political or economic pressure, and how much? If a country claims that the practices it is implementing are based on its religion, how should this affect the U.S. response? Should military force ever be used to promote human rights and justice? If so, how?

These and related questions are difficult issues to resolve in any context. In the Middle East, they are even more difficult to resolve because of the long histories and deep animosities that lie behind many of the conflicts, and because of the way politics and religion are intertwined throughout the region. These questions are also complicated by alliances and friendships that the U.S. has in the region and by the Western world's need for oil.

Since the September 11 terrorist attacks, the U.S. has increasingly linked its antiterrorism efforts in the Middle East and policy of regime change in Iraq with the cause of promoting freedom and democracy. U.S. officials frequently cite the lack of freedom and openness in Middle Eastern societies as a major cause of the frustration present among Arabs, which is widely seen as a key factor contributing to terrorism in the region.[12] The Bush administration has announced a Middle East Partnership Initiative (MEPI) designed to support democratization through sustained efforts to promote economic development, education, rights for women, and the funding of civil-society organizations.

Initiatives such as MEPI, however, are undercut by a perception in the Middle East and elsewhere that there is a gap between U.S. human-rights rhetoric and U.S. actions. American support for authoritarian regimes in Egypt, Saudi Arabia, and elsewhere in the region is not only a criticism leveled by moderate Arabs, but also a core reason given by Osama bin Laden for why his al Qaeda organization opposes the U.S. The U.S.'s handling of the situation in Iraq, support for Israel's crackdown against the Palestinian *Intifada* (uprising), and strategic interests in the region's oil further contribute to the Arab public's skepticism about the sincerity of the U.S.'s pro-democracy rhetoric. Often, the rhetoric is viewed as a means to extend American hegemony by lowering resistance to U.S. policies.

While Arabs may be wary of U.S. intentions, many recognize the urgent need to improve the human-rights situation in the region. In July 2002, the UN published the landmark Arab Development Report, which was notable for the fact that it was written entirely by Arabs. The report is highly critical, citing a "freedom deficit" and "women's empowerment deficit" as major causes of the region's relative lack of development. A follow-up report, published in 2003, also stressed a "knowledge deficit."

Some efforts are being made by Middle Easterners to improve the region's human-rights record. From the work of the Jordanian first lady, Queen Rania Al-Abdullah, to promote the rights of women, to the increasing political openness, though not democracy, seen in Jordan, Kuwait, Morocco, Qatar, and elsewhere, progress has been made. As the world grows ever more interconnected and the "globalization" phenomenon continues, it is hoped that more positive social, economic, and political change will be seen in the Middle East, with the recognition that this change will take place within the region's unique cultural context.

An Iraqi man places human remains in a plastic bag for identification at the site of a mass grave where over 3,000 bodies were unearthed at Hilla, 100 kilometers south of Baghdad, May 15, 2003. The discovery of graves across Iraq brought bitter relief for those desperate for closure after years of worrying about the fate of missing relatives.

President George W. Bush greets troops after arriving at Baghdad International Airport, Thursday, November 27, 2003. Bush paid a surprise Thanksgiving Day visit to American troops in Baghdad.

LESSON 1

U.S. INTERESTS IN THE MIDDLE EAST

Activity 1

Why is the United States interested in Middle Eastern affairs?

ACTIVITY OBJECTIVE

The student will identify and evaluate reasons for U.S. interest in the Middle East.

MATERIALS AND RESOURCES

❑ SCIS Background Reading, Lesson One, "U.S. Interests in the Middle East"
❑ SCIS Videotape, *The Middle East in Transition*, Lesson 1, "U.S. Interests in the Middle East"
❑ Worksheet 1.1, "U.S. Interests in the Middle East"

STRATEGIES

Although the Middle East is located thousands of miles from its borders, the United States has demonstrated considerable interest in Middle Eastern affairs. Reasons for this interest and involvement are many and varied. Five primary reasons are discussed in the background reading:

   1) regional stability and geostrategic concerns;
   2) maintenance of a free and independent Israel;
   3) availability of and access to oil;
   4) preventing the spread of weapons of mass destruction; and
   5) human rights and justice issues.

Familiarize students with these reasons by dividing the class into groups of five students. Provide each group with a single copy of the SCIS Background Reading, Lesson One, "U.S. Interests in the Middle East" and have each student in the group become an "expert" on one of the five reasons in order to teach the reason to other members of the group. The group will need to cut the essay into its five sections so that each student has access to one of the five reasons. Students from across all the groups who have the same reason should meet in "expert groups" to come to a consensus regarding the main points in the essay. Worksheet 1.1, "U.S. Interests in the Middle East," provides a form for recording the major points of the essay.

After reviewing the essay, show students the SCIS videotape, *The Middle East in Transition*, Lesson 1, "U.S. Interests in the Middle East." This will provide students with the perspectives of former U.S. Secretaries of State and Defense on U.S. interests in the Middle East. Each student expert will then return to his or her original group to teach his or her classmates.

To conclude this activity, the teacher should lead a class discussion to clarify any points which students find unclear. At the end of the videotape, former Secretary of State George Shultz acknowledges the continued importance of Persian Gulf oil to the United States, but goes beyond this issue to speak of the creation of a "new world order," which is forming in the post-Cold War era. Have students discuss what this new world order might be and place the Gulf Wars in the context of these newly emerging alliances.

Reuters/Raheb Homavandi

Iranian women fill in their ballots for the parliamentary elections in Tehran, February 20, 2004. Voting was overshadowed by a ban on most reformist candidates and a crackdown on pro-reform media.

U.S. INTERESTS IN THE MIDDLE EAST

Directions: Use the section of the Background Reading for Lesson 1 to answer the related questions.

I. Regional stability and geostrategic concerns

    A. What was U.S. policy in the Middle East from the 1940s through the 1960s?

    B. What was the "Twin Pillar" strategy?

    C. How did the United States address the collapse of the "Twin Pillar" strategy?

        1.

        2.

        3.

II. Maintenance of a free and independent Israel

    A. Why has the United States been closely identified with Israel?

        1.

        2.

        3.

        4.

    B. In what areas do the United States and Israel disagree?

        1.

        2.

        3.

III. Availability of and access to oil

A. How dependent is the world on oil from the Middle East?

1. Middle East Reserves —

2. U.S. Dependency —

3. Western European Dependency —

4. Japanese Dependency —

B. What was the role of oil in the Iraqi invasion of Kuwait?

IV. Weapons of mass destruction

A. What Middle Eastern countries have the ability or are trying to develop the ability to make nuclear, chemical, and/or biological weapons?

B. What discovery has guaranteed the continuation of the U.S. policy objective of preventing the spread of weapons of mass destruction?

V. Human rights and justice issues

A. What are the two central difficulties involved with promoting human rights and justice in the Middle East?

1.

2.

B. Why are these issues difficult to resolve?

LESSON 1

U.S. INTERESTS IN THE MIDDLE EAST

Activity 2

What is the significance of Middle Eastern oil?

ACTIVITY OBJECTIVE

The student will identify the major sources of oil in the Persian Gulf region and analyze their importance in the world market.

MATERIALS AND RESOURCES

❑ SCIS Videotape, *The Middle East in Transition*, Lesson 1, "U.S. Interests in the Middle East"
❑ Worksheet 1.2, "The Flow of Oil"
❑ Worksheet 1.3, "Oil Production and Consumption Comparisons"

STRATEGIES

The largest oil deposits in the world are located in the Persian Gulf region of the Middle East. Former Secretary of State Cyrus Vance acknowledges that the uninterrupted flow of oil from the region is of vital interest to the U.S. and to many other countries. Worksheet 1.2, "The Flow of Oil," provides students the opportunity to chart the flow of oil from the Gulf and identify strategic geopolitical "choke points" where the oil flow could be stopped. Distribute the worksheet to students and assist them in identifying the countries that control the oil reserves and the routes which tankers follow when shipping oil from the Gulf to various parts of the world. Students should conclude that the flow of oil can be stopped at several different locations.

It is also important that students recognize that oil production in the Persian Gulf represents a significant percentage of the world oil market. Students should also understand the extent to which the United States economy is dependent on Persian Gulf oil. Distribute Worksheet 1.3, "Oil Production and Consumption Comparisons," to provide students a statistical comparison of:

1) total energy consumption and imports in the United States, and
2) estimated world oil production and oil reserves.

The teacher should conclude this activity by showing the SCIS videotape, *The Middle East in Transition*, Lesson 1, "U.S. Interests in the Middle East," and by leading a discussion of the political implications of the data previously analyzed and the commentary of the former Secretaries on oil issues. Be sure to ask students to evaluate former Secretary of State George Shultz's proposal that the way to reduce America's energy consumption is "to get gasoline priced somewhere near where it's priced in all the rest of the developed world . . . so I think we should impose a great big tax on gasoline."

A Norwegian-flagged oil tanker, Kronviken, sails past Istanbul's Ottoman-built Ortakoy Mosque, which juts out into the Bosphorus Strait, May 11, 2002.

THE FLOW OF OIL

Directions: Read the following text and record the information requested on the appropriate map.

Where the Oil is Located

The largest oil deposits in the world are in the Middle East. Several members of the 13-member Organization of Petroleum Exporting Countries (OPEC) are located in the region. Find the countries on the map of the Middle East and enter the data regarding the percentage of the world's known oil reserves found in that country.

Algeria* 0.9%	Kuwait 9.4%	Saudi Arabia . . . 25.4%
Egypt* 0.3%	Libya 2.9%	United Arab
Iran 8.7%	Oman* 0.5%	Emirates 9.5%
Iraq 10.1%	Qatar 1.5%	Yemen* 0.4%

*Non-OPEC member

Source: Energy Information Administration, *International Energy Annual* 2001, Table 8.1

Shade all the countries with 5 percent or more of the world's known oil deposits. What percentage of the world's oil is found in those states located near the Persian Gulf?

Three Major Shipping Routes

Oil from the Persian Gulf region is carried by tankers through the Gulf to the Arabian Sea to states around the globe. The oil from the Gulf follows three main routes.

Route One. Locate the point at which the Persian Gulf joins the Arabian Sea. Draw a line from this point southwest to the Red Sea. Continue the line through the Red Sea, northwest to the Mediterranean Sea. The Suez Canal, in Egypt, connects these two seas. After leaving the canal, many tankers take their oil to ports in the Mediterranean such as: Naples, Italy; Marseilles, France; and Barcelona, Spain. Draw lines from the Suez Canal to these cities. Other tankers continue westward across the Mediterranean and into the Atlantic Ocean. They deliver their oil to ports such as Antwerp, Belgium and Hamburg, Germany. Continue your lines to these port cities.

Route Two. Begin where the Persian Gulf joins the Arabian Sea. Draw a line southward along the east coast of Africa to the Cape of Good Hope. Continue northward along the coast of Africa to the equator. At the equator, split your line into two branches. Draw the first as an arrow pointing toward Europe and the second as an arrow from the equator to the east coast of the U.S.

Route Three. Begin at the Persian Gulf. Draw a line toward Mumbai (Bombay), India, then toward the southeast to Malaysia through the Strait of Malacca. Continue your line northeast to Japan and to China.

THE FLOW OF OIL

Summary

More than one-half of the world's oil is found near the Persian Gulf. Every tanker passes through the strait that connects the Gulf and the Arabian Sea—the Strait of Hormuz. If this strait were blocked, the flow of oil from the Gulf would stop. If the oil were stopped for long, all the countries that depend on it would be in trouble. "Choke points" where the oil flow could be stopped are listed below. Locate them on the world map. For each, decide which parts of the world would be most affected if the oil were stopped there.

• Strait of Hormuz (at the south end of the Persian Gulf)

• The Suez Canal (between the Red Sea and the Mediterranean)

• The Strait of Gibraltar (between Spain and Morocco)

• Bab el Mandeb (at the south end of the Red Sea)

• Strait of Malacca (near Malaysia)

THE FLOW OF OIL

Outline Map of the Middle East

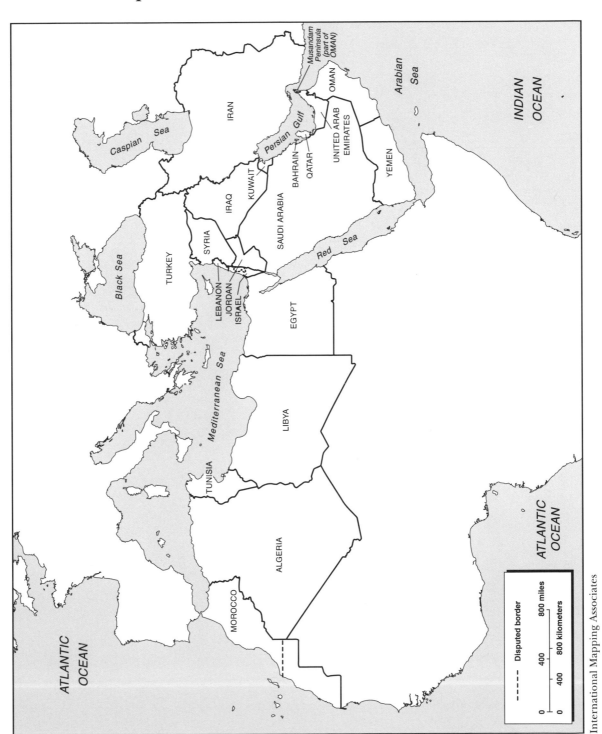

International Mapping Associates

THE FLOW OF OIL

Outline Map of the World

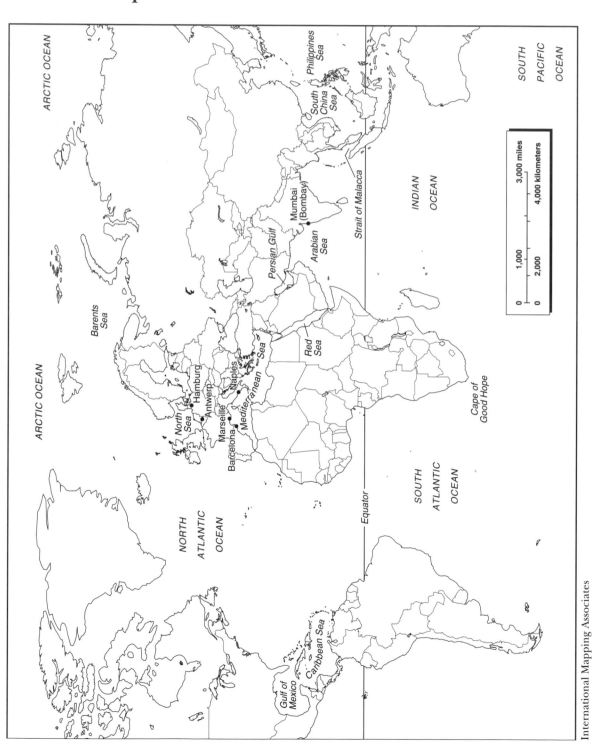

International Mapping Associates

OIL PRODUCTION AND CONSUMPTION COMPARISONS

Total U.S. Energy Consumption, 2002

Source: Energy Information Administration, *Monthly Energy Review,* October 2003.

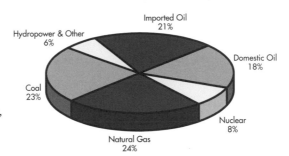

Imports of Crude Oil into the U.S. by Import Group

Source: Energy Information Administration, *Petroleum Supply Annual,* 2001, Vol. 1.

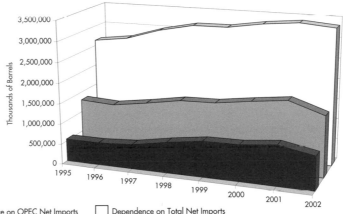

■ Dependence on Arab OPEC Net Imports   ■ Dependence on OPEC Net Imports   □ Dependence on Total Net Imports

World Crude Oil Flow

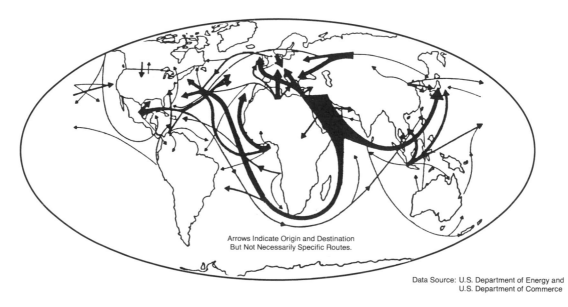

Arrows Indicate Origin and Destination But Not Necessarily Specific Routes.

Data Source: U.S. Department of Energy and U.S. Department of Commerce

OIL PRODUCTION AND CONSUMPTION COMPARISONS

World Oil Production, 2001

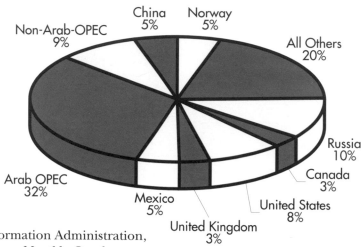

Source: Energy Information Administration, *International Petroleum Monthly,* October 2003.

Source: Energy Information Administration, *International Petroleum Monthly,* October 2003.

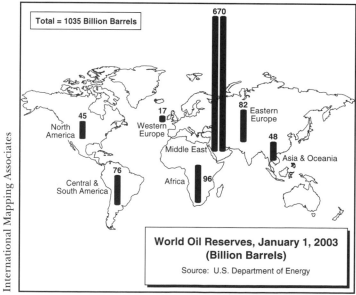

International Mapping Associates

Arab OPEC Countries	World Production
Algeria	2.0%
Iraq	3.0%
Kuwait	2.8%
Libya	2.0%
Qatar	1.0%
Saudi Arabia	11.4%
United Arab Emirates	3.1%
Total	**24.8%**

Non-Arab OPEC	World Production
Indonesia	1.9%
Iran	5.2%
Nigeria	3.2%
Venezuela	3.9%
Total	**14.1%**

OIL PRODUCTION AND CONSUMPTION COMPARISONS

Study Questions

Total Energy Consumption and Imports in the United States

1) Oil accounts for what percentage of total U.S. energy consumption? According to the map of crude oil flow, from what parts of the world does the U.S. import oil?

2) What percentage of U.S. oil imports come from OPEC countries? What percentage of U.S. oil comes from Arab OPEC countries? Given these data, how do oil needs become matters of concern in international politics, particularly countries bordering the Persian Gulf?

3) During what years did the U.S. import the largest percentage of oil? During what years were imports the lowest? Who were the U.S. presidents during these years? What policies were in effect which might have affected these changes? What is the current status of oil imports? What are the political, economic and environmental implications of these figures?

4) What other energy sources are available in the U.S.? What are the political, economic, and environmental implications of these alternatives? Of all the energy sources, which do you feel holds the most promise for the future? Why?

Estimated World Oil Production and Oil Reserves

1) What is the total oil production of both Arab and non-Arab OPEC countries? Why is Iran listed as a non-Arab OPEC country?

2) What percentage of the world's oil comes from the Gulf region?

3) Which of the Middle Eastern OPEC countries have traditionally been allies of the United States? With which of the Middle Eastern OPEC countries has the United States had difficult relations in recent years?

4) The world map clearly shows the predominant position of the Middle East with regard to oil reserves. What percentage of the world's known oil reserves are located in the Middle East? in North America?

5) What are the political implications of these data?

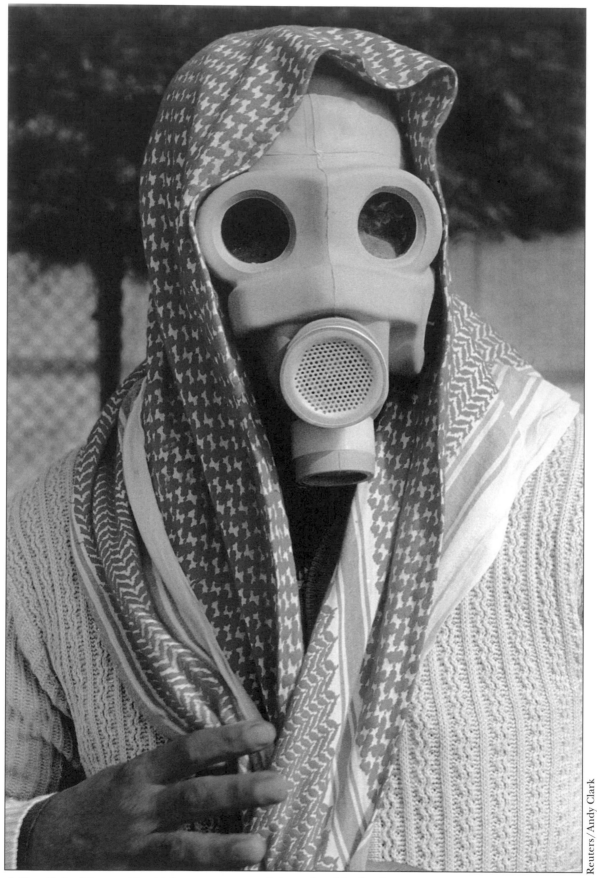

A Saudi Arabian resident tries on a gas mask issued to him by the government in Dhahran, Saudi Arabia on January 10, 1991. Residents were issued gas masks just prior to the Gulf War in the event Iraq used chemical weapons during the conflict.

LESSON 1

U.S. INTERESTS IN THE MIDDLE EAST

Activity 3

What should U.S. policy be with respect to weapons of mass destruction (WMD) in the Middle East?

ACTIVITY OBJECTIVE

The student will examine the issue of weapons of mass destruction in the Middle East and write a position paper on the topic.

MATERIALS AND RESOURCES

❑ SCIS Videotape, *The Middle East in Transition*, Lesson 1, "U.S. Interests in the Middle East"
❑ Teacher Resource 1.1, "Weapons of Mass Destruction"
❑ Teacher Resource 0.1, "Political Map of the Middle East"
❑ Handout 1.1, "Iran: Nuclear Weapons"
❑ Handout 1.2, "Iraq: Whodunnit?"
❑ Handout 1.3, "Israel's Arsenal Is Point of Contention"

STRATEGIES

Given the hostilities that exist in the Middle East, preventing the spread of weapons of mass destruction in the region is an extremely high U.S. priority. In 2003, the issue of WMD in the Middle East became the focus of world attention as the decade-long battle with Iraq over weapons inspections came to a head. Convinced that Saddam Hussein possessed WMD and was subverting the inspections process, the U.S. and Britain invaded Iraq and overthrew Saddam's regime. In 2004, international pressure led Iran and Libya to allow international inspections of their nuclear programs. In much of the Middle East, however, the U.S. focus on the proliferation of WMD in Persian and Arab states is seen as hypocritical, since Israel is the only Middle Eastern state known to possess nuclear weapons. The Israelis also have chemical and biological weapons. This activity allows students to explore the complex issues surrounding efforts to control the spread of WMD in the Middle East.

Start this activity by showing the class the discussion on weapons in the Middle East by the former Secretaries of Defense on the SCIS Videotape, *The Middle East in Transition*, Lesson 1, "U.S. Interests in the Middle East." Point out to the students that this discussion took place in 1992, just after the collapse of the Soviet Union. Ask the class:

- What does James Schlesinger think about nuclear weapons?
- Who does David Gergen point to as the primary distributor of conventional weapons to Iran?
- What is said about the U.S. sale of conventional weapons?

Next, introduce students to the concept of WMD by projecting Teacher Resource 1.1, "Weapons of Mass Destruction." Ask the class: Why are nuclear, chemical, and biological weapons singled out? [*Answer: As is implied by the term "weapons of mass destruction," they are singled out because their capacity to inflict death and destruction is far greater than that of conventional weapons.*]

After the class understands the concept of WMD, project a transparency of Teacher Resource 0.1, "Political Map of the Middle East." Using Table 1, fill in the countries that have pursued programs to develop weapons of mass destruction. First mark the countries that have had a biological weapons program. With a second colored pen, mark the countries that have had a chemical weapons program. With a third color, mark the countries that have had a nuclear program. As an alternative, the teacher may distribute the map and chart to the students, so that they can fill in/color maps individually.

Note to students that not all countries suspected of developing a nuclear program are believed to have produced nuclear weapons. For example, some countries may still be in the research and development stage. Others may have a functioning nuclear power plant used to produce energy, but lack the ability to enrich uranium, which is necessary to produce nuclear weapons. While Israel is the only country in the Middle East believed to have produced nuclear weapons, the existence of a nuclear program is one indication that a country may be pursuing nuclear weapons.

Table 1: **Weapons of Mass Destruction in the Middle East**

Country	Biological Weapons Program	Chemical Weapons Program	Nuclear Program
Algeria			X
Egypt	X	X	
Iran	X	X	X
Iraq	X	X	X
Israel	X	X	X*
Libya	X	X	X
Sudan		X	
Syria	X	X	

*Believed to have developed weapons

Source: "States Possessing, Pursuing, or Capable of Acquiring Weapons of Mass Destruction," Federation of American Scientists, http://www.fas.org/irp/threat/wmd_state.htm (accessed March 16, 2004).

To conclude this portion of the activity, ask the students such questions as:

- How many countries in the Middle East are believed to have pursued WMD? [8]
- Which countries have pursued more than one type of WMD? [6]
- Why do you think these countries want to have WMD? [*Answers will vary.*]
- What are the geopolitical implications? [*Answers will vary.*]
- What is the Non-proliferation Treaty (NPT) and why is it important? [*The NPT is an international treaty whose objective is to prevent the spread of nuclear weapons and weapons technology, to promote cooperation in the peaceful uses of nuclear energy, and to further the goal of achieving nuclear disarmament. In the treaty, nuclear states agree not to assist states not possessing nuclear explosives in obtaining or producing them. Non-nuclear states pledge not to pursue nuclear weapons. The treaty does, however, permit the exchange of equipment, materials, and scientific and technological information for the peaceful uses of nuclear energy. The treaty also establishes a safeguards system in which inspections by the International Atomic Energy Agency (IAEA) are used to verify compliance. The treaty is based on the understanding that, in exchange for compliance by non-nuclear states, nuclear states will gradually work to destroy their nuclear arsenals and to refrain from developing new nuclear weapons.*]
- Why do you think that more countries have pursued chemical/biological weapons than nuclear? [*They are less expensive and easier to produce. The technology and skill required to enrich uranium or process weapons-grade plutonium is extremely advanced.*]
- In general, what is the United States' relationship to these countries? [*Answers will vary.*]

To continue the activity, divide the class into three groups, each of which will focus on a different country suspected of having pursued WMD. Distribute to each group one of the following: Handout 1.1, "Iran: Nuclear Weapons," Handout 1.2, "Iraq: Whodunnit?," or Handout 1.3, "Israel's Arsenal Is Point of Contention." Each student in the group will need his or her own copy of the group article. The groups should designate a discussion leader, a recorder, and a presenter. Remind the groups that they should follow the rules of cooperative learning.

The groups should read and discuss their article, and then prepare a presentation for the class that answers the following questions, which can be projected:

- What is the history of WMD in this country?
- How advanced is this country's nuclear program?
- Why should the U.S. and other countries be concerned about the spread of WMD in this country?
- How have the U.S. and the international community reacted to WMD in this country?
- What are the pros and cons of the way the international community has responded to the development of WMD?
- Are there any biases noted in your article?
- Has the U.S. turned a blind eye to some programs and not to others?

The group recorder will write the answers prepared by the group, but each group member should take his or her own notes for use later in the activity. After all the groups have made their presentations, the teacher should ask the class:

- What are the similarities in the ways that the international community has responded?

- What are the differences?
- Does there seem to be a best way to respond to these situations or is each situation so unique that it needs to be handled differently?

Note that as an extension, the groups can research their country online before making their presentations. A good starting point for research is the Infolinks page on www.southerncenter.org.

To conclude the activity and to assess students' understanding of WMD and U.S. policy in the region, have the students write a one-page, single-spaced, five-paragraph position paper on what they think the U.S. should do, if anything, to prevent the proliferation of WMD in the Middle East. In order to write the paper the students will need their notes from the group discussion and presentations as well as copies of the three articles. The teacher should tell the students how their papers will be graded.

WEAPONS OF MASS DESTRUCTION

Nuclear Weapons

Incredibly powerful bombs that derive their force from either the fission or the fusion of atomic nuclei. Examples include atomic bombs and thermonuclear bombs. A ten-megaton nuclear bomb has the power to destroy everything within an 11-mile radius, an area the size of New York City.

Chemical Weapons

Weapons that release toxic gases or liquids that attack the body's nervous system, blood, skin, or lungs. Chemical weapons have been in use since World War I. Examples include mustard gas, Agent Orange, sarin, and VX.

Biological Weapons

Weapons that infect humans, animals, or plants with disease-producing biological agents, such as bacteria and viruses. The use of biological weapons goes back hundreds of years. Examples include anthrax, botulinum toxin, and smallpox.

IRAN: NUCLEAR WEAPONS

By Sharon Otterman

What steps are being taken to curb Iran's nuclear program?

Iranian officials have admitted to the United Nations International Atomic Energy Agency (IAEA) that they have been secretly developing a broad range of nuclear capabilities for the past 18 years. The IAEA board decided not to sanction Iran for these disclosures. Instead, on November 26 [2003] it adopted a resolution that condemned Iran's past violations of IAEA rules and welcomed Iran's new pledges of cooperation. In recent weeks, Iran has agreed to snap weapons inspections and a temporary halt to its uranium enrichment program.

What is the Bush administration's reaction to this deal?

Secretary of State Colin Powell said November 26 he was "very happy" with the IAEA resolution. But U.S. officials had been pushing for stronger action against Iran. Specifically, they wanted Iran to be declared in breach of the 1968 Nuclear Non-proliferation Treaty (NPT) and for the matter to be referred to the UN Security Council, which could then impose sanctions. U.S. officials failed to convince a majority of countries on the 35-member IAEA board that this step was required. According to *The New York Times*, only Canada, Australia, and Japan agreed to support the U.S. position.

Why did most countries push for a compromise?

One reason was that the IAEA did not consider Iran's many violations of specific nonproliferation rules proof that Iran had a nuclear weapons program. This conclusion led to outrage on the part of the U.S. representative to the IAEA, Kenneth Brill, who said the Iranian government had "systematically and deliberately deceived the IAEA and the international community about these issues for year after year after year" to further its "pursuit of nuclear weapons." Many international nuclear experts have agreed that the types of experiments Iran was conducting—such as uranium enrichment by laser—strongly suggest the existence of a nuclear weapons program.

Another reason was that officials from France, Germany, and Britain were eager to encourage so-called pragmatic leaders in Iran who are pressing for greater engagement with the international community, rather than continued isolation. Hardliners in Iran have argued that their country—which the State Department classifies as the leading state sponsor of terrorism—should drop out of the NPT and speed up development of a nuclear bomb. This path, similar to the one pursued by North Korea, would have escalated the crisis, proponents of engagement say.

What does the new IAEA resolution say about Iran's nuclear program?

It "strongly deplores Iran's past failures" to disclose its nuclear program and calls on Iran "to undertake and complete the taking of all necessary corrective measures on an urgent basis," according to press reports. The IAEA's latest analysis of Iran's nuclear program found "that Iran has failed in a number of instances over an extended period of time to meet its obligations" with respect to the reporting, processing, and use of nuclear materials. However, it found "no evidence" that Iran was pursuing nuclear weapons—a phrase IAEA head Mohammed El Baradei later explained meant "no proof" in a legal sense.

What would happen if Iran violates more IAEA rules?

The agency would then be able to use "all options at its disposal" to punish Iran, according to the IAEA resolution. U.S. diplomats say this language is a veiled reference to UN Security Council action.

Does Iran have a program to build nuclear weapons?

Many international officials and weapons experts believe it does. The Bush administration is concerned that a nuclear-armed Iran, one of the three nations in the group President Bush labeled the "axis of evil," would further destabilize the Persian Gulf region and possibly give terrorists access to weapons of mass destruction.

Why does Washington suspect Iran is seeking nuclear weapons?

Iran's secret nuclear program included all the steps needed to make fissile material for a nuclear bomb. U.S. officials argue that Iran would not have denied the existence of a peaceful nuclear energy program. Iran also has the world's sixth-largest oil reserves, raising suspicions about why it would spend billions of dollars to develop nuclear power plants. Iranian officials, however, say their program is committed to nuclear power and other peaceful uses.

Will the new agreement prevent Iran from getting a nuclear weapon?

It's unclear. Some experts and international officials argue that the new, more rigorous IAEA inspection protocol, coupled with Iran's desire to engage with the international community, will dissuade it from seeking nuclear weapons. Others point out that powerful elements within the Iranian govern-ment, including the leadership of the Revolutionary Guards, remain intent on acquiring the capability to develop atomic weapons, raising concerns that Iran might continue to conceal parts of its nuclear program. Nuclear experts also warn that, under the terms of the NPT, Iran can legally develop a peaceful nuclear power program, then drop out and rapidly convert it to an illegal weapons program. According to the NPT, Iran may build any nuclear facility, including uranium enrichment plants to create nuclear fuel, as long as the facility is devoted to peaceful uses and subject to IAEA safeguards and inspections.

When could Iran have a nuclear weapon?

The Bush administration has been operating on the assumption that Iran could have a nuclear bomb by 2006 if no steps are taken to slow the program, says Kenneth Katzman, a specialist in Middle East affairs for the Congressional Research Service. On June 11 [2003], Secretary of Defense Donald H. Rumsfeld said, "The assessment is that they [the Iranians] do have a very active program and are likely to have nuclear weapons in a relatively short period of time." Previous administration forecasts—made before Iran's stepped-up uranium enrichment activities were discovered in February 2003—indicated Iran could go nuclear by the end of the decade.

Sharon Otterman is a staff writer at cfr.org, the Web site of the Council on Foreign Relations.

Source: Council on Foreign Relations, November 25, 2003,
http://www.cfr.org/background/iran_nuclear.php.

IRAQ: WHODUNNIT?

WHEN many were sceptical, David Kay* was once confident that some dodgy trailers found in Iraq were mobile biological facilities. He was likewise sure that some aluminium tubes were evidence of Saddam Hussein's pursuit of nuclear weapons. That such a hawkish analyst should now say—as Mr. Kay has done since resigning last week as America's chief weapons-hunter in Iraq— that there is probably not much more to find, is more than a little awkward for George Bush. "We were all wrong," Mr. Kay told senators, "and that is most disturbing." He has changed his mind about the trailers and the tubes.

The first findings that Mr. Kay reported to Congress last October, though slim, did give some succour to advocates of the war. Mr. Kay's team had found some undeclared laboratories that might have been suitable for WMD research, evidence of work on illegal missiles, and

other violations of UN resolutions. But the post-war inspectors had turned up minimal evidence of chemical and nuclear activity, and no actual weapons. Mr. Kay now believes that Iraq's WMD stockpiles were destroyed during the 1990s. The chemical-protection suits discovered by advancing American soldiers, Mr. Kay told *The New York Times*, were intended for protection against possible chemical attack by Israel, rather than one launched by Iraq itself.

If the ex-inspector is right, two questions arise. Why on earth did Mr. Hussein act as guiltily as he did— and why did Britain and America think he was such a menace? Mr. Kay has thoughts on both issues. He speculated that Mr. Hussein may have been deceived by his own scientists into financing, and believing in, non-existent weapons programmes, as Iraq descended into what he described as a "vortex

of corruption" in the late 1990s. Some in the intelligence world doubt that theory; the idea that ingratiating scientists promised Mr. Hussein more than they were able to deliver may be more plausible.

Mr. Kay has also mentioned the possibility that Mr. Hussein was the architect of the deceit, rather than its victim. To maintain international prestige, to deter invasion, or for some other half-baked reason, he may have wanted the world to believe he retained a capacity to inflict massive destruction, while at the same time hoping that international sanctions against Iraq might be lifted if there were no tangible proof of his arsenal. The targets of his deception may have been his internal underlings and enemies, as well as international ones: Iraqi commanders, Mr. Kay has reported, seemed to believe that other units were armed with "special" weapons to help them

---

* In June 2003 President Bush directed the Central Intelligence Agency to hunt for Iraqi weapons of mass destruction, and CIA Director George Tenet appointed Dr. David Kay to lead that search and direct the activities of the 1,400-member Iraq Survey Group. In January 2004, having concluded that there had been no stockpiles of weapons of mass destruction in Iraq at the time of the war, Dr. Kay reported that conclusion and resigned his position.

fend off the invaders, even though they themselves had none.

Distressingly for the spooks, Mr. Kay's answer to the other question—about the Anglo-American case for war—is that the intelligence on which it relied was faulty. Like others, he thinks that after the UN inspectors left Iraq in 1998, the intelligence agencies were over reliant on satellite images, intercepted communications, foreign spies, and Iraqi defectors and exiles. Without the UN inspectors' help, the resulting hypotheses could not be checked on the ground. (Other explanations include an over-compensation for having under-estimated Iraq's WMD progress before the Gulf War of 1991; hyper-sensitivity induced by September 11th; and a failure by the CIA to correct the worst imaginings of Mr. Bush's administration.) A major overhaul of the intelligence system looks necessary.

There is little sign yet of either the CIA or MI6 (Britain's foreign-intelligence service) retracting their pre-war assessments. The Brits still think Iraq did indeed retain a capability to make chemical agents "just-in-time" (something Mr. Kay now doubts), and that it had mobile biological facilities, leftover Scuds and active plans to import "yellowcake" uranium from Niger. MI6's yellowcake allegation derives from information shared by the intelligence services of two other countries, and not passed on to the Americans. Mr. Kay reportedly said he found no evidence to substantiate that claim. But if, in the Kay view, the spies got it largely wrong, the American and British air forces got it right, since bombing in 1998 destroyed much of Iraq's residual WMD infrastructure. The UN inspectors, he believes, also had a more disabling impact on Mr. Hussein's schemes than their detractors have maintained.

Mr. Kay has not alleged any "sexing-up" or bullying by politicians, a small mercy for Mr. Bush. But his remarks, seized on by the president's Democratic rivals, leave the president in a tight spot. In October, Mr. Kay had observed that "our understanding of Iraq's WMD programme was always bounded by large uncertainties and had to be heavily caveated." Such caveats, most necessary in relation to Iraq's supposed nuclear programme, were largely dropped by Mr. Bush and his aides in their pre-war statements. Some in his administration—though not the robustly unapologetic vice-president—now seem to be inserting them retrospectively, and Mr. Bush himself is emphasizing Mr. Hussein's general badness. But the questions raised by Mr. Kay's volte-face may only go away if an independent inquiry is set up to answer them.

Source: *The Economist*, January 29, 2004.

ISRAEL'S ARSENAL IS POINT OF CONTENTION

By Douglas Frantz

Israel has modified American-supplied cruise missiles to carry nuclear warheads on submarines, giving the Middle East's only nuclear power the ability to launch atomic weapons from land, air and beneath the sea, according to senior Bush administration and Israeli officials.

The previously undisclosed submarine capability bolsters Israel's deterrence in the event that Iran—an avowed enemy—develops nuclear weapons. It also complicates efforts by the United States and the United Nations to persuade Iran to abandon its suspected nuclear weapons program. . . .

Arab diplomats and UN officials said Israel's steady enhancement of its secret nuclear arsenal, and U.S. silence about it, has increased the desire of Arab states for similar weapons.

"The presence of a nuclear program in the region that is not under international safeguards gives other countries the spur to develop weapons of mass destruction," said Nabil Fahmy, Egypt's ambassador to the United States. "Any future conflict becomes more dangerous." . . .

Israel will not confirm or deny that it possesses nuclear arms. Intelligence analysts and independent experts have long known that the country has 100 to 200 sophisticated nuclear weapons.

Israel, India and Pakistan are the only countries with nuclear facilities that have not signed the Nuclear Nonproliferation Treaty, which was initiated in 1968 to stop the spread of nuclear weapons through inspections and sanctions. India and Pakistan also have nuclear bombs.

Iran and Arab states with civilian nuclear programs have signed the treaty. The Arab countries have refused to agree to tougher inspections because Israel will not sign it, UN officials said.

"A big source of contention is Israel," said a senior official trying to win acceptance of the additional inspections. "This is a magnet for other countries to develop nuclear weapons." . . .

While not acknowledging the country's nuclear capability, Israeli officials have promised they would not "introduce" such weapons to the Middle East. Israeli and U.S. officials said that means Israel would not launch a first strike using the weapons. They argue that other countries have nothing to fear from Israel's nuclear arms, whereas Israel has everything to fear from its neighbors. . . .

Since 1969, Washington has accepted Israel's status as a nuclear power and not pressured it to sign the nonproliferation treaty.

"We tolerate nuclear weapons in Israel for the same reason we tolerate them in Britain and France," a senior administration official said. "We don't regard Israel as a threat." . . .

Growing Vulnerability

Israel is smaller than New Jersey and its population of 6 million is within reach of missiles from Iran and other neighbors. As Iran and other countries in the region improved their long-range missiles in the

65

1990s, Israel's land-based nuclear weapons became vulnerable to attack.

The strategic alternative was to develop nuclear-armed submarines, which would be almost invulnerable, said Robert S. Norris, a nuclear historian at the Natural Resources Defense Council in Washington.

Israel ordered three specially designed submarines from Germany in the mid-1990s and they were delivered in 1999 and 2000. The diesel-powered vessels have a range of several thousand miles and can remain at sea for up to a month.

The attempt to arm them with nuclear missiles was first disclosed in a book published in June 2002 by the Carnegie Endowment. . . .

The consensus in the U.S. intelligence community and among outside experts is that Israel, with possibly 200 nuclear weapons, has the fifth- or sixth-largest arsenal in the world.

Under the nonproliferation treaty, five countries are permitted nuclear weapons. Britain has 185, the smallest number among the five, according

to the Stockholm International Peace Research Institute. The group estimated that Russia has 8,232 weapons; the United States, 7,068; China, 402; and France, 348.

Israel has about double the number of India and Pakistan. North Korea claims to have nuclear weapons, but U.S. intelligence officials are uncertain whether that is true. Estimates of the number have ranged from one or two to six.

A Deal With France

Israel began building a nuclear bomb in the mid-1950s when hostile neighbors surrounded the young country and the Holocaust was fresh in the minds of its leaders.

A secret agreement with the French government in 1956 helped Israel build a plutonium nuclear reactor. . . .

The reactor site was in a remote corner of the Negev desert, outside the village of Dimona.

It was a massive project, with as many as 1,500 Israeli and French workers building the reactor and an extensive underground complex on 14 square

miles. French military aircraft secretly flew heavy water, a key component of a plutonium reactor, from Norway to Israel, according to the Federation of American Scientists in Washington.

American U-2 spy planes spotted the construction soon after it began in 1958. Israel initially said it was a textile plant and later a metallurgical research facility. Two years later, U.S. intelligence identified the site as a nuclear reactor and the CIA said it was part of a weapons program, according to documents at the National Archives in Washington.

In December 1960, Israeli Prime Minister David Ben Gurion told the Israeli parliament that a nuclear reactor was under construction, but he said it was exclusively for peaceful purposes. . . .

American teams visited Dimona seven times during the 1960s and reported that they could find no evidence of a weapons program. . . .

By early 1968, Carl Duckett, then deputy director of the CIA office of science and technology, had concluded that Israel had nuclear weapons, according to testimony he gave to the Nuclear Regulatory Commission in 1974. . . .

The proof surfaced 17 years later. On Oct. 5, 1986, *The Sunday Times* of London published an article in which a former Dimona technician, Mordechai Vanunu, provided a detailed look at Israel's nuclear weapons program. His cache included diagrams and photographs from inside the complex, which he said had produced enough plutonium for 100 bombs since it went online in 1964.

To conceal the weapons work from U.S. inspectors, a false wall had been built to hide elevators that descended six stories beneath the desert floor to facilities where plutonium was refined and bomb parts were manufactured, Vanunu said.

Shortly before the article was published, a female agent from Israel's intelligence service lured Vanunu from London to Rome. He was kidnapped and smuggled back to Israel, where he was convicted of treason in a

secret trial and sentenced to 18 years in prison. . . .

Israel has never openly tested nuclear weapons. Experts said the Israelis have used supercomputers, some supplied by the U.S., to conduct simulations for designing weapons. Components also can be tested using conventional explosives.

An Open Secret

Israel's nuclear program remains shrouded by a policy it calls "nuclear ambiguity." The phrase means Israel does not acknowledge its nuclear capability and suffer the accompanying political and economic fallout, yet it gains the benefit of deterrence because other nations know the weapons exist. . . .

Some experts contend Israel no longer needs nuclear weapons because Iraq is no longer a threat and Israel's conventional forces are superior to any combination of Arab armies. Israel's problems with Palestinian extremists, they argue, cannot be remedied by nuclear strikes.

"Israel has a direct interest in making sure no Muslim state acquires the one weapon that could offset its conventional superiority, a nuclear bomb," said Cirincione, the nonproliferation director at the Carnegie Endowment. "One way to do that is by putting its own nuclear weapons on the table."

Some Arab leaders advocate declaring the Middle East a zone free of weapons of mass destruction. The process would be long, starting with mutual pledges to give up weapons and the creation of a mechanism to verify compliance.

Few Israelis think this is the right time to discuss it, because of the level of violence with the Palestinians.

"Israel could accept the idea after two years of comprehensive peace in the Middle East," said Ephraim Kam, deputy director of the Jaffee Center for Strategic Studies in Tel Aviv. "Only then could we consider changing our nuclear position."

Source: *Los Angeles Times*, October 12, 2003. © 2003, *Los Angeles Times*. Reprinted with permission.

About 500 community members along with family and friends of torture victims gathered outside the United Nations House with anti-government banners in the Bahraini capital of Manama during a rally held to mark the International Day in Support of Victims of Torture, June 25, 2004.

LESSON 1

U.S. INTERESTS IN THE MIDDLE EAST

Activity 4

Should human rights be a factor in U.S. Middle Eastern policy?

ACTIVITY OBJECTIVE

The student will evaluate the role of human rights issues in foreign policy decisions.

MATERIALS AND RESOURCES

❑ Worksheet 1.4, "Human Rights"
❑ Handout 1.4, "United Nations Universal Declaration of Human Rights"

STRATEGIES

The issue of democracy and human rights is identified by many people as a complicating factor in our dealings with many Middle Eastern allies. President Jimmy Carter made human rights a cornerstone of his presidency. Carter found this policy controversial, as some people criticized it as being an inappropriate involvement in the affairs of other countries. Others felt the U.S. had an obligation to consider such issues. The question of human rights has also been addressed by the United Nations through the Universal Declaration of Human Rights, issued in 1948.

A lesson designed around human rights issues in other countries must be balanced so that students recognize that, regarding this issue, no country is totally blameless. The United Nations Declaration of Human Rights is even open to discussion as all states have not agreed on the provisions to be included. In order to assemble data on human rights abuses, have students obtain reports from the following organizations:

Amnesty International
600 Pennsylvania Avenue, S.E.
5th Floor
Washington, DC 20003
(202) 544-0200
www.amnesty.org

Human Rights Watch
350 Fifth Avenue, 34th Floor
New York, NY 10118
(212) 290-4700
www.hrw.org

U. S. Department of State
2201 C St., N.W.
Washington, DC 20520
www.state.gov

After the reports arrive or have been downloaded off the Internet, divide the class into seven groups and have each group study the sections on human rights situations in one of the following countries: Egypt, Iraq, Iran, Israel, Jordan, Saudi Arabia, and Syria. As they read, students should compile a list of incidents of human rights violations in the country they are studying using Worksheet 1.4, "Human Rights." Students should then evaluate this information in light of the provisions of Handout 1.4, "United Nations Universal Declaration of Human Rights."

The teacher should explain to students that although the UN Declaration of Human Rights has been ratified, countries consider the document an ideal and few follow all of its principles. Next, have students research the political situations in each of these countries to place the allegations of human rights violations in a contemporary context (e.g. the Israeli occupation of the West Bank and Gaza, Egypt's attempts to contain the Muslim Brotherhood, and violence against women in the region).

Next, have students return to their groups and search the publications from the organizations for information dealing with human rights issues from the following countries: the United States, the United Kingdom, Germany, South Africa, Colombia, Japan, and China. Students should also apply the UN Declaration of Human Rights and determine a political context for the information related to the violations attributed to each of these countries.

As a followup activity, have students search through magazines and newspapers for additional information regarding human rights concerns in the countries studied. These articles may either support or contradict the positions taken by the human rights organizations. As a concluding activity, have students write a position paper in which they determine whether or not human rights considerations have an appropriate place in the making of U.S. foreign policy. They should also include an evaluation of the United Nations Universal Declaration of Human Rights. If they feel that human rights is an appropriate factor to consider, how would they suggest such policies be effectively enforced? Examples from recent history should be included to illustrate their point.

HUMAN RIGHTS

Directions: Use the chart below to identify and document examples of human rights violations.

State	Description of Incident	Right Involved	Declaration of Human Rights Article

71

UNITED NATIONS UNIVERSAL DECLARATION OF HUMAN RIGHTS [Abbreviated Version]

Article 1. All people are free and equal in dignity and rights.

Article 2. No distinction shall be made on the basis of race, color, sex, language, religion, political or other opinion, national or other status.

Article 3. Right to life, liberty, and the security of person.

Article 4. No slavery.

Article 5. No torture or cruel, inhuman, or degrading treatment or punishment.

Article 6. Right to recognition as a person before the law.

Article 7. Right to equal protection before the law.

Article 8. Right to an effective remedy by a competent tribunal for acts violating fundamental rights.

Article 9. No arbitrary arrest, detention, or exile.

Article 10. Right to a fair and public trial.

Article 11. Innocent until proved guilty; cannot be charged *ex post facto.*

Article 12. No arbitrary interference with his/her privacy, family, home or correspondence, nor attacks upon his/her honor and reputation.

Article 13. Freedom of movement and residence within the borders of each nation; the right to leave any country and return.

Article 14. Right to seek asylum from persecution.

Article 15. Right to a nationality.

Article 16. Right to marry and found a family.

Article 17. Right to own property and not be arbitrarily deprived of same.

Article 18. Freedom of thought, conscience, and religion.

Article 19. Right to freedom of opinion and expression; this includes freedom to express opinions without interference and through any media.

Article 20. Right to a peaceful assembly; no one may be compelled to belong to an association.

Article 21. Right to vote, participate, and influence government.

Article 22. Right to economic, social, and cultural security.

Article 23. Right to work, free choice of employment, favorable working conditions and the right to join trade unions.

Article 24. Right to rest and leisure, including reasonable limitations of working hours and holidays with pay.

Article 25. Right to an adequate standard of living, including food, clothing, housing, and medical care.

Article 26. Right to an education.

Article 27. Right to participate in the cultural life of the community, to enjoy the arts and to share in scientific advancement and its benefits.

LESSON 2

THE PERSIAN GULF WAR AND ITS CONTINUING AFTERMATH

Lesson 2 of 5 Lessons for the
Southern Center for International Studies'
Multimedia Educational Package
THE MIDDLE EAST IN TRANSITION

After Iraq invaded Kuwait, the United States deployed nearly a half million troops to the Middle East. In January 1991, the United States and its coalition allies launched Operation Desert Storm to expel Iraq from Kuwait.

AP Wide World Photo, Inc.

Background Reading for

LESSON 2

of the SCIS Educational Package
THE MIDDLE EAST IN TRANSITION

THE PERSIAN GULF WAR AND ITS CONTINUING AFTERMATH

On August 2, 1990, over 100,000 Iraqi troops invaded Kuwait, a small, oil-rich state just south of Iraq. In less than 14 hours, Iraq had conquered all of Kuwait. Shortly thereafter, Iraq formally annexed Kuwait as its 19th province.

Much of the international community responded with outrage. The United Nations passed a series of resolutions that condemned Iraq and authorized, first, international economic sanctions and, later, military action against Iraq. Within days of the original invasion, the United States began to deploy its military forces in Saudi Arabia, just south of Kuwait and Iraq, to prevent further Iraqi aggression. Eventually, 430,000 U.S. servicemen and women and 245,000 military personnel from 29 other countries were deployed to the area around Kuwait and Iraq.

On January 16, 1991, this 30-state alliance led by the United States went into action, beginning a month of sustained air attacks against Iraq and Iraqi forces in Kuwait. Then, on February 23, the alliance launched a ground assault against Iraqi forces in Kuwait and Iraq. Within 100 hours, Iraq was defeated and driven from Kuwait.

Why did these events take place? Why did Iraq invade Kuwait? Why did the United States respond so quickly and intensely to the Iraqi invasion, sending its largest military force overseas since the Vietnam War? Why did the international community believe it so important to expel Iraq from Kuwait? How was the alliance held together? Should anything have been done differently?

Answers to these questions are critical to our understanding of the Persian Gulf War and what caused it. Perhaps even more importantly, they also will help us understand the dynamics of ongoing events, including the 2003 U.S.-led war in Iraq and its aftermath.

BACKGROUND TO THE IRAQI INVASION

Why did Iraq invade Kuwait? There are several answers to this question, but the place to begin is with the history of both countries.

Kuwait and Iraq are both oil-rich countries whose histories and cultures have been intertwined for centuries. Before the 20th century, the territory that makes up Kuwait and Iraq was ruled by the Ottoman Empire and, on occasion, by local independent tribal rulers. Nevertheless, despite a number of shared characteristics, the past histories and present realities of the two countries differ in many ways.

In the 1700s, local rulers in what is today Kuwait sought to obtain independence from the Ottoman Empire. One effort was led by the al-Sabah family, which succeeded in negotiating autonomy, but not complete independence, for Kuwait from the Ottoman Empire.

Kuwait retained this autonomy for a century and a half. Then, in 1899, fearing that the Ottoman Empire intended to curtail Kuwait's autonomy, the head of the al-Sabah family concluded a treaty with Great Britain under which Britain received concessions in Kuwait in return for its promise to protect Kuwait from the Ottoman Empire. This treaty was the basis for Britain's 1914 recognition of Kuwait as an independent country under British protection, a response to the Ottoman Empire's entry into World War I on Germany's side.

Kuwait remained a British protectorate until 1961, when it received formal independence. The al-Sabah family continued to rule Kuwait, keeping most political control in its own hands. It also distributed a sizeable percentage of the country's oil-produced wealth to Kuwaiti citizens via education, training, housing, telephone service, and health care, all of which the government provided for free.

However, the Kuwaiti government had a very narrow definition of citizenship. In 1990, only 28 percent of the 2.1 million people living in the country were Kuwaitis. Eighteen percent were Palestinians, 21 percent were other Arabs, 9 percent were South Asians, 4 percent were Iranians, and 20 percent were other nationalities.

Iraq followed a considerably different course during this time. Before World War I, the territory that is now Iraq was part of the Ottoman Empire. When the Ottoman Empire collapsed after the war, Great Britain assumed control of Iraq under a League of Nations mandate. In 1932, Iraq received its independence from Britain. Ruled as a constitutional monarchy, Iraq followed an essentially pro-British course for the next 26 years.

In 1958, a military coup overthrew the constitutional monarchy. For the next decade, Iraq experienced a series of coups and countercoups led alternately by the Arab Socialist Resurrection Party (the Baathist Party) and the Iraqi military. Finally, in 1968, the Baathist Party under the command of General Ahmed Hassan al-Bakr and his subordinate, Saddam Hussein, firmly established control in Baghdad.

For most of the 1970s, al-Bakr was little more than a figurehead president. Actual power was in Saddam's hands. In 1979, al-Bakr resigned, leaving Saddam in control of the Iraqi government, the military, and the Baathist Party. Saddam moved quickly to eliminate challenges to his rule, executing 21 ministers for "treason" shortly after al-Bakr's resignation. Thereafter, political executions and intimidation within Iraq continued. Amnesty International estimated that 100 people per year were executed for political reasons throughout the 1980s.

Like Kuwait, Iraq sits atop immense oil reserves. During the 1980s, Saddam's government exported more and more oil. Indeed, by 1988, oil made up two-thirds of Iraq's $12.5 billion of exports. By comparison, Kuwait in 1988 exported $7.1 billion of goods and products, $6.4 billion of which was oil.

Unlike Kuwait, Iraq devoted a significant percentage of its export earnings to building its military. Between 1978 and 1988, Saddam's government spent $61 billion of its export earnings on military hardware, equipment, and supplies. This was 45 percent of the total value of Iraq's imports between 1978 and 1988.

One reason why Saddam needed this military force was because in 1980 he initiated a war with Iran, Iraq's neighbor to the east. The Iran-Iraq War continued for eight years. Together, the two sides suffered over one million casualties. By the end of the war, Iraq had virtually destroyed the Iranian military. In addition, Iraq had incurred an immense economic burden, borrowing at least $20 billion from Kuwait to help finance its war effort.

When the Iran-Iraq War ended in 1988, Saddam Hussein viewed himself as the rightful leader of Arab peoples in the Persian Gulf region. On several occasions, he declared himself to be the man who could return international prestige and power to the Arab peoples, likening himself to Babylonian King Nebuchadnezzar, who in 587 B.C. sacked Jerusalem, and to Saladin, who in the late twelfth century A.D. drove the Christian crusaders out of Jerusalem.

In late July 1990, Saddam ordered Iraqi forces to mass at the Iraqi-Kuwaiti border. At first most analysts believed that Iraq only intended to pressure Kuwait for concessions on disagreements that the two countries had regarding oil production and pricing. These assessments proved wrong. On August 2, Iraqi forces rolled into Kuwait.

UN RESOLUTIONS AND ECONOMIC SANCTIONS

The international community reacted quickly to the Iraqi invasion. The United Nations Security Council condemned Iraq's action immediately and called for Iraq's immediate and unconditional withdrawal from Kuwait. In less than a week, the UN also voted to place economic sanctions against Iraq. Meanwhile, within four days of Saddam's invasion of Kuwait, the United States froze all Iraqi and Kuwaiti bank assets, stopped all U.S. trade with Iraq, and began to send U.S. troops and planes to Saudi Arabia to prevent a possible Iraqi assault on Saudi Arabia.

Before the end of November, the UN passed 12 different resolutions relating to Iraq's invasion of Kuwait. Hoping to avoid the use of military force and obtain a peaceful Iraqi withdrawal from Kuwait, the UN at first emphasized economic sanctions on Iraq. Earning 95 percent of its 1989 and 1990 foreign exchange from oil exports, Iraq appeared vulnerable to economic sanctions. To those who believed that economic sanctions would force Iraq to quit Kuwait, the only question was how long it would take before Iraq was forced to withdraw.

Others were less optimistic. On the two previous occasions when the UN voted for economic sanctions, in 1967 against Rhodesia (now Zimbabwe) and in 1977 against South Africa, sanctions failed to achieve their objectives for two reasons. First, not all countries enforced and followed UN sanctions. Second, there was no guarantee that economic pressures would lead to the desired alterations in policy.

Concerned that some countries might not enforce or follow sanctions, the UN, three weeks after sanctions were approved, passed another resolution that authorized member countries to stop ships and aircraft bound for Iraq or occupied Kuwait. Three months later, in late November, the United Nations took the next step, voting to authorize the use of "all necessary means," including military force, to drive Iraq from Kuwait if Saddam's forces had not departed by January 15, 1991.

THE MILITARY BUILDUP

The day after Iraq invaded Kuwait, U.S. President George H.W. Bush concluded that the Iraqi action was a threat to U.S. interests and that the U.S. must act. The U.S. government quickly identified four objectives:

1) complete and unconditional Iraqi withdrawal from Kuwait;
2) restoration of Kuwait's government;
3) protection of American citizens in the region and elsewhere abroad; and
4) establishment of regional stability.

The Saudi government, having seen U.S. satellite photos that showed an extensive Iraqi military buildup inside Kuwait, only 175 miles away from the Saudi oil fields at Dhahran, was also alarmed. Both countries feared that Saddam might try to take Saudi Arabia's Dhahran fields. The Saudi government, therefore, asked the U.S. to send troops to Saudi Arabia to deter Iraq. Wanting to protect its own oil interests in Saudi Arabia, the U.S. responded with "Operation Desert Shield." Within days of the Iraqi invasion, the U.S. began the fastest large-scale, intercontinental deployment of troops in military history. Eventually, the U.S. deployed nearly a half million military personnel to the Saudi peninsula and the Persian Gulf region.

The United States was not the only country that provided military forces to counter Iraq. Twenty-nine other countries, including seven Arab states, also joined the anti-Iraq coalition. Many countries sent only token forces, but it was nevertheless politically significant that so many countries participated. In addition, 18 other countries provided economic, humanitarian, or related assistance to the coalition. Diplomatically, economically, and militarily, Iraq was virtually isolated.

The anti-Iraq coalition was assembled through skillful diplomacy by U.S. President George H.W. Bush and his Secretary of State, James Baker. In the month after the crisis began, Bush talked with 62 foreign heads of state in an effort to form the coalition. Sometimes the coalition members made strange bedfellows. For example, the United States and Syria were longtime opponents on many Middle Eastern issues. Nevertheless, both opposed Iraq's presence in Kuwait, and both were members of the alliance.

THE IRAQI OCCUPATION AND LAST-DITCH DIPLOMACY

Following its invasion of Kuwait, Iraq moved to consolidate its position there. Within days of the invasion, Iraq's legislature voted to annex Kuwait as Iraq's 19th province. All foreign diplomatic missions in Kuwait were told to relocate to Baghdad or leave Kuwait. Those that did not, including the American embassy, had their water and electricity cut off and were placed under what amounted to siege. Some embassies were militarily occupied. Iraq also began building bunkers, barricades, and other permanent military facilities in Kuwait. In addition, Iraqi troops placed explosive charges in and around Kuwait's oil wells to try to deter attack. Also, the Baghdad government abrogated its debts to Kuwait and began transporting all movable property in Kuwait to Iraq.

Even worse, Iraqi troops engaged in massive human-rights violations. Torture, rape, and murder against Kuwaitis became everyday occurrences. Many observers concluded that Iraq was trying to drive the Kuwaitis out of their country and repopulate it with Iraqis.

As it became clear that the international community would not accept Iraq's annexation of Kuwait, Saddam moved to prevent international action against Iraq by refusing to allow foreigners to leave Iraq. For all practical purposes, this meant that foreigners living in or visiting Iraq were hostages. Some of the hostages were moved to industrial and military sites to prevent attacks against those potential targets. These actions outraged much of the world. Although the hostages were eventually permitted to leave, the international community unanimously condemned Saddam's hostage-taking.

At the same time, Iraq declared that it was willing to discuss the Kuwait situation in the context of the resolution of other Middle Eastern issues, specifically the Palestinian problem and Israel's occupation of the West Bank and the Gaza Strip. The U.S. and most other countries rejected this ploy, stressing that the Iraqi invasion of Kuwait was not linked to other Middle Eastern problems. To the alliance, only a complete and unconditional Iraqi withdrawal from Kuwait would be acceptable.

During the weeks before January 15, 1991 (the date when the UN had decreed the use of military force would be authorized), the international community undertook several last-ditch diplomatic efforts to avert war. The most significant was a January 9 meeting in Geneva between U.S. Secretary of State James Baker and Iraqi Foreign Minister Tariq Aziz. Shortly after this meeting, UN Secretary-General Javier Perez de Cuellar journeyed to Baghdad to try to resolve the conflict. In addition, Algeria, the European Community, and France all initiated last-ditch efforts to avert war and to achieve an Iraqi withdrawal from Kuwait. In every case, these efforts failed.

Diplomacy had run its course. Iraq and the U.S.-led UN coalition had staked out their positions, and neither had wavered. As January 15 passed, the world wondered when war would begin.

WAR: OPERATION DESERT STORM

The wait was not long. On January 16, 1991, the United States and other coalition countries initiated "Operation Desert Storm," a two-phased assault on Iraq and Iraqi forces in Kuwait designed to expel Iraq from Kuwait.

The first phase of Operation Desert Storm was a month-long air assault. At 7 PM E.S.T. on January 16 (3 AM on January 17 in Baghdad), U.S.-led coalition planes and U.S. cruise missiles began to attack Iraq and Iraqi-held positions in Kuwait. The first targets were antiaircraft sites, Scud missile launchers, airfields and aircraft, and communications centers. The target list soon grew to include Iraq's nuclear, chemical, and biological weapons production facilities, oil refineries, transportation and supply systems, and ground forces.

The coalition lost few aircraft in the first air attacks, and claimed that its raids were highly accurate and highly successful. High-tech cruise missiles, laser-guided bombs, stealth aircraft, and other weapons proved extremely effective. Iraq showed little ability to defend itself against the air attacks. Indeed, during the first four weeks of Operation Desert Storm, coalition aircraft averaged over 2,000 flights a day against Iraq without encountering significant opposition.

Even so, the air assault did not destroy all its targets. Beginning on the second day of the conflict and continuing throughout the war, Iraq launched Scud missiles against

Israel, which was not a combatant, and Saudi Arabia. Although the Scuds were not very accurate and had no great military value, they represented a significant psychological threat to the populations of Israel and Saudi Arabia. Given Iraq's chemical weapons capabilities and Saddam's proven willingness to use such weapons (he had used them against Iran during the 1980–1988 Iran-Iraq War and against Kurdish rebels living in Iraq in 1988), the threat of an Iraqi chemical attack using Scuds was worrisome. Fortunately, the poorly designed Scuds frequently missed their targets or broke up in flight.

The air phase of Operation Desert Storm was the most intensive bombing campaign in history. It continued unabated for over a month. Disagreement remains about the number of casualties and the extent of destruction the air attacks caused, but all bomb damage assessments agree that they were extensive.

As speculation mounted in mid-February about when the ground phase of Operation Desert Storm would begin, the Soviet Union tried to persuade Saddam to withdraw from Kuwait. Like previous efforts to end the conflict diplomatically, this last-chance effort to avert a ground war failed.

On February 23 (February 24 in the Middle East), the United States and its coalition partners began the ground war. It commenced on a 300-mile front that stretched from the Persian Gulf inland. Aircraft continued to bomb Iraqi positions in Iraq and Kuwait, and battleships shelled dug-in Iraqi units in Kuwait as coalition ground forces led by U.S. Army units began their attack into Iraq and occupied Kuwait. Off Kuwait's coast, 31 ships laden with Marines waited to launch an amphibious attack.

The amphibious attack never came. During the weeks leading up to the ground war, the U.S. commander, General Norman Schwarzkopf, had moved over 150,000 U.S., British, and French troops far inland beyond the 138-mile-long Kuwait-Saudi border and beyond the entrenched Iraqi positions in Kuwait. The Iraqis, whose intelligence capabilities had been destroyed during the air war, did not know that the move had taken place, and remained concentrated along the Kuwait-Saudi border and on the Kuwait coast, waiting for a direct assault into Kuwait from Saudi Arabia and an amphibious landing into Kuwait from the sea. Eight coalition divisions were thus poised to strike northward, unopposed, directly into Iraq. If they succeeded in their drive to the Euphrates River, all Iraqi forces in Kuwait would be cut off.

The plan worked perfectly. In only two days, coalition armored units raced across 200 miles of desert, reached the Euphrates River, turned east, and rolled toward Kuwait and the Iraqi city of Basra, headquarters of Iraq's elite Republican Guard. During their advance, U.S. and coalition forces swept away everything in their path, destroying hundreds of Iraqi tanks and taking thousands of prisoners. Pounded by weeks of air attacks and thoroughly demoralized, many Iraqi soldiers surrendered without a fight.

The coalition offensive across the Kuwait-Saudi border also proceeded smoothly as U.S. and Arab forces advanced ahead of schedule into a devastated Kuwait and Kuwait City. The retreating Iraqis set nearly 1,000 oil wells on fire across the country, causing immense environmental damage.

Trapped to the west by advancing coalition armored forces and pushed from the south by other coalition armored forces, the Iraqis retreated northward toward Basra, only to be pounded by allied air power. The road leading northward out of Kuwait toward Basra became a highway of destruction as coalition aircraft destroyed hundreds of vehicles and killed thousands of Iraqi troops.

In 100 hours, the ground war was over. The fourth-largest armed force in the world had been defeated in what some analysts called the most one-sided war in world history. Exact figures will never be known, but Iraq probably lost more than 100,000 people while the U.S. suffered 152 combat deaths. The rest of the coalition forces combined had a similarly small number of combat casualties.

Iraq had been pushed out of Kuwait, and the Persian Gulf War was over. The United Nations, the United States, and the U.S.-led coalition had achieved their war objectives. Having won the war, it remained to be seen whether they could construct a stable peace.

DID DESERT STORM STOP TOO SOON?

The ground phase of Operation Desert Storm stopped after only 100 hours, with U.S.-led coalition forces deep inside Iraq and in complete control of Kuwait, and Iraqi forces seriously damaged and in complete retreat. No serious analyst of military affairs believes that Iraqi forces could have survived had the war continued, and none doubt that U.S. forces could have marched into Baghdad and removed Saddam from power. With U.S.-led coalition forces in complete command of the situation, many people wondered why the U.S. did not "finish the job" by destroying what was left of the Iraqi military and then removing Saddam Hussein.

President George H.W. Bush and the U.S. government had several reasons for stopping Operation Desert Storm. *First*, the United Nations resolution under which authority the coalition was operating authorized only the expulsion of Iraqi forces from Kuwait. It did not authorize overthrowing the Iraqi government. Hence, the U.S. government was unwilling to go beyond the limits of UN approval.

Second, several of the states within the coalition opposed any effort to change the Iraqi government. Continuing the war against Iraq and adding the overthrow of Saddam to the United States' war objectives list therefore had the potential to destroy the coalition.

Third, with its objectives limited to expelling Iraq from Kuwait, the U.S. had been extremely successful in the Arab and Islamic worlds in portraying itself as a defender of a rightfully ruling Arab government. Had the United States tried directly to overthrow Saddam, opponents in the Arab and Islamic worlds may have been more successful than they were in portraying the United States as a dangerous and expansionist outsider that was an enemy of the Arab peoples and Islam.

Fourth, the U.S. reasoned that if its troops marched into Baghdad, then U.S. forces would probably have to stay in Baghdad for an extended period to maintain order and run Iraq. In addition, once U.S. forces withdrew, any Iraqi government that was left in power would probably be perceived as having been imposed on Iraq by the United States. The possibility of stability in Iraq would thus have been eliminated.

Fifth, the U.S. was also concerned that if its forces destroyed the Iraqi military, then Iran or Syria might become the dominant political-military power in the region. Iran remained hostile toward the United States, and despite Syria's membership in the anti-Iraq coalition, the U.S. and Syria had had a long history of confrontation and opposing interests. The U.S. did not want either of these two anti-American regional powers to dominate the region.

Sixth, as Desert Storm neared its 100th hour, it had become a massacre. Iraqi forces were in complete retreat, in most cases completely unable to defend themselves. The carnage was immense, particularly on the road leading northward out of Kuwait toward Basra. Much of the death and destruction on this "highway of death" had been photographed and broadcast by the international media, including CNN. Thus, pressure was building on the U.S. government to stop the war.

Finally, and an extremely important consideration, the U.S. intelligence community believed that there was a strong possibility that Iraq's senior military officers, having been led into a humiliating conflict by Saddam and virtually certain of being accused by Saddam of being the cause of failure, might rise up against him and overthrow him. For the U.S., then, the preferred solution to the Saddam problem was that the Iraqi military would overthrow Saddam without direct U.S. involvement. It appeared that there was a good chance that this might occur.

No single reason from the above list may have been sufficient to stop Desert Storm when it was stopped. But together, this list presented a persuasive case to end the fighting after 100 hours of ground warfare. So on February 28, 1991, Operation Desert Storm ended.

SADDAM AND WEAPONS OF MASS DESCTRUCTION[1]

Some of the terms of the cease-fire that ended the Persian Gulf War were that Iraq had to reveal the location of its biological, chemical, and nuclear weapons research and production facilities; allow United Nations teams to inspect those sites; provide information to UN inspection teams about Iraqi weapons of mass destruction (WMD) programs; and when instructed by the United Nations, destroy WMD research and production facilities and stockpiles.

The first UN inspection team arrived in Iraq in May 1991. Over the next two years, one UN inspection team after another combed Iraq looking for information about Iraqi non-conventional weapons programs, inspecting Iraqi non-conventional weapons research and production sites, and recommending to the United Nations the destruction of certain types of facilities and weapons.

Despite having agreed to cooperate with UN inspectors and to follow UN directions on destroying non-conventional weapons research and production facilities and weapons, Iraq frequently tried to prevent UN teams from carrying out their tasks. Sometimes, Iraq refused to grant UN teams access to a facility. Other times, Iraq altered or destroyed records. On still other occasions, Iraqi officials simply lied to UN inspectors. And on still other occasions, Iraqi officials, military personnel, and security officers harassed, detained, or tried to intimidate UN inspectors. Nevertheless, because of persistence and occasional UN threats of military force, the UN teams discovered more and more about Iraq's biological, chemical, and nuclear programs.

As inspections progressed, two things became clear. First, Iraq had sophisticated and broad-based programs in all three non-conventional weapons areas (chemical, biological, and nuclear). Second, before the inspections began, no one outside Iraq realized how advanced Iraq was in its non-conventional weapons programs, especially in nuclear

weapons. More than one member of the UN nuclear inspection teams observed that
had Israel not attacked and destroyed Iraq's "Osirak" nuclear reactor in 1981, Iraq may
have had nuclear weapons by 1991. These were disconcerting discoveries that made the
need to prevent the spread of WMD into the Middle East all the more obvious.

CONTINUING CONFLICT

Throughout the decade following the Persian Gulf War, Saddam Hussein attempted
to rebuild his strength and reassert his authority in Iraq. Over time he became
increasingly defiant toward the international community, which attempted to contain
him through diplomatic and economic sanctions as well as periodic military action.
Recurrent crises, offset by sporadic periods of cooperation, kept relations between
Iraq and the outside world at a status best described as low-level conflict.

In March 2003, despite widespread international criticism, the U.S., along with
Britain and a few other allies, launched a war that toppled the Iraqi government,
essentially finishing the job left undone by the Persian Gulf War. The U.S., the Iraqi
people, and the international community now face the tremendous challenge of
rebuilding the country into a stable, secure, and free society. As discussed below, the
question is no longer "Did Desert Storm end too soon?" More relevant questions now
include: "Were the U.S. and Britain justified in taking military action against Iraq?
Will Iraq be reshaped into a stable, democratic society? How will the change in Iraq
affect the rest of the region and the world?"

Inside Iraq After the Persian Gulf War

In the early 1990s, Saddam Hussein's regime appeared to have a tenuous grip on power.
At the urging of the U.S., groups of Iraqi Shia Muslims in the south and Kurds in the
north rebelled against the Iraqi government. However, when the U.S. did not provide
support, Saddam brutally crushed the rebellions. In response, the UN Security Council
established "no-fly zones" (see Map 1) in both areas, preventing Baghdad from fully
reestablishing its sovereignty.
Hemmed in between the northern
and southern no-fly zones and cut off
from much of the world by the UN
embargo, Saddam Hussein's regime
seemed vulnerable.

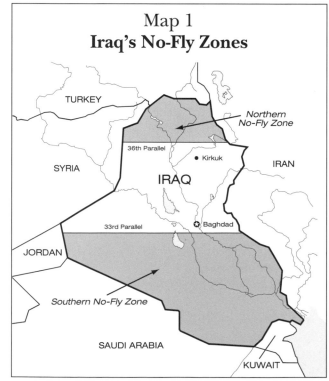

Map 1
Iraq's No-Fly Zones

In 1995, with the economy collapsing, Iraqi dissidents made several
(albeit unsuccessful) coup and/or
assassination attempts. With each
failure came a new purge. In August
1995, Saddam's two daughters and
their husbands defected to Jordan.
Hussein Kamil, one of the sons-in-
law, had headed Iraq's secret weapons program and was a key presidential advisor. Many analysts assumed
that the defection of Saddam's
daughters and sons-in-law meant
that the regime was finally seeing its
last days.

Yet Iraqi opposition groups operating out of Jordan and elsewhere did not rally to Hussein Kamil. In fact, they regarded him as little better than Saddam himself. In the end, Saddam offered the defectors amnesty and they elected to return to Iraq. Saddam then pardoned his daughters and had them immediately divorce their husbands. In the grisly episode that followed, the husbands were executed by their own relatives.

In 1996, Saddam sent forces into northern Iraq, where rivalry between the leading Kurdish factions had led one of them, the Kurdish Democratic Party (KDP), to turn to Saddam for help. In the battles that followed, Iraqi forces backing the KDP launched a successful offensive against dissident factions, capturing a key city. In retaliation, the U.S. launched cruise missile attacks and extended the southern no-fly zone to the 33rd parallel. Tensions deescalated only after Iraqi troops withdrew from the area.

As the 21st century began, opposition groups remained disorganized and feuded among themselves, enabling Saddam to consolidate his power. He rewarded those loyal to him (sometimes lavishly), purged those opposed to him (at times using mass executions), and used the ongoing UN sanctions to justify his consolidation of power. Nevertheless, Saddam's ongoing battle with the UN continued to place pressure on his regime.

Iraq and the Outside World

Throughout the 1990s, Iraq's foreign relations were characterized by continuing conflict with its neighbors, as well as the U.S. and UN. Indeed, between 1991 and 2002, the U.S. and Britain flew roughly 374,000 sorties (missions by a single plane) over Iraq, the equivalent of fighting Desert Storm every three years.[2]

In October 1994, the movement of Iraqi troops toward the Kuwaiti border heightened tensions. The Iraqis backed down only after the U.S. sent an aircraft-carrier battle group, additional warplanes, and 54,000 troops to the region.

In 1995, the Iraqi government's policy of obstructing international attempts to uncover its WMD programs was undermined by the defection of Saddam Hussein's son-in-law, Hussein Kamil, the head of Iraq's secret weapons program. Baghdad, perhaps to preempt whatever Hussein Kamil planned to tell the Western powers, immediately released extensive documentation showing a far more extensive biological weapons program than previously admitted. In 1996, with the Iraqi economy in shambles, Saddam surprised observers again by agreeing for the first time to accept UN Security Council Resolution 986, which allowed limited sales of Iraqi oil, but gave the UN control over the revenue. Under UN direction, the money was used to purchase food and medicine for the Iraqi people, finance the UN weapons inspection program, and compensate victims of the Persian Gulf War.

But occasional examples of apparent cooperation were offset by other events. In 1996, the Iraqi army moved into the northern no-fly zone on several occasions. During the late 1990s, recurring confrontations between Iraq and the United Nations Special Commission (UNSCOM), charged with investigating and dismantling Iraq's WMD program, kept tensions high. American arms inspectors were first expelled in 1997. By December 1998, relations with the international community were so poor that Iraq had cut off ties with the UN weapons inspection teams, UNSCOM personnel had been evacuated, and the Americans and British had launched a massive air campaign against Iraqi military targets.

Unlike previous actions against Iraq, the air strikes of December 1998 did not have the backing of the UN Security Council. France, Russia, and China—the other three permanent members of the Security Council—opposed the strikes and favored loosening or even lifting the sanctions against Iraq. Disagreement within the Security Council intensified in early 2000, as Hans von Sponeck, the top UN humanitarian official concerned with Iraq, resigned, complaining that international sanctions caused widespread suffering and made it impossible to meet minimum humanitarian requirements for Iraq's 24 million people. Also, planes from several countries, including Russia, France, Jordan, and Morocco, began flying to Iraq in violation of a UN travel ban in order to promote the easing of UN sanctions. These events proved to be early signs of the growing conflict within the UN Security Council over how to deal with Iraq.

IRAQ POLICY UNDER GEORGE W. BUSH AND THE WAR ON TERRORISM

Upon taking office, the Bush administration continued U.S. efforts to isolate Iraq and undermine Saddam Hussein's government. The U.S. and U.K. continued to enforce UN economic sanctions and other restrictions, such as no-fly zones, against the country. Indeed, not long after President Bush's inauguration in January 2001, U.S. and British warplanes bombed Iraqi air defenses near Baghdad. Unlike most previous strikes, the assaults were against targets outside the no-fly zones and were preventive in nature, rather than being prompted by antiaircraft fire or other provocation. The attacks immediately drew criticism from France, Russia, China, India, Pakistan, and other countries.

Following the 9/11 terrorist attacks on the U.S. and the subsequent drive to remove the Taliban and al Qaeda from Afghanistan, the Bush administration focused on Iraq as the next target in the war on terrorism. While American and European intelligence officials did not believe that Saddam and his government played a role in the 9/11 attacks, Bush argued that the Iraqi government was developing links with al Qaeda and, if left unchecked, could one day provide terrorist organizations with WMD. By mid-2002, the Bush administration was stating that it would make sure Iraq was disarmed of its unconventional weapons, and that it would go to war to do so if necessary, with or without UN approval.

In response to growing criticism of U.S. unilateral action, both from within the U.S. and abroad, President Bush took his case to the UN in September 2002, arguing that the UN must do more to enforce its resolutions on Iraq. In November, after intense negotiations, the UN Security Council approved a strongly worded resolution (Resolution 1441) calling on Saddam to allow unconditional weapons inspections. Within weeks, UN monitors were on the ground in Iraq. With the resumption of inspections, opposition to military action grew within the Security Council and the world community. But the Bush administration expressed skepticism over the effectiveness of UN inspections and emphasized regime change, rather than simple disarmament, as a fundamental goal.

In February 2003, U.S. Secretary of State Colin Powell made a dramatic presentation to the Security Council in an attempt to persuade its members that Iraq had WMD, that Saddam was subverting the inspections process in violation of Resolution 1441, that Saddam had links to al Qaeda, and that military action should therefore be authorized. However, chief UN weapons inspector Hans Blix questioned U.S. intelligence reports and described increasing cooperation from the Iraqi government as well as satisfaction with the pace of disarmament. In the absence of clear evidence of Iraqi noncompliance or the existence of WMD, the majority of Security Council members opposed military action and argued that weapons inspectors should be given more time and resources to do their job. Only Britain stood steadfast with the U.S. in advocating the use of force to remove Saddam from power. While negotiations continued for several weeks, in mid-March the U.S. and Britain abandoned efforts to obtain a UN mandate for war against Iraq after France announced it would veto any such resolution.

THE SECOND WAR IN IRAQ

On March 20, 2003, the U.S. led a "coalition of the willing" in a war to overthrow Saddam Hussein, stating that his pursuit of WMD and alleged connections with al Qaeda constituted an imminent threat to U.S. and global security. The coalition, comprised mainly of U.S. and British forces, moved through the country with lightning speed. British forces quickly controlled the southern port of Basra while U.S. forces raced on to Baghdad. In less than a month, allied forces had captured Tikrit, the last stronghold of Saddam's regime. By mid-April, the U.S. had installed a civil administration in Baghdad, later named the Coalition Provisional Authority (CPA), tasked with governing the country and overseeing the transition to an interim Iraqi government.

Unfortunately, the job of restoring stability to Iraq proved much more difficult than defeating Saddam's army. In the immediate aftermath of the war, rioting was widespread, and U.S. forces, unprepared to serve as policemen, stood by and watched as looters ransacked government and commercial institutions, utility companies, warehouses, hospitals, and even museums. Of particular concern was the looting of a nuclear site, which raised fears that the radioactive material stored there could pose health and environmental risks or be used to create a "dirty bomb." For many Iraqis, awe at the ease with which the U.S. defeated Iraq's military quickly turned to anger over its inability to provide security or restore order.

REBUILDING IRAQ

After the war, the U.S. faced a difficult dilemma. To provide the stability needed to rebuild the country, the U.S. often had to assert its authority to fill the power vacuum, including through the use of force when necessary. But this only fueled resentment and suspicion among some Iraqis that the U.S. had come to dominate, rather than liberate, the country. As a result, the CPA had to maintain a delicate balancing act between transferring power and authority to Iraqis as quickly as possible while trying to do so in a way that would not jeopardize the country's security or political and economic development. By mid-2004, some progress had been made in rebuilding Iraq's political and economic systems as well as enhancing security, but in all three areas serious challenges remained.

Politics

While it remains to be seen if Iraq can be turned into a stable democracy, the seeds of an independent Iraqi government have been planted. In July 2003, the CPA, under the leadership of U.S. Administrator L. Paul Bremer, abandoned plans for a large national conference of Iraqi leaders, which was to lay the groundwork for a representative Iraqi interim government, and instead appointed a 25-member Iraqi Governing Council (IGC). Bremer argued that the new plan was necessary to bring Iraqis into government leadership positions as soon as possible. Critics countered that it was simply a way for the U.S. to put an Iraqi face on the current administration while ensuring its control over the development of a new Iraqi government.

Importantly, the CPA took care to make sure the IGC reflected the country's demographic make-up. It included 13 Shias, five Sunni Arabs, five Kurds, one Assyrian Christian, and one Turkmen. To help ensure the creation of a secular and Western-oriented democracy, the CPA appointed nine expatriate Iraqis, several of whom had been quite visible in advising the Bush administration in the months preceding the U.S. invasion of Iraq. While the IGC was representative of the country's ethnic diversity, the fact that the CPA had the ultimate authority to approve or veto decisions taken by the IGC undercut its legitimacy in the eyes of many Iraqis.

Originally the IGC was established simply as an advisory council, but over time it acquired some real power. The Council was granted the ability to appoint and dismiss ministers and to draft the budget for 2004. It was also tasked with supervising the creation of a congress to draft a new Iraqi constitution, which the Americans insisted was a necessary precondition for national elections to be held. However, this plan soon fell victim to a major challenge facing Iraq's political transition—competing visions held by the country's various ethnic and religious groups as to what a democratic Iraq should look like and how it should be realized.

The quarrel centered around differences between Iraq's Shia majority and the plethora of minorities over important constitutional questions, such as the degree of federalism, the role of religion in state affairs, and how the constitutional process should move forward. Shias, who were long oppressed under the rule of Sunni Arabs, felt they had a right to play a leading role in the country's political process, and favored direct elections for both a national government and a constitutional assembly. Shia leaders argued that only an elected assembly would have the legitimacy to write a constitution and the independence to protect it from American interference.

With 60 percent of the population, Shias would likely dominate elections, and some U.S. leaders feared that they might elect Islamists who would write a constitution more along the lines of Iran's Islamic Republic. Leaders of Iraq's minorities, particularly Sunni Arabs and Kurds, also feared such a scenario and argued that a religiously moderate, federal system was necessary to protect their interests. Despite these fears, there was no consensus among Iraqi Shias that a system modeled on Iran's should be adopted. In fact, Iraq's most senior Shia leader, the Grand Ayatollah Ali al-Sistani, remained a powerful advocate for democracy and the separation of religion and politics.

In November 2003, with attacks against Americans increasing and pressure to transfer authority to Iraqis intensifying, CPA Administrator Bremer bypassed the debate by separating the political transition from the constitutional process. He announced that authority would be handed over to a provisional Iraqi government by July 2004, while elections for a constitutional assembly, and later for a government, would be postponed until 2005. Under the new plan, representatives selected by the Iraqi Governing Council and by local councils across Iraq would choose members of a national assembly that in turn would select a provisional government. The IGC, in consultation with the CPA, would also decree a "basic law," providing for a fixed interim constitution that, among other things, would stipulate the extent of federalism and the role of religion in state affairs.

The plan soon faced strong opposition from Iraq's Shia population, who feared that the caucuses might be rigged to limit their influence. By January 2004, the plan was on the verge of collapse after Grand Ayatollah al-Sistani issued a *fatwa*, or religious decree, stating that the interim legislature must be chosen through direct elections and that only directly elected representatives could negotiate an agreement to allow U.S.-led forces to remain in Iraq. The decree prompted more than 100,000 Shias to demonstrate in Baghdad and Basra, demanding elections. Importantly, Sistani made it known that if elections were not held, he would urge Shias, who so far had largely been cooperating with the CPA, to begin resisting the American presence.

The U.S. resisted the idea of elections, arguing that it would be impossible to organize them in time to transfer power by the July 1 deadline. The U.S. enlisted the help of UN Secretary-General Kófi Annan to negotiate a compromise plan that would keep to the timetable but also satisfy the basic concerns of Iraq's various groups. As the deadline approached, the prospects for such a plan grew dimmer.

An important step was achieved in March 2004, when members of the IGC signed an interim constitution. However, the Shia members of the council immediately voiced strong opposition to several aspects of the constitution and said they only approved it to preserve the unity of the country in the short term. They insisted that their concerns had not yet been addressed and that the constitution would never have legitimacy until it was amended and approved by a democratically elected national assembly. Regardless of what process is ultimately adopted, Iraqi politics will be defined for some time to come by competition among Iraq's various ethnic and religious groups and attempts to develop a national identity acceptable to all. The U.S. faces a difficult challenge as it tries to simultaneously guide and disentangle itself from the country's political process.

Economics

When the CPA and Iraqi Governing Council took power, they inherited an economy severely damaged by war, a decade of international sanctions, and years of neglect by Saddam Hussein. However, by the beginning of 2004 there was evidence that Iraq's economy was slowly recovering despite obstacles such as sabotage, crime, violence, and fear. Much of this was due to the massive amount of international aid that was forthcoming. In November 2003, the U.S. Congress authorized $18.6 billion to rebuild Iraq on top of the more than $2 billion already spent. Other countries pledged another $14 billion.[3] As a result, money poured into the country to rebuild the infrastructure, including sewage and communications systems, health clinics, railways, ports, and oil fields. By early 2004, living standards for some Iraqis had increased since President Bush declared the war over. While at least half the workforce remained unemployed, those who could find work earned as much as four times their prewar wages. Roughly 2,000 new schools had been built.[4] Electricity, while still erratic, was roughly to its prewar level. And, perhaps most important, oil production was slowly returning to its prewar level.

Still, the Iraqi economy faced many challenges. Persistent acts of sabotage and attacks on coalition forces and their supporters continued to disrupt reconstruction efforts. The difficult situation faced by international aid agencies was dramatically illustrated by the August 2003 bombing of the UN's Baghdad headquarters, which caused the UN and many nongovernmental organizations to pull out of Iraq. Private foreign investors were reluctant to provide much-needed investment until the violence abated and a legal framework existed to protect them. Similarly, international lenders were waiting to see if the new Iraqi government would be held responsible for the many debts incurred by Saddam's regime.

Security

Coalition leaders acknowledged that ultimately the success of reconstruction efforts in Iraq would depend on their ability to reestablish security. Indeed, the political, economic, and security environments were closely intertwined. As mentioned above, insecurity in Iraq continued to hinder political and economic development. At the same time, political infighting among Iraq's fractious ethnic and religious groups as well as the economic hardship faced by a majority of Iraqis threatened to produce new sources of conflict and insecurity if not properly managed.

By the beginning of 2004, the coalition had achieved some notable successes on the security front, particularly in its attempts to stamp out the remnants of Saddam Hussein's regime. The most notable of these were the killing of Saddam's sons, Uday and Qusay, in July 2003 and the capture of Saddam Hussein himself in December 2003. In all, the U.S. had captured 43 of the most-wanted 55 Iraqis that appeared in its infamous "deck of cards." The U.S. had also taken steps toward rebuilding Iraq's security forces by training police, border guards, and soldiers for a new Iraqi army. In all, roughly 90,000 U.S.-trained Iraqi security personnel were deployed throughout Iraq assisting coalition forces.[5]

Despite these achievements, the U.S. and its allies still struggled to restore order. Attacks against coalition forces were intense, averaging around 40 per day at a peak in November 2003.[6] The coalition also had to contend with widespread acts of sabotage, rampant crime, fighting among rival Iraqi factions, and clashes between coalition forces and Iraqi citizens who had become disillusioned with the occupation. The security environment was such that very few members of the CPA left their barricaded complex in the heavily fortified "Green Zone" without armed escort.

It was not entirely clear to what extent there was an organized insurgency orchestrating the violence or who exactly was involved. Certainly, many of the insurgents were former members of Saddam Hussein's Baath Party who opposed the occupation and the emerging Shia-led political order. The degree to which foreigners, particularly radical Islamists, were involved in the insurgency was a matter of debate. Some of the attacks, such as the suicide bombings against the UN headquarters in August and Italian soldiers in November, bore the markings of Islamist terrorists, perhaps connected to al Qaeda. U.S. military officials believed that a few hundred foreign terrorists were likely in Iraq.[7] While they had no ideological connection with Saddam loyalists and there appeared to be little cooperation between the two groups, they shared the common goal of creating instability in an attempt to force the withdrawal of coalition troops. Rampant crime only exacerbated the situation by adding to the sense of fear and insecurity.

American military officials were also concerned about Iraqis who were not Saddam loyalists, but had become disillusioned and increasingly opposed the occupation.[8] Some of these were former members of Saddam's Baath Party who were alienated by the CPA's policy of "de-Baathification." Upon taking power, the CPA stripped hundreds of thousands of former Baath Party members from their jobs and blocked them as much as possible from participating in reconstruction efforts. These former soldiers, government bureaucrats, businessmen, and teachers provided ample recruiting fodder for the more extreme insurgents. In other cases, coalition military operations against insurgents had the unintended effect of galvanizing resistance among ordinary Iraqis not previously opposed to the occupying forces. The accidental killing of civilians, humiliating searches and detentions, and cultural miscommunication led to resentment and new sources of opposition.

CONCLUSIONS

At the beginning of 2004, U.S. officials expressed hope that the capture of Saddam Hussein would ultimately silence the remnants of his regime and lead to a process of national reconciliation. While the violence continued, there was some reason for cautious optimism. Slow but steady progress was being made in rebuilding Iraq's infrastructure and economy, and concrete steps were being taken to return control of the country to Iraqis. Nevertheless, the future of Iraq was far from certain, and a number of key questions remained, including:

- How long will violent attacks in Iraq continue?
- How long will U.S. forces have to stay?
- Can democracy be brought to Iraq?
- What would a stable, democratic Iraq mean for the rest of the Middle East?
- What should Americans think about anti-Americanism in the Middle East?
- What about anti-Americanism in Europe among traditional U.S. allies?
- How has the war in Iraq affected the "war on terrorism"?
- Was the second war in Iraq justified? Was it worth the cost?
- Will the second war in Iraq have a positive or negative influence on the Arab-Israeli conflict?

During Iraq's occupation of Kuwait, Iraqi President Saddam Hussein, center, shakes hands with a soldier during a visit to inspect Iraqi troops stationed in Kuwait on October 4, 1990.

LESSON 2

THE PERSIAN GULF WAR AND ITS CONTINUING AFTERMATH

Activity 1

How should the United States have responded to Iraq's invasion of Kuwait?

ACTIVITY OBJECTIVE

The student will identify varying opinions regarding the timing of the coalition forces' attack against Iraq.

MATERIALS AND RESOURCES

❑ Index cards with the name of each former Secretary of Defense
❑ SCIS Videotape, *The Middle East in Transition*, Lesson 2, "The Persian Gulf War"

STRATEGIES

After Iraq's invasion of Kuwait, the world community was divided over whether to take military action or impose economic sanctions against Saddam Hussein's regime. In late 1990, before the war against Iraq began, the former U.S. Secretaries of Defense considered the implications of these same alternatives and arrived at varying conclusions as to what the most appropriate U.S. response might be.

This activity allows students to weigh the alternatives proposed by the former Secretaries and then evaluate those alternatives in light of President Bush's subsequent decision in January 1991. Begin the activity by dividing the class into 7 groups and assigning each group one former Secretary of Defense (Brown, Carlucci, Laird, McNamara, Richardson, Rumsfeld, or Schlesinger) to focus on while viewing the SCIS videotape, *The Middle East in Transition*, Lesson 2, "The Persian Gulf War." Students should determine the position taken by their assigned former Secretary on the issue of what the appropriate U.S. response to Iraq's invasion of Kuwait should have been. At the conclusion of the videotape, have students place their former Secretary's recommendation at the appropriate place on the following Likert scale:

Immediate Military Action	Non-committal	Long-Range Economic Sanctions

Students should be able to explain why they placed their former Secretary where they did by citing his opinions as expressed on the videotape.

Reuters/Oleg Popov

Kuwaiti men and boys race their camels during a "Liberation Tournament" camel race, part of a celebration marking the twelfth anniversary of the liberation of Kuwait from Iraqi occupation in the desert near Kuwait City.

LESSON 2

THE PERSIAN GULF WAR AND ITS CONTINUING AFTERMATH

Activity 2

Why did Iraq invade Kuwait?

ACTIVITY OBJECTIVE

The student will identify reasons for the Iraqi invasion of Kuwait.

MATERIALS AND RESOURCES

❑ Handout 2.1, "Iraq: Outlets for Oil"
❑ Worksheet 2.1, "Iraq and Kuwait—A Quick Comparison"

STRATEGIES

On August 2, 1990, Iraq's army overran Kuwait after negotiations between the two countries had broken down over differences involving oil, money, and borders. Although most countries in the world community were quick to dismiss Iraq's claim that Kuwait was historically its "19th province," few understood the complicated areas of disagreement between the two countries. This activity gives students an opportunity to examine the strategic and economic factors that contributed to the 1990 invasion.

Establish groups of students and distribute copies of Handout 2.1, "Iraq: Outlets for Oil," to each group along with Worksheet 2.1, "Iraq and Kuwait—A Quick Comparison." Ask students to use the map and the statistics to answer the questions on the worksheet related to Iraq's economic and strategic situation prior to the invasion of Kuwait.

IRAQ: OUTLETS FOR OIL

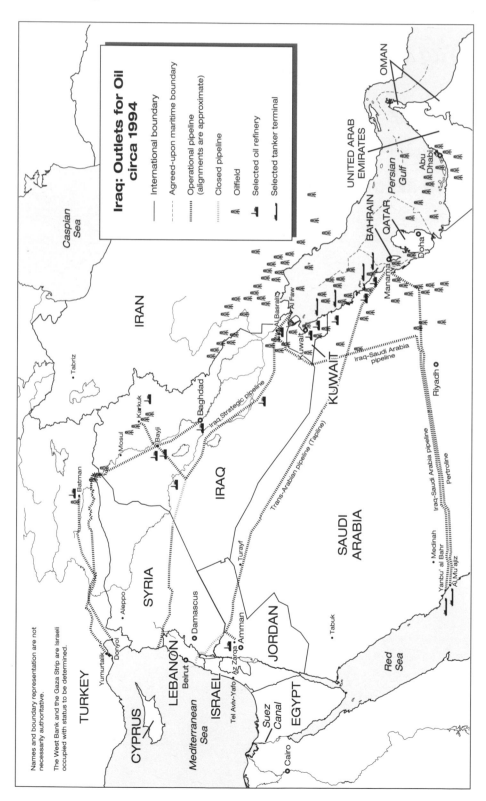

IRAQ AND KUWAIT—*A Quick Comparison*

Directions: Use the map "Iraq: Outlets for Oil" and the data below to draw conclusions about the factors leading to the Iraqi invasion of Kuwait.

Summer 1990	Iraq	Kuwait
Population	19,525,000	2,100,000
Oil Reserves (barrels)	100,000,000,000	94,000,000,000
% GNP from Oil Exports	67%	90%
% GNP Spent on Military	32%	5.2%
Per Capita Income	$2,213	$13,594
National Debt	$80 billion	$7.2 billion

1) What are the differences between the two states in terms of population and per capita income?

2) Do the figures regarding national debt reflect a problem for Iraq? What caused this large debt?

3) What do the figures on military expenditures indicate about Iraq's and Kuwait's military forces?

4) How do the two countries compare in terms of oil reserves? With similar oil reserves available, what conclusions can you draw about per capita income?

5) If oil exports were disrupted, what would be the impact on the economies of the two states?

6) Locate the borders of Iraq on the map. Where is Iraq's outlet on the Persian Gulf? How does this compare with access to water enjoyed by other countries bordering the Gulf? What problems would be associated with using Basra as Iraq's main port city?

7) Where is Kuwait in relationship to Iraq? How does its coastline compare to Iraq's?

8) Do Iraq and Kuwait share oil fields? What disputes might arise from shared natural resources?

9) Locate the major oil pipelines leading out of Iraq. The pipeline leading to a port on the Red Sea goes through what country? The Trans-Arabian Pipeline ends in what country? The pipelines that follow the Tigris and Euphrates Rivers pass through what countries and end where? What strategic and diplomatic difficulties does this pose for Iraq?

10) In light of this information, why did the invasion of Kuwait come as such a surprise to everyone who followed events in the region?

During the Gulf War, a Kuwaiti helicopter herds Iraqi prisoners of war across a stream in southeastern Kuwait, February 25, 1991.

LESSON 2

THE PERSIAN GULF WAR AND ITS CONTINUING AFTERMATH

Activity 3

Why was it in the strategic interest of the United States and the UN coalition to liberate Kuwait?

ACTIVITY OBJECTIVE

The student will evaluate coalition and United Nations efforts to force Iraq's withdrawal from Kuwait.

MATERIALS AND RESOURCES

❑ Teacher Resource 2.1, "A Line Has Been Drawn in the Sand: A Chronology"
❑ Teacher Resource 2.2, "Balance of Power: Troops in the Persian Gulf"

STRATEGIES

With the Iraqi invasion of Kuwait, a chain of events began that led to the launching of Operation Desert Storm by a UN coalition made up of countries from all over the world. (See Teacher Resource 2.1, "A Line Has Been Drawn in the Sand" for a timeline of events from Iraq's invasion to the launching of the allied attack.) The greatest share of the effort was carried by the United States and Saudi Arabia. (See Teacher Resource 2.2, "Balance of Power: Troops in the Persian Gulf.") Former Secretary Brown refers to this as a "remarkable achievement, partly made possible by the end of the Cold War." Distribute Handout 2.1, "Iraq: Outlets for Oil" and lead a class discussion focusing on the following questions:

- Of all the countries in the coalition, why do you think the United States and Saudi Arabia committed the largest numbers of troops?
- If Iraq's invasion of Kuwait had been allowed to stand, what oil resources would the Iraqis have controlled?
- Why was the United States particularly concerned with safeguarding the Gulf coast of Saudi Arabia from potential Iraqi expansion?
- How would an "enlarged" Iraq change the balance of power in the Gulf region? What other countries would have been affected?
- Why was maintaining free access to the Strait of Hormuz important to the U.S.?
- How would an enlarged Iraq and a victorious Saddam Hussein have altered the balance of power in other parts of the Middle East? What concerns might Turkey, Syria, Jordan, Israel, and Egypt have had about an Iraqi victory?
- Why were U.S. interests compatible with the interests of many other states in the international community in maintaining open access to the oil in the Gulf?

The teacher should next explain that there were other countries in the world community that did not send troops to the Gulf but supported Operation Desert Storm financially (e.g. Germany and Japan).

Reuters/Andrea Comas

A Marsh Arab woman walks with a bucket filled with water in the Iraqi village of Eaz, May 26, 2003. The government of Saddam Hussein mounted a campaign in the 1990s to destroy the lifestyle of the Marsh Arabs, who had farmed the area for thousands of years. The marshes were drained of water and hundreds of thousands of Marsh Arabs were forced to flee to villages like Eaz, where they live in poverty.

A LINE HAS BEEN DRAWN IN THE SAND
A Chronology

1990

July 17   Iraqi President Saddam Hussein accuses Kuwait and the United Arab
           Emirates of flooding the oil market, driving prices down, and costing Iraq
           $14 billion

July 31   Iraq and Kuwait begin negotiations to resolve oil and border differences;
           Iraq masses 100,000 troops at Kuwaiti border

Aug. 1   Iraq quits negotiations

Aug. 2   Iraq invades Kuwait

Aug. 3   Iraqi troops advance toward Saudi border;
           UN Security Council votes 14-0 demanding Iraqi withdrawal

Aug. 7   George H. W. Bush orders U.S. troops and planes to Saudi Arabia

Aug. 8   The United Kingdom agrees to join multinational force against Iraq;
           Bush declares, "A line has been drawn in the sand."

Aug. 9   First U.S. troops arrive in Saudi Arabia;
           Iraq closes its borders, trapping thousands of foreigners;
           UN Security Council votes 15-0 declaring Iraq's annexation of Kuwait
              null and void

Aug. 16   U.S. orders Navy ships to intercept ships bound for Iraq

Aug. 18   Security Council votes 15-0 demanding Iraq free foreigners

Aug. 20   Iraq says Western detainees moved to strategic sites as human shields to
              guard against bombing

Aug. 22   Bush orders reservists to active duty

Sept. 13   Security Council votes 13-2 to allow food aid into Iraq and Kuwait

Sept. 17   Defense Secretary Dick Cheney fires Air Force General Michael Dugan
              for discussing war plans

Sept. 27   Iraq threatens to hang diplomats sheltering Westerners

Oct. 25   U.S. announces it will send 100,000 more troops to Saudi Arabia

Nov. 8   Bush orders another 150,000 troops to the Persian Gulf region

Nov. 9   Former German Chancellor Willy Brandt departs Baghdad with 117 hostages

Nov. 19   Iraq orders 250,000 more troops into Kuwait; 136 more hostages leave Iraq

Nov. 22   Bush visits U.S. troops in Saudi Arabia on Thanksgiving

Nov. 29   UN Security Council approves resolution authorizing "all necessary means" to expel Iraq from Kuwait after January 15

Dec. 2   Boxer Mohammed Ali departs Baghdad with 15 hostages

Dec. 4   Saddam releases all Soviets still in Iraq

Dec. 24   Saddam says Tel Aviv, Israel will be his first target if war begins

Dec. 28   Iraq increases defenses along its border with Turkey, a NATO member

1991

Jan. 2   U.S. Vice President Dan Quayle visits U.S. troops in Saudi Arabia

Jan. 4   Bush offers to send U.S. Secretary of State James Baker to Geneva to meet with Iraqi Foreign Minister Tariq Aziz

Jan. 6   Iraq accepts U.S. offer to send Baker to Geneva to meet with Aziz

Jan. 9   Baker and Aziz meet for 6 hours in Geneva, but there is no progress

Jan. 10   U.S. Congress begins debate on whether to authorize use of military force

Jan. 12   Congress approves the use of force

Jan. 13   UN Secretary-General Javier Perez de Cuellar meets with Saddam, but there is no progress toward an Iraqi withdrawal

Jan. 14   France and Yemen try to convince Saddam to withdraw, but fail

Jan. 15   Deadline permitting use of military force to expel Iraq from Kuwait is reached

Jan. 17   War begins with air raids against Iraq

BALANCE OF POWER:
TROOPS IN THE PERSIAN GULF

The Allied Coalition

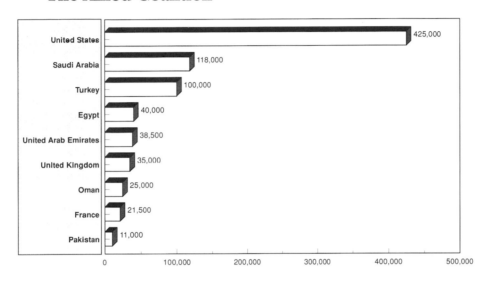

OTHER ALLIED FORCES			
Kuwait	7,000 troops	Czechoslovakia	200 troops (anti chemical unit)
Morocco	5,000 troops	Germany	18 fighter jets sent to Turkey
Syria	21,000 troops	New Zealand	2 planes (46 crew members)
Bahrain	3,350 troops	Italy	3 frigates 8 fighter planes
Bangladesh	5,000 troops	Netherlands	2 frigates 1 supply ship
Canada	1,700 troops 3 warships	Belgium	2 minehunters 1 support ship
Australia	600 troops 3 ships	Argentina	2 ships 100 troops
Niger	500 troops	Poland	2 rescue ships
Senegal	500 troops	Soviet Union	2 ships
Spain	3 frigates 2 corvettes	Greece	1 frigate 200 troops
Sweden	390 troops (field hospital unit)	Denmark	1 corvette
Bulgaria	276 troops offered	Norway	1 coast guard ship

IRAQ FORCES

1,000,000 troops [including 500,000 in and around Kuwait]

The above numbers include only ground combat forces. Countries such as Belgium, Denmark, Germany, Italy, the Netherlands, New Zealand, Norway, Poland, the Soviet Union, Spain, and Sweden sent planes, ships, and/or noncombat ground personnel.

British Lance Corporal Graeme Church, 27, sits on top of the remains of a Saddam Hussein statue as it is lifted into the air in Al Zubayr, southern Iraq, April 2, 2003. The 17-foot statue was toppled and beheaded by members of Britain's Royal Electrical Mechanical Engineers in the 25th Armoured Engineer Squadron.

LESSON 2

THE PERSIAN GULF WAR AND ITS CONTINUING AFTERMATH

Activity 4

How did the United Nations attempt to resolve the situation diplomatically?

ACTIVITY OBJECTIVE

The student will evaluate coalition and United Nations efforts to force Iraq's withdrawal from Kuwait.

MATERIALS AND RESOURCES

❑ Handout 2.2, "UN Security Council Resolutions Condemning Iraq's Invasion of Kuwait"

❑ Handout 3.6, "United Nations Security Council Resolution 242"

STRATEGIES

In the SCIS videotape, *The Middle East in Transition*, Lesson 2, "The Persian Gulf War," former Secretary McNamara mentions the first resolution passed by the United Nations Security Council condemning the Iraqi invasion of Kuwait, UN 660. Iraq's failure to comply with UN 660 and other resolutions that followed was subsequently used as a basis for the allied counterattack in January 1991. This activity will provide students the opportunity to read the text of UN Resolution 660, analyze its provisions, and draw comparisons between this resolution and UN Resolution 242 which dealt with the Arab-Israeli conflict.

If the students have not already viewed the SCIS videotape, *The Middle East in Transition*, Lesson 2, "The Persian Gulf War," begin the activity by showing this portion of the video. Next distribute Handout 2.2, "UN Security Council Resolutions Condemning Iraq's Invasion of Kuwait." As the students read Handout 2.2, which contains the text of the resolution and a synopsis of the other 11 resolutions about the Iraqi situation passed by the UN Security Council between August 2, 1990 and November 29, 1990, they should prepare to answer the following questions:

- What is the UN position regarding the Iraqi invasion of Kuwait?
- What is Iraq called upon to do regarding its occupation of Kuwait?
- What are Iraq and Kuwait urged to do to solve this conflict?
- What UN action will follow this declaration?

After debriefing this portion of the activity, have students read Handout 3.6, "United Nations Security Council Resolution 242" located in Lesson 3, Activity 3. After the students have had a chance to read the resolution, ask them the following questions:

- What conflict led to the passage of UN Resolution 242?
- What is Israel called upon to do in Resolution 242?
- What was the Israeli response to this Resolution?
- What were the U.S. and world responses to Resolution 242?
- Why do you think the United States and the world community were adamant in insisting that Saddam Hussein comply with UN Resolution 660?
- What argument could the Israelis make that their territorial acquisition of the West Bank and Gaza was different than Iraq's occupation of Kuwait?
- What leverage in the world community did Kuwait have that Palestinians lacked?

UN SECURITY COUNCIL RESOLUTIONS
CONDEMNING IRAQ'S INVASION OF KUWAIT

1990

Aug. 3 **Resolution 660: Passed 14-0** the day after Iraq invaded Kuwait, with Yemen abstaining because it "did not have instructions." The resolution read:

> The Security Council: Alarmed by the invasion of Kuwait on August 2, 1990 by the military forces of Iraq; determining that there exists a breach of international peace and security as regards the Iraqi invasion of Kuwait; acting under Articles 39 and 40 of the Charter of the United Nations:
>
> 1) Condemns the Iraqi invasion of Kuwait;
> 2) Demands that Iraq withdraw immediately and unconditionally all its forces to the positions in which they were located on August 1, 1990;
> 3) Calls upon Iraq and Kuwait to begin immediately intensive negotiations for the resoution of their differences and supports all efforts in this regard, and especially those of the Arab League;
> 4) Decides to meet again as necessary to consider further steps to ensure compliance with this resolution.

Aug. 6 **Resolution 661: Passed 13-0**, with Cuba and Yemen abstaining. Ordered a trade and financial embargo of Iraq and occupied Kuwait.

Aug. 9 **Resolution 662: Passed 15-0.** Declared Iraq's annexation of Kuwait null and void.

Aug. 18 **Resolution 664: Passed 15-0.** Demanded that Iraq free all detained foreigners.

Aug. 25 **Resolution 665: Passed 13-0,** with Cuba and Yemen abstaining. Empowered the U.S. and other naval powers to enforce the economic embargo against Iraq and Kuwait by stopping shipping bound there.

Sept. 13 **Resolution 666: Passed 13-2,** with Cuba and Yemen opposed. Allowed food and humanitarian aid to be sent to Iraq and Kuwait.

Sept. 16 **Resolution 667: Passed 15-0.** Condemned Iraq's aggressive acts against diplomatic missions in Kuwait.

Sept. 24 **Resolution 669: Passed 15-0.** Declared that only the Security Council's Sanctions Committee could permit food and other humanitarian assistance to be sent to Iraq and Kuwait.

Sept. 25 **Resolution 670: Passed 14-1,** with Cuba opposed. Expanded economic embargo to include air cargo.

Oct. 29 **Resolution 674: Passed 13-0,** with Cuba and Yemen abstaining. Held Iraq liable for all war damage and demanded release of hostages.

Nov. 28 **Resolution 677: Passed 15-0.** Condemned Iraq's attempts to drive Kuwaitis out of Kuwait and repopulate the country with Iraqis.

Nov. 29 **Resolution 678: Passed 12-2,** with Cuba and Yemen opposing and China abstaining. Provided Iraq with "one final opportunity" until January 15 to comply with all previous resolutions, after which "all necessary means" could be used to drive Iraq from Kuwait.

LESSON 2

THE PERSIAN GULF WAR AND ITS CONTINUING AFTERMATH

Activity 5

Did Desert Storm end too soon?

ACTIVITY OBJECTIVE

The student will evaluate the timing of the decision to stop Operation Desert Storm.

MATERIALS AND RESOURCES

❑ SCIS Videotape, *The Middle East in Transition*, Lesson 2, "The Persian Gulf War"
❑ Worksheet 2.2, "Evaluating the Outcome of Desert Storm"
❑ SCIS Background Essay, *The Middle East in Transition*, Lesson 2, "The Persian Gulf War and Its Continuing Aftermath," section entitled, "Did Desert Storm Stop Too Soon?"

STRATEGIES

The allied decision to end Operation Desert Storm after only 100 hours has been the subject of extensive debate. This lesson will ask students to examine and evaluate the reasons for halting Desert Storm before Saddam Hussein was removed from power.

The second half of Lesson 2 of the SCIS videotape was filmed shortly after the conclusion of the Persian Gulf War in 1991. In it, former Secretaries of State Haig and Shultz discuss the end of the ground phase of Operation Desert Storm after 100 hours. Have students watch this portion of the videotape and construct a list of positions and rationales offered by each of the former Secretaries on this issue.

Students should then be provided with a copy of the SCIS Background Essay, *The Middle East in Transition*, Lesson 2, "The Persian Gulf War and Its Continuing Aftermath," section entitled, "Did Desert Storm Stop Too Soon?" and Worksheet 2.2, "Evaluating the Outcome of Desert Storm." Have students identify seven rationales given by the coalition for ending Desert Storm immediately after the liberation of Kuwait.

Students should evaluate each point in terms of its consequences, both positive and negative, using information from both the reading and the video. At the conclusion of this lesson students should be asked to write a position statement expressing their own opinion of the coalition decision.

EVALUATING THE OUTCOME OF DESERT STORM

Directions: Read the section of the background essay "Did Desert Storm Stop Too Soon?" and use the information to complete the chart. You may not find both pros and cons for each position in the reading and the video of the former Secretaries, but from your own knowledge of events during the war generate items for both columns.

	Reasons For Ending Desert Storm Before Toppling Saddam Hussein	**Pro**	**Con**
1			
2			
3			
4			
5			
6			
7			

What do you think? Did the United States stop too soon? Write a position statement giving your own opinion.

LESSON 2

THE PERSIAN GULF WAR AND ITS CONTINUING AFTERMATH

Activity 6

What is the future of government in Iraq?

ACTIVITY OBJECTIVE

The students will assess the current political situation in Iraq.

MATERIALS AND RESOURCES

❑ Teacher Resource 2.3, "Map of Iraqi Ethnoreligious Groups"
❑ Teacher Resource 2.4, "Iraq's Oil Infrastructure"
❑ Handout 2.3, "Iraq's Major Ethnoreligious Groups"
❑ Teacher Resource 2.5, "The Iraqi Governing Council"
❑ Teacher Resource 2.6, "Key Governmental Terms and Concepts"
❑ Worksheet 2.3, "Key Questions Facing an Iraqi Constitutional Convention"

STRATEGIES

In 2003, following the overthrow of Saddam Hussein, the U.S.-led Coalition Provisional Authority and Iraqi citizens faced the monumental task of creating a stable, democratic Iraq. The task was made more difficult by the fact that Iraq's various ethnic and religious groups often held competing opinions on fundamental constitutional questions, such as the degree of federalism that should be allowed, the role of religion in state affairs, and how the constitutional process should move forward. Divisions within these groups further complicated matters. This activity allows students to examine the various factions within Iraq and the complex issues associated with creating a democratic government.

The night before the class the teacher may want to have students read Federalist Papers 10 and 51 as a homework assignment. These primary documents, written by James Madison and Alexander Hamilton, discuss issues pertinent to the Iraqi people today, such as factions and federalism. However, they can be difficult to read and may not be appropriate for all students. In addition to being found in a number of published collections, these documents are available on the Internet by searching for Federalist 10 and Federalist 51.

Open the class by asking students: "What is a faction?" Tell the class that in 1787—as the U.S. was debating its own constitution—James Madison wrote that a faction is "a number of citizens, whether amounting to a majority or a minority of the whole, who are united and actuated by some common impulse of passion, or of interest." The teacher should ask the class, "What are some of the factions in the United States?" [*Factions in the U.S., sometimes called interest groups, include everything from the National*

Rifle Association to the Sierra Club, from labor organization to business associations, from women's groups to religious organizations.]

Continue the activity by projecting a transparency of Teacher Resource 2.3, "Map of Iraqi Ethnoreligious Groups." Ask students such questions as:

- Where do the Kurds live?
- What are the major religions of the Kurds?
- Where do the Sunni Arabs live?
- Where do the Shia Arabs live?
- What other groups are represented?
- What are the most populous groups?
- How do the various groups relate to peoples in other countries?

Overlay a transparency of Teacher Resource 2.4, "Iraq's Oil Infrastructure," and ask: "How does this information affect the interests of each group? How might economic issues affect the creation of a new government?"

The following questions can also be raised with the class:

- What are some of the factions in Iraq? [*Examples include, but are certainly not limited to, Shia Arabs, Sunni Arabs, Kurds, Turkmen, Christian Assyrians, Baath Party members, and returning exiles. The teacher should note that these factions frequently overlap. For example, Sunnis may include Arabs, Kurds, and Turkmen, while returning exiles may be Shia or Sunni Arabs, or indeed one of a variety of groups. There are also factions within factions. For example, in 2004 one faction of Shias included followers of the Grand Ayatollah Ali al-Sistani, while another included followers of Imam Muqtada al-Sadr.*]
- How have these factions interacted in the past? [*The teacher should distribute and review Handout 2.3, "Iraq's Major Ethnoreligious Groups."*]
- How does the Iraqi Governing Council reflect Iraqi factions? [*The teacher should project Teacher Resource 2.5, "The Iraqi Governing Council."*]
  - ○ Who are these representatives and how were they chosen? [*Council members include a diverse mixture of Iraqis—including recently returned exiles, tribal leaders, women, religious leaders, and secular political leaders. The ethnic and religious makeup of the Council is meant to be representative of Iraq as a whole. Members were appointed by the occupation authorities, who consulted with the major anti-Saddam groups that had worked with Washington before the Iraq war.*]
  - ○ What might be the benefits and drawbacks to how this council was assembled? [*Answers will vary. Possible benefits include being able to bring Iraqis into government leadership positions very quickly and the fact that the council reflects the ethnic and religious makeup of Iraq. Possible drawbacks include the fact that representatives were appointed by the occupying powers rather than elected by Iraqis, and many Iraqis do not feel the council represents their interests. In addition, the council contains many exiles who do not have popular support within Iraq.*]
- Outside economic interests, what other interests might be key as the Iraqis write their constitution? [*Answers will vary, but include many issues, from religious issues to the structure of government.*]

As an activity extension, prepare the class for a mock Iraqi constitutional convention by projecting Teacher Resource 2.6, "Key Governmental Terms and Concepts." Review the terms and concepts with the class. Explain that the writers of the new Iraqi constitution will have to create a system that addresses all such issues, as well as others, but that the class will only negotiate over the four key issues raised on Worksheet 2.3, "Key Questions Facing An Iraqi Constitutional Convention." However, at the teacher's discretion, a broader constitutional convention can be held.

Break the class into five groups, one for each of the main factions in Iraq. At the teacher's discretion, a group can also represent the Iraqi exile population. In addition, one student can be appointed or elected chair of the convention. The groups should use the background essays for Lessons 2 and 4, the Infolinks on www.southerncenter. org, and the school media center to research their groups' positions on the four issues to be discussed and to complete their worksheets, which should be distributed. Groups can also divide research tasks, with individual delegates focusing on specific topics.

Before the convention, groups should rank order their primary goals for the convention, and establish bottom lines on each issue that they feel they must achieve, turning in their lists of goals and bottom lines to the teacher.

Either the student chair or the teacher can call the convention to order. Groups should be sitting together so that they can confer with each other. The elected or appointed spokesperson for each group should be given five to seven minutes to present his or her group's general positions on the topics, without stating his or her group's possible areas of compromise.

Alternatively, the topics can be addressed one at a time, with each group presenting a topic before turning to the next topic. If this option is used, differing group spokespeople can make two-minute presentations—one for each of the four topics.

After the initial presentations, motions can be heard offering specific compromises for the new Iraqi constitution. This can be done randomly, in open debate fashion, with spokespersons asking the chair for permission to speak. Alternatively, negotiations can be held in a more structured, revolving fashion. At any point, groups can ask for a two-minute recess to consult privately (teachers may want to limit the number of recesses each group can ask for). Negotiations should continue until consensus is reached on the four issues.

To debrief this activity extension, raise the following questions with the class:

- How hard was it for the groups to reach a compromise on the issues?
- Should the groups that represented a larger percentage of the Iraqi population have been allowed more influence and/or debating time? If yes, how much more?
- Which groups did better at achieving their goals? Why? [*The class should review the stated goals and bottom lines.*]
- Which groups set the most realistic goals for their Iraqi faction?
- Given the many other issues that the Iraqis will have to negotiate, how hard will it be for them to write a new constitution?
- What influence will the U.S. or other outside actors have on the negotiations?

Please note, the dynamics surrounding the creation of a stable and democratic Iraqi government are changing rapidly in 2004. Teachers may want to choose alternate issues for students to discuss. If a new Iraqi constitution has been adopted, the students may want to compare their class discussions and compromises to the new constitution and discuss the pros and cons of the new Iraqi government.

MAP OF IRAQI ETHNORELIGIOUS GROUPS

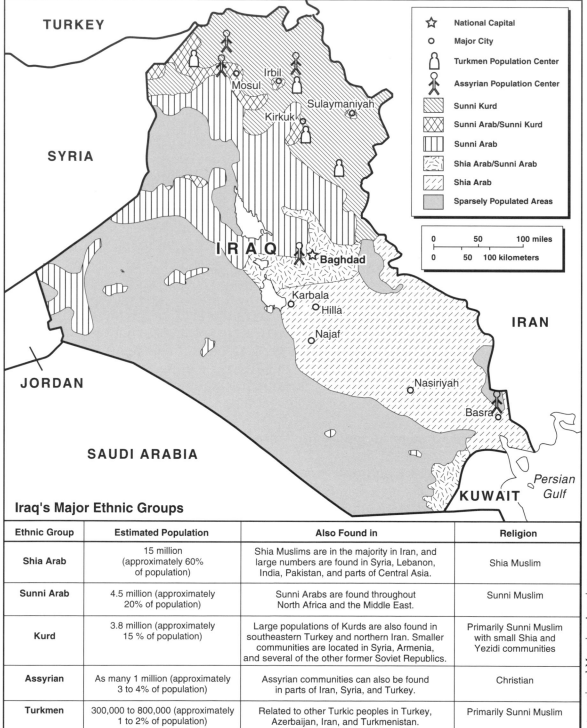

Iraq's Major Ethnic Groups

Ethnic Group	Estimated Population	Also Found in	Religion
Shia Arab	15 million (approximately 60% of population)	Shia Muslims are in the majority in Iran, and large numbers are found in Syria, Lebanon, India, Pakistan, and parts of Central Asia.	Shia Muslim
Sunni Arab	4.5 million (approximately 20% of population)	Sunni Arabs are found throughout North Africa and the Middle East.	Sunni Muslim
Kurd	3.8 million (approximately 15 % of population)	Large populations of Kurds are also found in southeastern Turkey and northern Iran. Smaller communities are located in Syria, Armenia, and several of the other former Soviet Republics.	Primarily Sunni Muslim with small Shia and Yezidi communities
Assyrian	As many 1 million (approximately 3 to 4% of population)	Assyrian communities can also be found in parts of Iran, Syria, and Turkey.	Christian
Turkmen	300,000 to 800,000 (approximately 1 to 2% of population)	Related to other Turkic peoples in Turkey, Azerbaijan, Iran, and Turkmenistan.	Primarily Sunni Muslim

International Mapping Associates

IRAQ'S OIL INFRASTRUCTURE

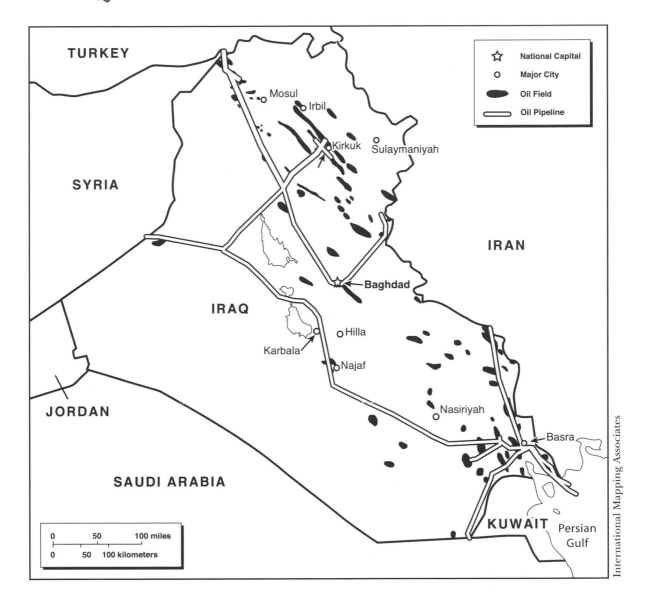

113

IRAQ'S MAJOR ETHNORELIGIOUS GROUPS

Shia Arabs

The Shia, estimated to compose some 60 percent of Iraq's population, live mostly in the south of the country and share religious, although not ethnic, ties with Iran. During Saddam's regime, Iraq's Shia majority was ruled by a Sunni minority and subjected to systematic discrimination. Thirteen of the 25 seats on the Iraqi Governing Council are allotted to Shia Arabs. In general, Shias favor a strong central government in Iraq, rather than a federal system, with representatives chosen through direct elections. The Shia also agree on the principle that a future Iraq should be based on Islamic law, although they range from extremists who advocate Islamist rule analogous to Iran, to moderates who are wary of mixing religion and politics. In a compromise between moderate Shias and religious conservatives, Iraq's interim constitution, signed on March 8, 2004, enshrined *Sharia* as "a source" of legislation, although not the primary one. The Shia largely obey the pronouncements of their religious leaders, the most prominent being Grand Ayatollah Ali al-Sistani. While they supported the overthrow of Saddam Hussein, Shias generally favor a quick end to the U.S. occupation.

Sunni Arabs

Sunni Arabs make up around 15 percent of Iraq's population and live mainly in the center of the country. During the rule of Saddam Hussein, himself a Sunni Arab, they enjoyed a privileged position. Since the overthrow of Saddam Hussein, Sunni Arabs have been forced to surrender their privileges, causing resentment and a sense of humiliation. Because of their involvement in Saddam Hussein's Baathist government, Sunni Arabs were an integral part of the country's bureaucracy. Yet the Coalition Provisional Authority, under a policy known as de-Baathification, prevented many Sunni Arabs from participating in the country's new government. While there are five Sunni Arabs on the Iraqi Governing Council, a majority of Iraqi Sunnis dismiss these representatives, particularly the Sunni Arab expatriates, as outsiders who are out of touch with their interests. It is the Sunni Arabs, particularly the upper echelon, who stand to lose the most in post-Saddam Iraq, a reality that explains why they have been the main culprits behind attacks against U.S.-led coalition forces. Resistance toward Allied troops has been particularly intense in an area known as the Sunni Triangle, with around 80 percent of the attacks in the first year of the occupation taking place there.

Sunni Kurds

Iraqi Kurds enjoyed a large degree of autonomy during the decade following the Persian Gulf War, due to the "no-fly zones" enforced by the United States and Britain. These no-fly zones kept Saddam's military from entering the northern portion of Iraq, protecting them from Saddam. As a result, the Kurds developed their own government and societal structures. The Kurds, who represent some 20 percent of the Iraqi population, believe they have little to gain from a unified Iraq if they have to sacrifice too much autonomy. As a result, they favor a federal system in which they would be given a high degree of control over their own affairs. For some Kurds, autonomy is not enough, and they still aspire to create an independent Kurdish state, a long-held ambition.

Turkmen

Turkmen comprise roughly one percent of the Iraqi population. While Turkmen are scattered throughout the country, the bulk live in the oil-rich area near Kirkuk, in northern Iraq. With only one representative on the Iraqi Governing Council, Turkmen feel they are underrepresented in the post-Saddam political environment. Turkmen are also displeased by the fact that the interim constitution gives Kurds a large degree of autonomy and control over territories claimed by Turkmen.

Assyrians

The Assyrian community comprises as many as one million inhabitants, or four percent of Iraq's population. They are located primarily in Baghdad and central Iraq, but large communities exist in the north and south as well. Assyrians are mainly Christian. While Assyrians lived in relative peace under Saddam Hussein, they now feel their interests are underrepresented in the emerging regime. Many feel threatened by an increasing emphasis on Islam, as reflected, for example, by the inclusion of *Sharia* in the interim constitution.

THE IRAQI GOVERNING COUNCIL

Faction Represented	Iraqi Governing Council Member	Description
Shia Exiles	Seyyid Muhammed Bahr ul-Uloom	Highest-ranking Shiite religious figure on the Council. Moderate cleric who fled to London in 1991 after Saddam killed some of his relatives.
	Ahmad Chalabi	Head of Iraqi National Congress, a collection of anti-Saddam political groups. A favorite of the Pentagon civilian leadership.
	Ayad Allawi	Head of the Iraqi National Accord, a group of former Iraqi army officers based in London. Involved in an unsuccessful 1996 CIA attempt to overthrow Saddam Hussein.
	Abdul Aziz al-Hakim	Political leader of the Supreme Council for Islamic Revolution in Iraq (SCIRI). Based in Iran since 1980, he cooperated with the U.S. to overthrow Saddam, but opposes the U.S.-led occupation.
	Ebrahim Jafari al Eshaiker	Spokesman for the Islamic Da'wa Party, a radical Shia movement. Exiled from Iraq in 1980.
	Mowaffak al-Rubaie	A former Da'wa spokesman in Britain, neurologist, and human-rights activist.
Shias from Inside Iraq	Wael Abdulatif	Judge in Basra since 1982. Imprisoned briefly by Saddam Hussein.
	Hamid Majeed Mousa	An economist and head of the Iraqi Communist Party since 1993. Originally from Babylon.
	Sheikh Ahmad Shyaa al-Barak	Leader of the Al-Bu Sultan tribe, a lawyer, and leader of an Iraqi human-rights association.
	Raja Habib Khuzai	One of three women on the Council, a doctor who heads a maternity hospital in southern Diwaniyah.
	Ezzedine Salim	Writer from the southern city of Basra and a local leader of the Da'wa Party. He was assassinated by Iraqi insurgents on May 18, 2004, while serving as president of the IGC, and not replaced.
	Abdul Karim al-Muhammadawi	Leader of a southern tribe who led guerrilla attacks against Saddam Hussein and has ties to Iran.
	Salama al-Khufaji	Female professor of dentistry at Baghdad University. She replaced Akila al-Hashimi, a former Iraqi diplomat who was assassinated in September 2003.

THE IRAQI GOVERNING COUNCIL

Faction Represented	Iraqi Governing Council Member	Description
Sunni Exiles	Adnan Pachachi	Foreign minister before Baath Party came to power in 1968; founded Independent Democratic Movement to work for a secular, democratic government. At 80 he is respected as the most senior political figure on the council.
	Samir Shakir Mahmoud al-Sumaidy	Owns a construction company in China. Leader of Sumaidy clan and opposition figure in Saddam era.
	Ghazi Ajil al-Yawar	Businessman from Mosul in the north. Member of powerful Shamar clan. Spent 15 years in Saudi Arabia.
Sunnis from Inside Iraq	Naseir al-Chaderchi	Lawyer and head of National Democratic Party of Iraq (NDP). Influential political figure before Baath Party came to power in 1968.
	Mohsen Abdul Hameed	Professor at Baghdad University and head of Iraqi Islamic Party. Authority on the interpretation of the Koran.
Kurds	Masood Barzani	President of Kurdistan Democratic Party (KDP), one of the two largest Kurdish political parties. Controls northwest portion of the autonomous Kurdish region of Iraq.
	Jalal Talabani	Head of Patriotic Union of Kurdistan (PUK), the other large Kurdish party. Controls southwest portion of the autonomous Kurdish region of Iraq.
	Salahaddin Muhammad Bahaddin	Secretary General of Kurdistan Islamic Union, a religiously based Sunni party and the third-most-powerful Kurdish group.
	Dara Nor al-Din	Judge on the Iraqi Court of Appeals, imprisoned by Saddam Hussein; from the northern city of Kirkuk.
	Mahmoud Othman	Independent politician and long-time leader of the Kurdish National Struggle.
Turkmen	Songul Chapouk	Head of Iraqi Women's Organization and teacher of fine arts in Mosul. Survived an assassination attempt in November 2003.
Assyrians/Chaldeans	Yonnadam Kanna	Secretary General of Assyrian Democratic Movement. Represents Christian minority made up of ethnic Assyrians and Chaldeans.

Source: Iraqi Coalition Provisional Authority, May 27, 2004,
http://www.cpa-iraq.org/government/governing_council.html.

KEY GOVERNMENTAL TERMS AND CONCEPTS

Bill of Rights—Legislation describing civil liberties that cannot be violated by the government in order to define the scope of individual freedom within a society. Civil liberties included in a bill of rights might include freedom of speech and expression, freedom of religion and belief, due process and equal protection under the law, and freedom to organize.

Checks and Balances—A system of government in which power is divided between the executive, legislative, and judicial branches of government, and the divided powers counterbalance each other.

Constitution—The fundamental system of laws that organize a country politically. These laws must be obeyed by the rulers and are generally embodied in a written document. A few countries, such as the United Kingdom, have unwritten or partially written constitutions.

Federal System—A political system in which power and resources are divided between central and regional governments. In the United States, for example, some powers are reserved for state governments while others are given to the federal government.

Parliamentary System—A system of government in which there are close ties between the executive and legislative branches of government. Executive power is vested in a cabinet that is composed of members of the legislature. The prime minister leads this cabinet and is head of government.

Presidential System—A system of government in which the executive branch is separated from the legislative branch and executive power is vested in one person, the president, who is elected independently of the legislature and has a fixed term.

Representative Democracy—A system of government where elected officials make decisions for the people.

Separation of Religion and State—The notion that religious practices and teachings should not play a direct role in politics, and that government should not intrude into religious life. Typically, this notion is meant to protect the freedom to practice any religion.

Unitary System—A political system in which one central authority holds political power. The central government may delegate duties to cities or other administrative units, but it retains final authority and can retract any tasks it has delegated.

KEY QUESTIONS FACING
AN IRAQI CONSTITUTIONAL CONVENTION

Faction Represented:_____

What role, if any, should religion play in Iraqi politics? (e.g., Should legislation be based on religious law? Should there be an official religion? Should protection be given to religious minorities?)

Should Iraq adopt a federal or unitary system of government? (e.g., Should a national government hold all the power or should specific powers be reserved for regional areas?)

Should the constitution give special protection to certain groups? (e.g., Should quotas be set for representatives of certain factions, such as women, Turkmen, Assyrians, or other minorities? Should representatives of minority interests be given veto power over certain legislation?)

Which civil rights should explicitly be protected in the constitution?

Reem Raiyshi, female suicide bomber, holds her son as she poses with weapons. On January 14, 2004, Raiyshi blew herself up at the major border crossing point between Israel and the Gaza Strip, killing herself and four Israelis.

Reuters/Hamas

LESSON 3

THE ARAB-ISRAELI CONFLICT

Lesson 3 of 5 Lessons for the
Southern Center for International Studies'
Multimedia Educational Package
THE MIDDLE EAST IN TRANSITION

A young Jewish settler boy, dressed up as an Israeli soldier, stands near an Israeli soldier in the West Bank city of Hebron, March 7, 2004.

Reuters/Gil Cohen Magen

Background Reading for

LESSON 3

of the SCIS Educational Package
THE MIDDLE EAST IN TRANSITION

THE ARAB-ISRAELI CONFLICT

Throughout the recent past, the Arab-Israeli conflict has been the single most prominent and dangerous confrontation in the Middle East. During the Cold War, with the United States generally supporting Israel and with the Soviet Union generally supporting the Arabs, the conflict had the potential to escalate to global warfare. Although the threat of global warfare growing out of the Arab-Israeli conflict has disappeared since the Cold War ended, the dangers of terrorism fueled by the Arab-Israeli conflict remain.

Many international actors, including the United States, several European powers, the former Soviet Union, and the United Nations, have attempted to negotiate a solution to the conflict. At best, these attempts have been only partially successful. Even the 1993 Israeli-PLO accord did not guarantee peace.

Why have the two sides been so opposed? Why has the conflict been so violent? Why has it been so intractable? Is there any hope of ending it? These are just a few of the questions we will explore here.

ISSUES IN THE ARAB-ISRAELI CONFLICT

The conflict between Arabs and Jews is hundreds of years old, and the issues that have kept it heated are many and complex. For our purposes here, the reasons behind it will be grouped into three issue-areas.

The first general issue-area deals with land, property, and water. Much of the land and property in the region has changed hands several times, and water, as always in the Middle East, is scarce.

The conflict over land is particularly complicated. Before the time of Christ, the Jewish people lived in their own kingdom, an influential Jewish-ruled state located where Israel is today. However, the Jewish state fell on hard times. In 586 B.C., the Babylonian Empire defeated Israel. Many Jews were brought to Babylon—in present-day Iraq—as slaves. Returning to their homeland after years of captivity, the Jewish people constructed a new state, only to be incorporated into the Roman Empire. Then, in 70 A.D., the Romans destroyed the Temple in Jerusalem, and the Jewish people were scattered throughout the Roman Empire and beyond. From this time until 1948, Jews had no state.

During the intervening centuries, Arab populations and the Islamic religion predominated in the territory where Israel had been. Indeed, for more than 1,000 years, the area has been the home of Arabs that came to be called Palestinians. This leads to a deceptively simple question, "Whose land is it?" There is no universally accepted answer.

Property issues are equally difficult. Before the modern state of Israel was founded, many Arabs owned property in what is today Israel and the Occupied Territories, as well as elsewhere in the region. From the beginning of the modern Jewish return to Palestine in the 1880s, Jews purchased some land from Arabs who owned land there. But when Israel was created in 1948, the Israelis abrogated many Palestinian property rights, and took over Arab land as well. This, of course, was the same thing that many Arab rulers had done to Jews living under their rule in earlier years. The same question, slightly modified, must again be asked, "Whose property is it?"

Water is another difficult problem in the Arab-Israeli conflict. Although a state's access to water resources is often overlooked as an issue, the aridity of the Middle East makes water a concern for all states in the region.

Arab states have long accused Israel of "water theft," especially in the Jordan River basin, where Israel and Jordan have conflicting policies on water use, and in the Occupied Territories, where Israel diverts a significant percentage of water for domestic use. Conversely, Israel has long been concerned about its extreme dependence on water resources whose flow can be interrupted by Arab states. This time the question is, "Whose water is it?"

The second issue-area in the Arab-Israeli conflict is history. It may be a statement of the obvious, but with the conflict between Arabs and Jews being of such long standing, and with both sides having long historical memories, past injustices, prejudices, discrimination, fighting, and killing remain very much on the minds of many Arabs and Jews. In the minds of many, bygones are not bygones but very much a part of the contemporary record.

History, then, is a deeply ingrained problem in the Arab-Israeli conflict. It adds fuel to the fires of current animosity as surely as present injustices, prejudices, discrimination, fighting, and killing. The historical record, combined with the assurance that many people on each side have that their own perspective on the conflict is accurate, is an extremely important factor that keeps the Arab-Israeli conflict smoldering.

The final issue-area relates to religion, ethnicity, and culture. This is a broad grouping, but even a casual observer must recognize that Islam and Judaism originally were centered respectively on Arabs and Jews. They also are religions that detail the cultural values and practices of the faithful. Many believers in both Islam and Judaism have adopted reform views that are more tolerant of the other than orthodox perspectives. Nevertheless—despite the fact that both Judaism and Islam stem from a common ancestor, Abraham—some members of both groups use their respective religion to rationalize their antipathy for the other side.

This does not mean that the Arab-Israeli conflict cannot be resolved. On occasion, Arabs and Jews have lived in peace before, for example in Spain during the ninth, tenth, and eleventh centuries or during the Ottoman Empire. While the 1993 Israeli-PLO agreement provides reason for optimism today, resolving the Arab-Israeli conflict remains an immense challenge.

THE CREATION OF MODERN ISRAEL

For almost nineteen centuries, the Jewish people had no state. Sometimes they became part of the societies in which they lived, and other times they maintained their traditional practices and customs. Often, Jews were persecuted in their adopted homelands.

As a result both of persecution and a longing for their own homeland, some Jews founded a movement to create a Jewish homeland. Called "Zionism," the movement gained little ground until World War I. Then, in an effort to solidify Jewish support behind the war, Great Britain in 1917 issued the Balfour Declaration, which promised to create a national home for the Jewish people in the territory of ancient Israel.

Following World War I, Great Britain received Palestine as a mandate from the League of Nations. In the 1920s, thousands of Jews moved to Palestine, expecting Britain to create a Jewish state. This migration inflamed anti-Jewish Arab nationalism in Palestine, but since Britain showed no real intention of creating a Jewish state, the impending conflict simmered on the back burners of world affairs.

World War II and the Holocaust changed this. Following Hitler's defeat, with millions of Jews having been massacred by the Nazis, Zionism became an immensely powerful force in the world's Jewish community. Having no desire to return to their adopted homelands in Europe, thousands of Jews again migrated to Palestine.

Britain was in a difficult situation. It had promised Jews a homeland in the Balfour Declaration, but it also had sizeable oil interests and strategic interests in Arab countries. Consequently, Britain slowed Jewish immigration to Palestine.

Some Jews responded to Britain's actions by resorting to terrorism to try to drive the British out of Palestine. Exhausted by World War II, the British had no desire to fight. They turned the Palestine problem over to the United Nations.

In short order, with the United States and the Soviet Union collaborating to forge a solution, the United Nations proposed that Palestine be partitioned, with a Jewish state being created along the Mediterranean coast and a Palestinian state inland. It was not a perfect solution, and few people, least of all the Arabs, were pleased with it.

But at least it was a solution, and both superpowers were behind it. Acting with that assurance, the Jews in the region moved quickly, proclaiming Israeli independence on May 14, 1948. The United States was the first country to recognize Israel, and the Soviet Union was just behind. Finally, the Jewish people again had their own state.

ISRAEL AT WAR

This did not mean that peace was at hand. Almost immediately, Arab states attacked Israel. At first, the outnumbered Israeli forces retreated before the Egyptian, Iraqi, Jordanian, Lebanese, and Syrian armies. Israel turned to the UN for help, and the U.S. and the Soviets again worked together, fashioning a four-week-long cease-fire.

During the cease-fire, Israel, with Soviet approval, obtained large quantities of weapons from communist Czechoslovakia. When the cease-fire ended, Israel pushed the Arabs back and pursued them into Arab territories. Egypt sued for peace, and the United States arranged a region-wide armistice. Modern Israel had passed its first trial by fire, and had emerged victorious. It had also acquired territory that under the UN partition had been intended for the Palestinians, keeping it despite U.S. pressure to return it. During the war, at least 750,000 Palestinians fled Palestine, moving to squalid refugee camps in surrounding Arab countries. The Arabs accused Israel of expansionism.

Since 1948, Arabs and Israelis have fought three more major wars. In 1956, France, Britain, and Israel attacked Egypt in a dispute over the Suez Canal. The three easily defeated Egypt, but the United States and the Soviet Union insisted that France and Britain withdraw and Israel return the land it acquired in the war to Egypt. All three complied.

In 1967, Israel won a stunning military victory in only six days. Israel acquired the Gaza Strip and the Sinai Peninsula from Egypt, the Golan Heights from Syria, and Jerusalem and the West Bank of the Jordan River from Jordan. This time, however, despite having agreed to UN Security Council Resolution 242, committing Israel to return virtually all Arab lands acquired in the war, Israel refused to return the territory it had captured. Israel argued that the new territory it now controlled gave it more defensible borders than it had before the Six Day War. Once again Arabs accused Israel of expansionism.

The Six Day War sowed the seeds for still more Arab-Israeli hatred. Whatever the legitimacy of Israel's need for more defensible borders, Israel now occupied land that was unarguably Arab. The Sinai Peninsula, for example, had been part of Egypt for almost 5,000 years. At the same time, thousands of Palestinian refugees flooded into Egypt, Jordan, Syria, and Lebanon. Meanwhile, Israel now controlled territory in which thousands of additional Palestinians lived. Many Palestinians now accepted the Palestine Liberation Organization and its leader, Yasser Arafat, as their spokesman. Worse yet, from the Israeli perspective, some Palestinians turned to terrorism to redress what they perceived as Israeli expansionism and injustice.

Six years later, in 1973, the fourth major Arab-Israeli war erupted as Egypt and Syria launched a surprise attack. Taken off guard, Israel suffered heavy losses and was almost overwhelmed. Only a massive U.S. airlift of materials and supplies averted disaster for Israel.

Within days, Israel recovered. Launching a counteroffensive, Israel drove the Egyptians and Syrians back. U.S. diplomacy once again constructed a cease-fire, and an uneasy truce fell over the Middle East.

For the United States, there was additional fallout. In retaliation for the U.S. airlift, Arab oil-producing states temporarily stopped shipping oil to the United States. The "oil weapon" had been unsheathed.

After the 1973 war ended, U.S. diplomats led by U.S. Secretary of State Henry Kissinger engaged in "shuttle diplomacy" for several years, flying back and forth between Washington, Israel, and several Arab states trying to arrange a more permanent peace. Kissinger achieved two significant interim agreements: the disengagement of hostile forces in the Sinai and in the Golan Heights, and an Israeli withdrawal from two strategic passes. Despite this, however, the Arab-Israeli conflict continued.

CAMP DAVID

When Jimmy Carter assumed the American presidency in 1977, he was alarmed that war in the Middle East might erupt once again. To forestall this, Carter proposed that all involved parties meet at Geneva to negotiate a solution to the Arab-Israeli dispute.

Unlike the previous U.S. shuttle diplomacy, the new U.S. initiative actively sought to involve the Soviet Union. Carter reasoned that the U.S.S.R. had influence with the Palestine Liberation Organization and radical Arab states, and that without their constructive participation, no lasting peace would be possible. Consequently, Carter approached the Soviets about cosponsoring the proposed Geneva meeting. The Soviets agreed.

This did not please Israel, which had been fighting against Soviet-armed Arab armies since 1956. Nor did it please Egypt's President Anwar Sadat, who in 1972 had ordered the Soviets to leave Egypt and who remained immensely distrustful of Soviet intentions. As a result, Sadat proposed to Israel that Washington be bypassed and Israel and Egypt negotiate directly. Israel agreed, and in November 1977, Anwar Sadat journeyed to Israel, hoping that his visit would lead to a peace treaty between Israel and the Arab states in which Israel would trade the land acquired in 1967 for diplomatic recognition, security, and peace. He also hoped that his visit would lead to self-determination for the Palestinians living in the West Bank and the Gaza Strip.

Sadat was overly optimistic. Even though the visit was a diplomatic success, Israel refused to trade land for peace except in the Sinai Peninsula. It also offered the West Bank and the Gaza Strip only limited self-rule, not self-determination. Israel's distrust of the Arab world was too great to do more. At the same time, the Israeli government continued to encourage Israelis to move to the West Bank to settle.

To Sadat and to the United States, Israel's settlement policy was a conscious Israeli effort to abrogate Security Council Resolution 242 and a direct slap in the face to both Egypt and the U.S. To show U.S. displeasure with Israel, Carter tied the sale of advanced U.S. fighter planes to Israel to a similar sale to Egypt and Saudi Arabia.

Meanwhile, the rest of the Arab world was furious with Sadat because of his trip to Israel. Arab states expelled Egypt from every Arab organization. Many Arab states broke diplomatic relations and boycotted trade with Egypt. Some called for Sadat's assassination.

In this charged atmosphere, Jimmy Carter made one last try for peace. He invited Sadat and Israel's conservative leader, Menachem Begin, to Camp David. For twelve days, the three men met. Carter later jokingly said that he held Begin and Sadat "virtual prisoners."

To the world's surprise, Begin and Sadat reached agreements—known as the Camp David Accords—on several issues. Begin promised to recognize the "legitimate rights of the Palestinians," to allow West Bank and Gaza Palestinians to participate in negotiations on these areas, and to freeze temporarily new settlements there. He also agreed to return the Sinai Peninsula to Egypt. Perhaps most importantly, Sadat and Begin also committed their countries to sign a peace treaty within three months. The Egyptian-Israeli treaty was actually signed in March 1979.

Israel was at peace with its most powerful Arab neighbor, and Egypt had recognized Israel's right to exist. In addition, Egypt had regained the Sinai Peninsula and no longer had to prepare for war with Israel. Camp David was thus a historic breakthrough in Arab-Israeli relations.

AFTER CAMP DAVID

From Egypt's perspective, however, there was a downside to Camp David as well. Egypt was now isolated within the Arab world. Egypt's position was made all the more tenuous as Menachem Begin announced that Israel would "never" withdraw from all the land it had acquired in 1967, as Begin made it clear that he had not altered Israel's position on Palestinian limited self-rule as opposed to self-determination, and as Israel resumed its settlement policies in the West Bank.

As the 1970s gave way to the 1980s, it became increasingly clear that the Arab-Israeli conflict would continue. In 1981, Israel attacked and destroyed Iraq's nuclear reactor. Later the same year, Islamic radicals assassinated Anwar Sadat, throwing the future of the Egyptian-Israeli treaty open to doubt. Fortunately, Sadat's successor, Hosni Mubarak, continued Sadat's policies.

Then, in 1982, in response to Palestinian attacks into Israel from Lebanon and in defense of Lebanese Christians under attack by Syria, Israel invaded Lebanon, thereby further confusing an already complex civil war. Israel also annexed the Golan Heights. At the same time, throughout the 1980s and into the 1990s, Israel pursued an accelerated settlements program in the West Bank.

Meanwhile, radical Palestinians and other Arabs launched attacks against Israel and Israeli interests. They sometimes also targeted U.S. interests because of U.S. support for Israel. In addition, in 1987, Palestinians began the *Intifada*, an uprising against Israeli occupation of the West Bank and the Gaza Strip, which continued into the 1990s.

As the 1990s opened, then, the Camp David Accords and the Egyptian-Israeli Treaty remained notable achievements, but they had not ended the Arab-Israeli conflict.

ARAB-ISRAELI NEGOTIATIONS IN THE 1990S

Following the 1991 Persian Gulf War, the United States initiated another effort to resolve the Arab-Israeli conflict. The basis for the new round of negotiations was the credibility that the United States developed in many anti-Iraqi Arab states as U.S. President George H. W. Bush assembled the alliance and conducted the war that drove Iraq out of Kuwait.

The first round in the post-Persian Gulf War negotiations began in October 1991 in Madrid. By July 1993, Israeli, Palestinian, Syrian, Jordanian, and U.S. negotiators had concluded ten rounds of talks, and there was room for both optimism and pessimism.

Pessimists pointed out that no breakthroughs had occurred. Arab negotiators still sought the return of land taken in the 1967 war, the end of Israeli settlements in the West Bank and the Gaza Strip, and Palestinian self-rule in those territories. In return, they promised peace, security, and an end to the state of war between Arabs and Israelis.

Israel, ever mistrustful of Arab intentions and not confident enough to accept a land-for-peace exchange, remained unwilling to take what it viewed as an extreme gamble. Instead, Israel put forward various suggestions for self-rule rather than independence for the Palestinians in the Occupied Territories, and hedged on returning the Golan Heights to Syria. In addition, the two sides could not even agree on what two key United Nations Security Council resolutions, 242 and 338, actually meant. Thus, to pessimists, the deadlock continued.

Optimists saw things differently. They noted that Israeli representatives to the talks were increasingly willing to talk with Palestinian representatives as equals rather than as subordinates, the Israeli government was moving toward willingness to talk with the PLO, sensitive issues such as water use and security arrangements were being discussed, and both sides had intimated that they understood the need to reach a historic compromise given the proper conditions.

Meanwhile, several other trends and events important to the Arab-Israeli conflict were also unfolding, some in public and some less obvious. First, in Israel, the Labor Party won the June 1992 elections, bringing Yitzhak Rabin to power as Israel's prime minister. As prime minister, Rabin pledged to explore every possible avenue toward peace. Second, in the wake of Iraq's invasion of Kuwait and the Persian Gulf War, the PLO's finances became increasingly tight. With much of the PLO's income before the invasion and war coming from Saudi Arabia, Iraq, and Kuwait, and with each of those three countries for different reasons slashing donations to the PLO in the wake of the war, PLO money sources were drying up. Third, many Palestinians, especially those living in the Gaza Strip, were increasingly opting to join Hamas, the Islamic Resistance Movement, which pledged the total destruction of the state of Israel and the creation of an Islamic state in its place. Thus, the PLO was losing influence, especially among younger Palestinians in the West Bank and the Gaza Strip.

Despite these trends and events, most observers expected progress toward peace in the Arab-Israeli conflict to be glacial, if it occurred at all. Virtually no one was prepared for the surprise that came in August and September 1993.

The Israeli-PLO Accords

Between January and August 1993, Israelis and Palestinians met 14 times in a series of extremely secret two- to three-day meetings in Oslo, Norway. These meetings were conducted at first by Israelis who did not officially represent their government and Palestinians who were only mid-level PLO officials.

The Oslo talks were one of four different back-channel negotiations between Israelis and Palestinians. No more than two dozen people ever knew that the Oslo talks were taking place. Away from the glare of publicity, the two sides were able to discuss each other's viewpoints and positions without posturing for political advantage and debating points. As the two sides talked, they slowly chipped away at the disagreements that separated them. They also worked on a draft agreement on Israeli-Palestinian relations. Throughout, relations between Israelis and Palestinians were friendly.

By May, work on the draft agreement had progressed far enough that the Israeli government sent two Foreign Ministry officials to Oslo to join the negotiations. PLO leader Yasser Arafat let it be known that he firmly supported the Oslo negotiations when Norwegian Foreign Minister Johan Holst visited Arafat in Tunisia in June. With both the Israeli government and the PLO now officially signed on to the Oslo channel, drafting a final agreement accelerated.

By August 20, the agreement was finalized and signed by the negotiating teams. On August 27, the Israelis briefed the United States about the amazing course of events. On September 9, Israel and the PLO exchanged letters recognizing the legitimacy of the other. On September 13, at the invitation of U.S. President Bill Clinton, Israeli Prime Minister Yitzhak Rabin and PLO Chairman Yasser Arafat signed the agreement, called the Declaration of Principles, on the White House lawn in Washington.

Under the terms of the 17 articles and four annexes of the Declaration of Principles, Israel promised to withdraw from the Gaza Strip and the West Bank town of Jericho. Palestinians were supposed to begin administering both locations within four months of the Israeli withdrawal. Israel would retain control over only external security of both places, and would also be responsible for the protection of Jewish settlers. Meanwhile, Palestinians would acquire limited authority over education, health, social services, taxation, and tourism in the rest of the West Bank. Eventually, Palestinians would elect an Interim Self-Government Authority, and the Israeli military and police would withdraw to guard Jewish settlements and the borders. A special Palestinian police force would be formed to provide security throughout the rest of the West Bank and the Gaza Strip.

In addition, the Israeli-PLO Accords, also known as the Oslo Accords, helped break the confrontational deadlock that existed between Israel and its two other immediate Arab neighbors, Jordan and Syria. Syria moved only reluctantly toward negotiating its differences with Israel, but Jordan was more favorably disposed toward resolving its disagreements with the Jewish state. In both cases, possibilities of peace began to emerge.

Finally, it appeared a new era in Israeli-Palestinian relations and Arab-Israeli relations was about to dawn.

Or was it? To many Palestinians and other Arabs, Yasser Arafat and the PLO had surrendered to Israel. One radical group in particular, Hamas, threatened to do everything it could to undermine the agreement. Indeed, Hamas, which claimed the allegiance of a significant percentage of Palestinians living in the Gaza Strip and the West Bank, had as one of its primary objectives the destruction of Israel.

Similarly, many conservative Israelis and West Bank settlers believed that with the Declaration of Principles the Rabin government had sold out to Arafat and the PLO. Some settlers warned that they would do anything necessary to protect and keep their property in the West Bank if they were told to relinquish it. Others warned that they would never accept Palestinian self-rule, and might fight to oppose it.

Over the next year, each side took initial steps toward fulfilling the Oslo Accords. Israeli troops withdrew from several villages and towns in the West Bank and from much of the Gaza Strip, turning these areas over to the Palestinians. The Palestinians developed the Palestinian National Authority (PNA)—with its own police force, president (Yasser Arafat), and elected parliament—to govern this territory. At the same time, violence continued to be carried out by Israelis and Palestinians opposed to the peace process. So despite the optimism brought about by the signing of the Declaration of Principles, there remained a long way to go.

After Oslo

The historic peace agreement forged between Israel and Jordan in 1994 was the next major event in the Middle East peace process. Israel's treaty with Jordan, which has a large Palestinian population, added momentum to the peace process, and Jordan's King Hussein became an important broker between Israelis and Palestinians.

By 1995, the Israelis and Palestinians were in the second stage of transferring West Bank territory to Palestinian control. But the Israelis were then, as they are now, increasingly divided over the peace process. Secular and moderate Israelis favor the land-for-peace process, while religious and ultranationalist Israelis strongly oppose it. For many, the depth of this division was symbolized by a single violent act, the November 1995 assassination of Israeli Prime Minister Yitzhak Rabin by a Jewish fundamentalist.

The 1996 election also showed the even split within Israeli society. With 50.5 percent of the vote, Likud candidate Benyamin Netanyahu barely beat then-Prime Minister Shimon Peres. Lacking a strong mandate, Netanyahu ruled with an uneasy coalition of right-wing nationalists and assorted religious parties. Given this coalition and the fact that Netanyahu was already on record as opposing "land for peace," it was not surprising that the peace process began to unravel.

Palestinians have also been divided over the issue of peace with Israel. While moderate Palestinians favor working toward a peace agreement with Israel, extremist groups such as the Hamas movement have opposed the peace process, arguing that negotiations have done little to improve the Palestinians' quality of life and that more can be gained through violent revolt. To this end, they have attacked Israelis and, at times, battled the PNA, led by Arafat.

In the late 1990s, attempts to strengthen security in the Occupied Territories led the PNA to become increasingly authoritarian. This, in turn, created a second major division within the Palestinian community: between those actively pushing for more democracy (including members of the Palestinian parliament) and those who see democracy as a luxury in the present context (including some in the PNA administration). These divisions—moderate and extremist, democratic and authoritarian—have only deepened as the peace process has shown little hope of leading to improvements in Palestinian economic well-being or human dignity.

The Wye River Memorandum

In October 1998, with the Oslo peace process foundering, the Clinton administration brokered a new set of negotiations between Israeli Prime Minister Netanyahu and Palestinian Authority President Yasser Arafat. These new talks were held at the Wye River Plantation in Maryland. After several false starts and the near collapse of the talks, King Hussein of Jordan, stricken with cancer, left his American hospital bed to intervene directly. That intervention, coupled with U.S. pressure and promises of increased aid, finally led to a new Israeli-Palestinian agreement.

The agreement, known as the Wye River Memorandum, outlined a new timetable for completing the implementation of the Oslo Accords and beginning negotiations on the most difficult issues, such as the final status of Jerusalem and the return of Palestinian refugees. The Memorandum also called for several intermediate steps, including the withdrawal of the Israeli army from a further 13 percent of the West Bank, the opening of an airport in Gaza, the opening of a "safe corridor" between the Gaza Strip and the West Bank, implementation of measures to combat terrorism, a reduction in the number of Palestinian police forces, and the release by Israel of some Palestinian prisoners.

Immediately following the signing of the Memorandum, the Palestinian Legislative Council renounced hostilities with Israel and revoked the articles of the Palestinian Charter that had called for the elimination of the Jewish state. The land-for-peace formula appeared to have been revived. However, Netanyahu, under pressure from the extreme right and religious parties opposed to the deal, repeatedly delayed implementation, eventually suspending the agreement altogether in December 1998. The Knesset, in turn, voted for early elections, which took place in May 1999.

In the 1999 Israeli elections, Labor candidate Ehud Barak overwhelmingly defeated incumbent Prime Minister Netanyahu, largely due to Netanyahu's unpopularity and Barak's promises to revive the peace process. Barak appeared to win a strong mandate to resume the land-for-peace formula and bring the Israeli army home from southern Lebanon (see below).

However, Barak found that attempts to negotiate peace were again hindered by Israel's divided government and society. Several right-wing parties opposed to the land-for-peace formula had increased their number of seats in the Knesset. One such party, the ultra-orthodox Shas Party, became an influential member in the coalition government, complicating Barak's attempts to forge a unified Israeli position.

ISRAEL'S WITHDRAWAL FROM LEBANON AND THE COLLAPSE OF THE PEACE PROCESS

Since Lebanon is largely controlled by Syria, Israel has traditionally seen peace with Syria as essential to any guarantee of security on its northern border. Beginning in the early 1980s, Israel secured this border by occupying a nine-mile-wide buffer zone in southern Lebanon. However, popular support for this presence in Lebanon had eroded by the late 1990s, as more and more Israeli soldiers were killed in attacks on security outposts by anti-Israeli Hezbollah guerillas. In March 2000, Barak announced Israel would unilaterally withdraw from southern Lebanon with or without a comprehensive peace agreement with Syria and Lebanon. In May 2000, the Israeli army completed this withdrawal.

Barak found it more difficult to fulfill his promise of peace with the Palestinians. In July 2000, U.S. President Bill Clinton—eager to achieve a settlement before the end of his term—hosted two weeks of intensive, face-to-face negotiations between Barak and Arafat at Camp David. With a self-imposed deadline for a "final settlement" of September 13 approaching and much work still to be done, pressure to resolve the most difficult remaining issues was intense.

In the end, opposing strategies and a mutual lack of trust undermined the negotiations. Barak believed that the best strategy was to abandon the process of gradual and reciprocal concessions as outlined in the Oslo Accords, and instead present all concessions and rewards in one comprehensive package. From his perspective, the Oslo process had allowed the Palestinians to extract Israeli concessions without revealing their final demands. As a result, the Israelis discarded many of the interim steps previously agreed to, and put all the chips back on the table. Barak believed that his willingness to make extraordinary concessions—including giving Palestinians control of some 90 percent of the West Bank and authority over parts of Jerusalem—in order to achieve a final agreement would in the end make interim steps unnecessary. This "all-or-nothing" approach placed tremendous pressure on the Palestinians.

For the Palestinians, however, the interim steps were very important for two reasons. First, they helped develop trust in Israel's commitment to honor any final agreement. From the Palestinian perspective, the Oslo process was seen as a series of deferred or unfulfilled Israeli promises. Six years after the agreement there were more Israeli settlements, less freedom of movement, and worse economic conditions. Second, Arafat viewed the interim steps as necessary for creating a more equal balance of power in advance of final-status negotiations. Unfulfilled interim obligations were interpreted as attempts to weaken the Palestinian position, since previously negotiated issues could once again be used as bargaining chips.

The end result was that, while the Israelis believed they had made a more than generous offer, the Palestinians viewed the proposals discussed as neither generous, nor even concrete, as the ideas discussed were never written down. While Arafat dismissed Israeli proposals as unjust, he failed to respond with a viable counteroffer, leading the Israelis to question his sincerity as a negotiating partner.

The talks collapsed amid disagreement over three of the most difficult issues: the permanent status of Jerusalem, the right of return of the Palestinian refugees, and the noncontiguous borders of the proposed Palestinian territory. Having been so close to an agreement, the situation reached a boiling point after the talks collapsed, with each side accusing the other of being unwilling to compromise.

In September 2000, Israeli opposition leader Ariel Sharon made a controversial visit to a Jerusalem shrine holy to both religions. Sharon's visit to the shrine, known as the Temple Mount to Jews and the Noble Sanctuary to Muslims, was provocative because Muslim clerics have generally had autonomy in administering the site, and the visit was seen as an attempt to demonstrate Israel's sovereignty over Muslim holy sites in East Jerusalem. Control over the site had been a stumbling block during the Camp David negotiations.

Violent clashes quickly erupted as Palestinians launched a second *Intifada*, or uprising, against Israeli occupation. By December, continued fighting had resulted in the deaths of hundreds of people, mostly Palestinians, and war-like conditions again prevailed. Under pressure from many sides, Barak called for new elections to be held in early 2001. The following month Israeli and Palestinian negotiators restarted peace talks in Taba, Egypt, as a last-ditch attempt to reach agreement. While the two sides came closer than ever before to bridging their differences, the talks ultimately failed amid increasing violence and statements by Ariel Sharon that he would not honor any agreement made in Taba if elected prime minister. Palestinian violence drove the Israeli public to the political right, and in February 2001 Ariel Sharon won a decisive victory. On March 7 he was sworn in as prime minister.

The Tenure of Ariel Sharon and the War on Terrorism

Upon taking office Ariel Sharon was able to form a broad-based national unity government with the opposition Labor Party, in part by promising to pursue an agreement with the Palestinians. However, the coalition members remained deeply divided over how to approach the negotiating process, with Sharon favoring a more hard-line approach. Attempts to jump-start negotiations were further complicated by the fact that many Palestinians deeply distrusted Sharon because of his role as defense minister in overseeing the 1982 Israeli invasion of Lebanon and the subsequent massacre of Palestinian refugees by Israeli-backed Christian militias.

Frustrated with Arafat's inability, or unwillingness, to stop repeated suicide bombings in Israel by Palestinian extremists, Sharon broke all contact with the longtime Palestinian leader, deployed Israeli forces in areas once controlled by the Palestinian Authority, and adopted a policy of assassinating militant Palestinian leaders. Following the September 11, 2001, terrorist attacks in the U.S., the Israeli government justified its military crackdown as part of the global war on terrorism. This view received support from the U.S., which branded Palestinian groups such as Hamas and Islamic Jihad as terrorist organizations. Palestinians, however, criticized this characterization. They argued that, unlike groups such as al Qaeda, they were fighting for national liberation against an occupying army. As positions hardened on both sides, the cycle of violence continued to escalate.

The situation came to a head in March 2002 when a series of horrific Palestinian suicide bombings in Israel provoked the Israeli army to launch its biggest military operation in over 20 years. Some 20,000 Israeli forces occupied areas throughout the West Bank and Gaza, including Ramallah, the capital of the Palestinian Authority. After Sharon declared the PA a "terror-supporting entity," the Israeli Army attacked and destroyed many PA institutions, including the organization's headquarters, where Israeli tanks trapped Arafat for more than a month. The army also attacked militant strongholds, including the Jenin refugee camp, which was largely reduced to rubble. Militant Palestinians responded to the attacks by continuing to launch suicide bombings in Israel, prompting a second Israeli incursion in September 2002. Israeli forces again laid siege to Arafat's headquarters and bulldozed buildings throughout Nablus and Ramallah. By May 2003, more than 3,000 people, including 2,287 Palestinians and 763 Israelis, had died since the "al-Aqsa *Intifada*" began.[1]

In response to the escalating violence, the European Union, the United Nations, Russia, and the United States (known as "the quartet") drafted a new peace plan dubbed the "road map" to peace. The plan calls for both sides to simultaneously carry out concessions, which over the course of three years would progress to the resolution of all disputes and the creation of an independent Palestinian state. Among other things, the first phase of the plan requires Palestinians to take "visible efforts on the ground" to stop violence, while Israelis are required to dismantle all settlements built since March 2001, as well as freeze all new settlement activity. However, introduction of the plan was postponed after Israel and the United States insisted that Palestinians first undertake major reforms in the institutions of the Palestinian Authority, in particular the replacement of its leader, Yasser Arafat.

Palestinian Reform

Indeed, pressure to reform the Palestinian Authority had been building for some time. On May 15, 2002, in response to international pressure, as well as pressure from Palestinians frustrated with the corrupt and authoritarian nature of Arafat's administration, Arafat announced a plan for reforming the Palestinian Authority. In addition to reforming institutions such as the security services and judicial system, the plan called for presidential and parliamentary elections to be held in January 2003. Recognizing that Arafat was likely to be reelected, the U.S. announced it would not support the presidential election and instead called on Palestinians to create a new post of prime minister, which could act as a counterweight to Arafat. Ultimately, the Palestinians indefinitely postponed the elections, saying they could not physically be carried out while the Israeli army occupied most of the West Bank and restricted movement in the Gaza Strip. Nevertheless, they did move ahead with political reform.

In March 2003, the Palestinian parliament created the post of prime minister, responsible for the day-to-day running of Palestinian affairs. The parliament's approval of the new prime minister, Mahmoud Abbas (also known as Abu Mazen), and his cabinet in April marked a tentative but symbolic power shift away from Yasser Arafat. The Palestinian reforms were widely viewed as a turning point in the peace process since they satisfied a key U.S. demand for moving ahead with the "road map" peace plan, which was formally introduced on April 30, 2003.

PROSPECTS FOR PEACE

Initially, there was reason for optimism that the peace process would finally move forward. Despite strong opposition by his most ardent supporters, in May Sharon forcefully persuaded his cabinet to accept the "road map," albeit with a list of 14 reservations. In June, Abbas persuaded the Islamist groups Hamas and Islamic Jihad, as well as Fatah, the largest Palestinian political movement, to declare a unilateral, three-month cease-fire. Abbas staked his political reputation on the cease-fire, telling Palestinians that it was necessary to induce the U.S. to pressure Israel to begin implementing the "road map" peace plan.

However, the truce proved to be short-lived. In late August, a Palestinian suicide bombing in Jerusalem and Israel's assassination of a Hamas political leader, Ismail Abu Shanab, effectively ended the cease-fire. Having lost much of his political support, Mahmoud Abbas resigned on September 6, and within hours the cycle of violence between Israelis and Palestinians was again in full swing. Officially, Abbas said his resignation was due to Israel's slowness in implementing its commitments under the "road map." After seven weeks of relative quiet, there had been no end to the Israeli occupation, settlement construction, or assassinations of leading Palestinians. He also blamed the U.S. for failing to exert pressure on the Israelis.

Abbas also made it clear, however, that his resignation was due in large part to a power struggle with President Yasser Arafat, which had hindered Abbas's ability to govern. Abbas accused Arafat of refusing to devolve power, particularly over the PA's security forces, and working behind the scenes to undermine his government. Arafat was able to portray attempts by Abbas to gain authority as part of an Israeli-American conspiracy to unseat him and install a regime that would give up Palestinian aspirations to self-determination, national sovereignty, and a right of refugees' return.

Yasser Arafat quickly nominated Ahmed Qurei, also known as Abu Alaa, as the new prime minister and reassumed much of his former power. Qurei, a trusted moderate and architect of the Oslo Peace Accords, announced his opposition to the armed *Intifada* and his commitment to the "road map." But he also made clear that Arafat would have to be involved if the peace process were to succeed. Despite gaining the trust of Arafat, the new prime minister faced the same fundamental dilemma as Mahmoud Abbas. Support from Israel and the U.S. was conditioned on his ability to crack down on Palestinian militants. But without some tangible benefits to show the Palestinian people, Palestinian public support would not tolerate a strong attack against the militants.

For its part, Israel has expressed many reservations about the "road map" peace plan. The current makeup of Israel's coalition government makes it difficult for Sharon to grant many of the concessions called for in the plan. After Israel's national unity government fell in October 2002, Sharon was reelected prime minister in January 2003, and he formed a new coalition government with several conservative parties opposed to the land-for-peace formula. Opposition within the cabinet, as well as Sharon's own Likud Party, to curbing settlement activity poses a significant obstacle to getting the "road map" peace plan off the ground.

Other obstacles include the Israeli government's threat to "remove" Yasser Arafat and Israel's steady construction of a barrier stretching more than 400 miles and sealing off the Palestinian-controlled part of the West Bank from Israeli-populated parts of Jerusalem. The wall is highly controversial both within Israel and abroad because it cuts deep into the Occupied Territories, effectively annexing Palestinian land that is meant to be the subject of future negotiations. The Israeli government says the wall is a necessary security measure to keep suicide bombers out of Israel. Palestinians say the barrier is turning their communities into prisons, as people are separated from family members and jobs, farmers are separated from their land, and children are separated from their schools.

There are signs, however, that a majority of Israelis and Palestinians are more prepared for a peace agreement than their leaders. At the end of 2003, several proposals for a final peace settlement were developed by former Israeli and Palestinian officials and academics acting in a private capacity in an attempt to show that agreement on even the most difficult issues is possible. The most prominent of these proposals, known as the Geneva Accord, received widespread support among Israelis and Palestinians, as well as the U.S., the European Union, and the United Nations. A November 2003 opinion poll showed that 53 percent of Israelis and 56 percent of Palestinians support a peace agreement along the lines of the "road map" or Geneva Accord, suggesting that Israeli and Palestinian leaders may be able to muster the political support necessary to make difficult decisions.[2]

Optimists also point to renewed interest by the U.S. in working to put the peace process back on track. For the U.S., progress in the Arab-Israeli peace process is important to two of its main goals in the region: fighting the war on terrorism and bringing stability to Iraq. The perception of the U.S. as being ardently pro-Israel in the conflict has helped contribute to the anti-Americanism seen in various corners of the world, particularly in the Middle East. U.S. officials are hoping that by helping to restart the peace process, they can regain some credibility with Arab governments and their citizens as they attempt to foster a friendly government in Iraq. More importantly, a final settlement would remove a major rallying cry used by terrorists to gain sympathy for their cause.

Sadly, the persistent conflict has had a tragic impact on the lives of both Israelis and Palestinians. Both societies are forced to live in constant fear, which has led to widespread frustration, anxiety, despair, and disillusionment. In Israel, the brutality and horror of all-too-frequent suicide bombings have taken a tremendous toll on the Israeli psyche. The conflict has also contributed to the country's worst recession in 25 years as tourism and direct investment have plummeted. With unemployment over ten percent and the government forced to cut welfare spending, the number of Israelis living in poverty has grown to 20 percent.[3] For Palestinians, the economic consequences have been even more devastating. With much of their infrastructure destroyed and freedom of movement restricted, it is extremely difficult for Palestinians to find access to work, adequate health care, or even food and water. As a result, more than two-thirds of Palestinians live below the international poverty line, unemployment is over 60 percent, and malnutrition is widespread and rising.[4] As the costs of continued violence and repression mount, one can only hope that both sides will instead turn to peaceful methods for improving their quality of life.

On September 13, 1993, Israeli Prime Minister Yitzhak Rabin and Palestine Liberation Organization Chairman Yasser Arafat signed a peace accord on the White House lawn, opening new possibilities for peace in the Arab-Israeli conflict; Left to right: Rabin, President Bill Clinton, Arafat.

LESSON 3

THE ARAB-ISRAELI CONFLICT

Activity 1

How did European decisions made during World War I set the stage for future conflict in the Middle East?

ACTIVITY OBJECTIVE

The student will identify the role that European politics played in creating modern boundaries in the Middle East.

MATERIALS AND RESOURCES

❑ Handout 3.1, "The Ottoman Empire, 1914"
❑ Handout 3.2, "The Balfour Declaration"
❑ Handout 3.3, "The San Remo Agreement, 1920"

STRATEGIES

To better understand the problems facing people in the Middle East today, students need to recognize that many of the current political boundaries were drawn at the end of World War I to meet the needs of the European victors. These boundaries were imposed on what had been the Ottoman Empire without regard to indigenous populations. To complicate matters further, Europeans created expectations that disappointed many Arabs and Jews when the final boundaries were drawn. This exercise is designed to allow students to draw conclusions about both diplomacy in general and this situation in particular by having them examine maps and a significant document on which final decisions were based.

Begin this activity by distributing Handout 3.1, "The Ottoman Empire, 1914." Briefly review with students the position of the Ottomans as allies of the Central Powers during World War I and European interests in gaining control of this region. The handout illustrates the extent of Ottoman power at the outbreak of the war. Have students identify areas of strategic concern to the Allies [*entrance to the Black Sea, Suez Canal, access to the Persian Gulf, access to the Indian Ocean*].

One document that is central to any attempt to reach a settlement between the Palestinians and the state of Israel is the Balfour Declaration. Distribute Handout 3.2, "The Balfour Declaration." Students should read the document and try to answer the question, "What is promised to whom?" Students should find that the Balfour Declaration presents a commitment to the establishment of some sort of homeland for the Jews in the area known as Palestine. Ask students to evaluate the implications of these promises and the subsequent expectation of Jewish settlers in Palestine. Ask students, "What might have been the reaction of Arab residents of Palestine? Why?"

After students have exhausted all the possibilities, distribute Handout 3.3, "The San Remo Agreement." This map shows the boundaries that were decided upon by the British and the French at the close of post–World War I negotiations. They are essentially the modern boundaries of the Middle East today. Have the students evaluate these boundaries from several different perspectives by asking such questions as:

- What has become of the old Ottoman Empire?
- What has become of the promise to the Jews? What was done with Palestine, and how might both Arabs and Jews living there react? [*Palestine becomes a British-controlled Mandate.*]
- What might have been the economic or political concerns of the French and British that led them to draw the boundaries for the newly created countries of Iraq, Lebanon, and Jordan? [*protection of colonial empires*]
- What was Britain's particular interest in holding on to Egypt? In having influence in Jordan and Iraq? [*access to India and protection of the Empire*]

THE OTTOMAN EMPIRE, 1914

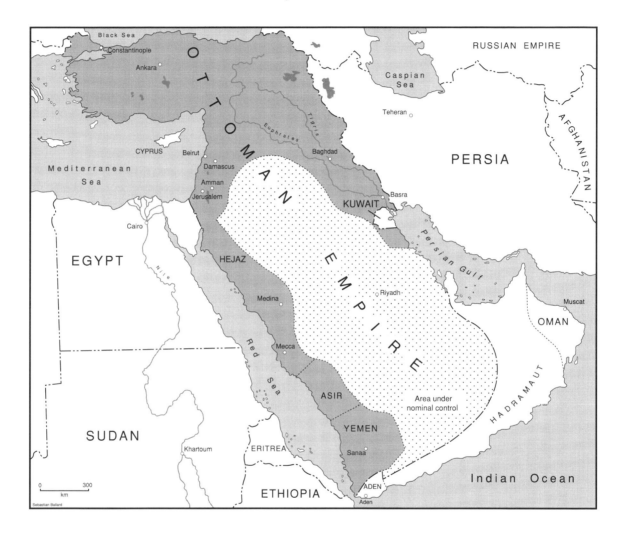

THE BALFOUR DECLARATION

Foreign Office
November 2nd, 1917

Dear Lord Rothschild,

I have such pleasure in conveying to you, on behalf of His Majesty's Government, the following declaration of sympathy with Jewish Zionist aspirations which has been submitted to, and approved by, the Cabinet.

"His Majesty's Government view with favour the establishment in Palestine of a national home for the Jewish people, and will use their best endeavors to facilitate the achievement of this object, it being clearly understood that nothing shall be done which may prejudice the civil and religious rights of existing non-Jewish communities in Palestine, or the rights and political status enjoyed by Jews in any other country."

I should be grateful if you would bring this declaration to the knowledge of the Zionist Federation.

Yours sincerely,

Arthur James Balfour

THE SAN REMO AGREEMENT, 1920

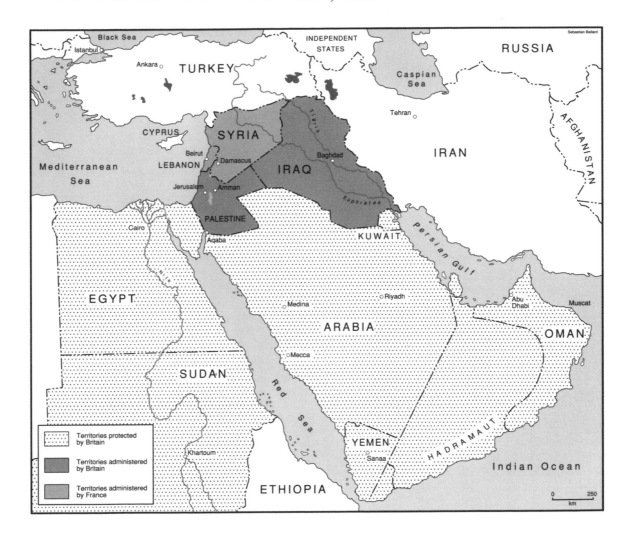

David Ben Gurion, Israel's founding father, declares Israel a state on May 14, 1948, hours before the British Mandate in Palestine is due to end. The following day the armies of Egypt, Syria, Jordan, and a contingent from Iraq attacked the new state, founded after six million European Jews were killed in the Holocaust.

Reuters

LESSON 3

The Arab-Israeli Conflict

Activity 2

How did the boundaries of Israel change between 1947 and 1949?

ACTIVITY OBJECTIVE

The student will evaluate the logic of UN boundary decisions and analyze the implications of the boundaries that existed after the 1948 war.

MATERIALS AND RESOURCES

❑ Handout 3.4, "Jewish Land Ownership and Population Distribution in Palestine"
❑ Handout 3.5, "1947 Partition and 1949 Armistice Lines"

STRATEGIES

The Arab-Israeli conflict has been an international concern since the creation of the state of Israel in 1948. This activity provides students the opportunity to evaluate the original United Nations decision to create the states of Israel and Palestine and to become familiar with the territorial disputes that have existed since the 1948 Arab-Israeli War.

Distribute Handout 3.4, "Jewish Land Ownership and Population Distribution in Palestine" to students and have them examine the boundaries suggested by the United Nations when it proposed an Arab and a Jewish state in Palestine in 1947. Explain that the UN boundaries were based loosely on the locations of major Jewish and Arab communities. Have students study the map and table and consider the following questions as they examine Handout 3.4:

- What happened to population and land ownership in Palestine between 1880 and 1947?
- What percentage of land did Jewish settlers own in 1917 at the time of the Balfour Declaration? What percentage of the population did they represent?
- Why do you think the Jewish population grew so quickly in relation to the Arab population from 1917 to 1946? What pressures do you think this created in Palestine?
- Examine the settlement patterns on the map. Approximately what percentage of the land was owned by Jewish settlers?

Next, distribute Handout 3.5, "1947 Partition and 1949 Armistice Lines." Ask students:

- What percentage of the population was Palestinian, Arab, and Jewish in 1947?
- Compare these figures to the total percentage of land owned by each group. Are

these boundaries logical? Why or why not?

- How did the 1947 UN map try to accommodate the settlement patterns? What potential problems are built into this plan?
- What was done with the city of Jerusalem in 1947? Why?
- How have the boundaries changed in the 1949 Armistice Plan?
- Using the information in the population and land settlement charts, evaluate the 1949 armistice lines from the vantage point of the Jewish residents. Do the same from the vantage point of Arab residents. What was the potential for future conflict?

Arab villagers flee from an unidentified area in Galilee in October 1948. Some 700,000 Palestinians fled their homes and villages during and following the War of Independence in what is known as "al-Nabka," or "The Catastrophe," in Palestinian culture.

144

JEWISH LAND OWNERSHIP AND
POPULATION DISTRIBUTION IN PALESTINE

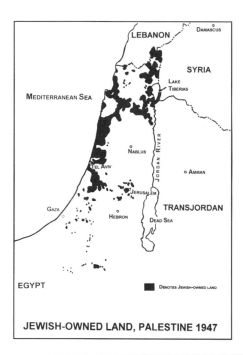

JEWISH-OWNED LAND, PALESTINE 1947

	Population				Jewish Land Ownership (Cumulative)	
	Arabs		**Jews**			
Year	Numbers	%	Numbers	%	Dunums	%
1880	300,000	94%	24,000	6%	N.A.	N.A.
1917 Balfour Declaration	504,000	90%	56,000	10%	650,000	<3%
1922	666,000	89%	84,000	11%	751,192	3%
1931	850,000	83%	174,096	17%	1,171,529	4%
1936	916,061	72%	384,078	28%	1,380,578	5%
1945 – 1946	1,242,000	69%	608,000	31%	1,588,365	6%
1947 UN Partition Plan	1,300,000	67%	640,298	33%	1,900,000	7%

Source: *Facts and Figures About the Palestinians.* The Center for Policy Analysis on Palestine, Information Paper Number 1, Washington, DC, 1992, p. 7.

NOTE: One dunum equals .25 acres

1947 PARTITION AND 1949 ARMISTICE LINES

1947 Partition

1949 Armistice

LESSON 3

THE ARAB-ISRAELI CONFLICT

Activity 3

How has the UN attempted to resolve the Arab-Israeli conflict?

ACTIVITY OBJECTIVE

The student will describe unrest in the Middle East and efforts of various groups to mediate and resolve the conflict.

MATERIALS AND RESOURCES

❑ SCIS Videotape, *The Middle East in Transition*, Lesson 3, "The Arab-Israeli Conflict"
❑ Handout 3.6, "United Nations Security Council Resolution 242"
❑ Handout 3.7, "Israel and the Occupied Territories, 1967"

STRATEGIES

World opinion has always played a role in attempts to resolve the Arab-Israeli conflict. The United Nations has tried to play the role of mediator and has passed numerous resolutions in an effort to bring about an equitable settlement for all parties concerned. This activity gives students an opportunity to work with United Nations Security Council Resolution 242 that was passed during the 1967 Arab-Israeli War.

Begin this activity by showing the SCIS videotape, *The Middle East in Transition*, Lesson 3, "The Arab-Israeli Conflict." On the videotape, the former Secretaries of State discuss the United States's involvement as a mediator in the Arab-Israeli conflict in the years since World War II.

Distribute Handout 3.6, "United Nations Security Council Resolution 242." Have students read the resolution and consider the following questions:

- What are all parties in the conflict called on to do?
- What mention is made of waterways and what are the waterways involved?
- What mention is made of the Palestinians?
- How might the Israelis and the Palestinians have reacted to this resolution and why?
- What other countries in the region would have been affected by this resolution and why?

Distribute Handout 3.7, "Israel and the Occupied Territories." Lead a discussion by asking such questions as: "What are the areas controlled by the state of Israel on this map? How have the strategic and economic concerns of both the Israelis and the

Arabs been affected by this expansion? How have the countries of Jordan, Egypt, and Syria become involved? What has happened to the city of Jerusalem? Why are these changes significant for Jews, Christians, and Muslims alike? To conclude this discussion, point out to the students, as did former Secretary Dean Rusk, that the wording of these resolutions, like most diplomatic language, is intentionally vague. What are the advantages and disadvantages to this approach? What does former Secretary Rusk feel was the intent of UN Security Council Resolution 242?"

After completing this discussion, students should be aware of the territorial changes and claims that are central to an understanding of modern-day Arab-Israeli negotiations. Areas that should be pointed out include the Sinai, the West Bank, the Gaza Strip, the Golan Heights, and the city of Jerusalem, all priorities for Middle Eastern diplomats today. On the videotape, former Secretary Dean Rusk points out that the U.S. has made no commitments to assist Israel in retaining the territory seized in June 1967. How has the issue raised by former Secretary Rusk been partially resolved with the signing of the Camp David Accords in 1978 and the Palestinian-Israel Agreement in September 1993? Ask students to hypothesize about what Rusk might feel should come next in the ongoing negotiations between the Palestinians and the Israelis.

UNITED NATIONS SECURITY COUNCIL RESOLUTION 242

22 November 1967

The Security Council,

Expressing its continuing concern with the grave situation in the Middle East,

Emphasizing the inadmissibility of the acquisition of territory by war and the need to work for a just and lasting peace in which every State in the area can live in security,

Emphasizing further that all Member States in their acceptance of the Charter of the United Nations have undertaken a commitment to act in accordance with Article 2 of the Charter,

1. *Affirms* that the fulfillment of Charter principles requires the establishment of a just and lasting peace in the Middle East which should include the application of both the following principles:

> (i) Withdrawal of Israeli armed forces from territories occupied in the recent conflict;

> (ii) Termination of all claims or states of belligerency and respect for and acknowledgment of the sovereignty, territorial integrity and political independence of every State in the area and their right to live in peace within secure and recognized boundaries free from threats or acts of force;

2. *Reaffirms* further the necessity

> (a) For guaranteeing freedom of navigation through international waterways in the area;

> (b) For achieving a just settlement of the refugee problem;

> (c) For guaranteeing the territorial inviolability and political independence of every State in the area, through measures including the establishment of demilitarized zones;

3. *Requests* the Secretary-General to designate a Special Representative to proceed to the Middle East to establish and maintain contacts with the States concerned in order to promote agreement and assist with efforts to achieve a peaceful and accepted settlement in accordance with the provision and principles in this resolution;

4. *Requests* the Secretary-General to report to the Security Council on the progress of the efforts of the Special Representative as soon as possible.

Adopted unanimously at the 1,382nd meeting.

ISRAEL AND THE OCCUPIED TERRITORIES, 1967

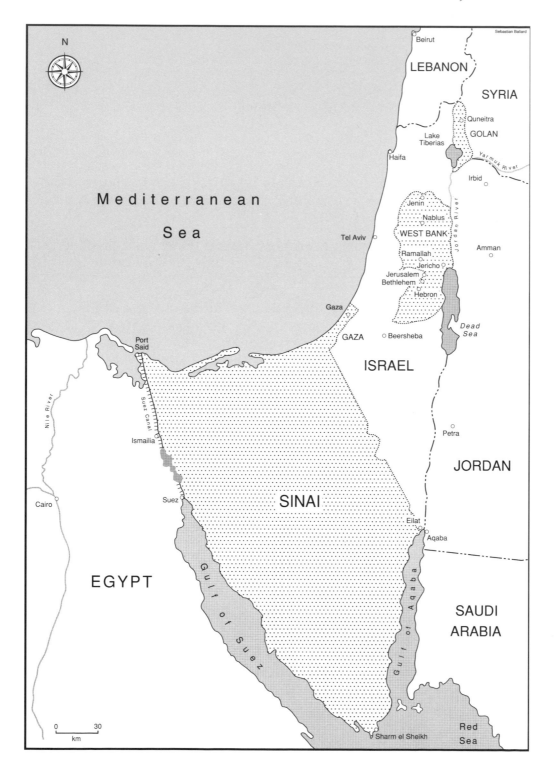

LESSON 3

THE ARAB-ISRAELI CONFLICT

Activity 4

What impact have the Camp David Accords and the Declaration of Principles had on the Middle East peace process?

ACTIVITY OBJECTIVE

The student will analyze and evaluate recent Middle East peace proposals.

MATERIALS AND RESOURCES

❑ Handout 3.7, "Camp David Accords [Excerpts]"
❑ Handout 3.8, "Declaration of Principles on Interim Self-Government Arrangements and Timeline for Implementation"

STRATEGIES

The 1978 Camp David Accords resulted in the first peace treaty signed between an Arab country, Egypt, and Israel. Many people see Camp David as the first step in the process that led to the dramatic breakthroughs in 1993 between the PLO and Israel, and subsequently between Israel and other Arab countries. Much of the 1993 negotiating between Israel and the PLO follows the outline of the Camp David framework relating to the West Bank and Gaza by focusing on the least complicated problems first and leaving the more complex issues for later. In order to understand the direction and goals of the current negotiations, students should be familiar with the portion of the Camp David Agreement dealing with the Occupied Territories.

Distribute Handout 3.7, "Camp David Accords [Excerpts]," and Handout 3.8, "Declaration of Principles on Interim Self-Government and Timeline for Implementation." Have students review these documents and then discuss the following questions regarding the Declaration of Principles:

• What mention is made of UN Resolution 242?
• What areas of the occupied territories are to come under Palestinian control first?
• What areas will the Palestinians be allowed to administer immediately?
• What security forces will the Palestinians be allowed to administer?
• What role is to be played by the PLO in the implementation of this agreement?
• What provisions are made for Palestinians living outside the territories?
• What role is to be played by Jordan and Egypt in the implementation of these principles?

- What mention is made of Jerusalem? Why or why not?
- What is the deadline for the signing of a permanent agreement between the Palestinians and the Israelis?
- What is to become of the Israeli military in the geographic areas covered by these principles?
- Compare the language of this agreement with the language of the excerpt from the Camp David Accords. In what ways is the 1993 agreement more specific and why do you think that was possible?

Continue this activity by providing students the opportunity to evaluate potential solutions that might develop from the Declaration of Principles. Divide the class into five groups and assign each group one of the following possible outcomes of the peace process:

- Group 1: Two-state solution
- Group 2: Palestinian federation with Jordan
- Group 3: Palestinian state in Gaza and Jericho only
- Group 4: Creation of one secular state in the region
- Group 5: Talks collapse; maintain status quo

Have students evaluate the positive and negative aspects of each potential solution. In doing so, they should consider the following issues:

- borders
- maintaining security
- economic concerns
- access to water
- utilities
- relationships with neighboring countries
- minority rights
- access to religious sites
- implementation
- other regional issues

After the groups complete their analysis, they can report their findings to the class. Students should reach consensus as to which solution holds the most potential for success.

CAMP DAVID ACCORDS
[EXCERPTS]

Framework

The parties are determined to reach a just, comprehensive, and durable settlement of the Middle East conflict through the conclusion of peace treaties based on Security Council Resolutions 242 and 338 in all their parts. Their proposal is to achieve peace and good neighborly relations. They recognized that, for the peace to endure, it must involve all those who have been most deeply affected by the conflict. They therefore agree that this framework, as appropriate, is intended by them to constitute a basis for peace not only between Egypt and Israel, but also between Israel and each of its other neighbors which is prepared to negotiate peace with Israel on this basis. With that objective in mind, they have agreed to proceed as follows:

A. West Bank and Gaza

1. Egypt, Israel, Jordan and the representatives of the Palestinian people should participate in negotiations on the resolution of the Palestinian problem in all its aspects. To achieve that objective, negotiations relating to the West Bank and Gaza should proceed in three stages:

(a) Egypt and Israel agree that, in order to ensure a peaceful and orderly transfer of authority, and taking into account the security concern of all the parties, there should be transitional arrangements for the West Bank and Gaza for a period not exceeding five years. In order to provide full autonomy to the inhabitants, under these arrangements the Israeli military government and its civilian administration will be withdrawn as soon as a self-governing authority has been freely elected by the inhabitants of these areas to replace the existing military government. To negotiate the details of a transitional arrangement, Jordan will be invited to join the negotiations on the basis of this framework. These new arrangements should give due consideration both to the principle of self-government by the inhabitants of these territories and to the legitimate security concern of the parties involved.

(b) Egypt, Israel and Jordan will agree on the modalities for establishing elected self-governing authority in the West Bank and Gaza. The delegations of Egypt and Jordan may include Palestinians from the West Bank and Gaza or other Palestinians as mutually agreed. The parties will negotiate an agreement which will define the powers and responsibilities of the self-governing authority to be exercised in the West Bank and Gaza. A withdrawal of Israeli armed forces will take place and there will be a redeployment of the remaining Israeli forces into specified security locations. The agreement will also include arrangements for assuring internal and external security and public order. In addition, Israeli and Jordanian forces will participate in joint patrols and in manning of control posts to assure the security of the borders.

(c) When the self-governing authority (administrative council) in the West Bank and Gaza is established and inaugurated, the transitional period of five years will begin. As soon as possible, but not later than the third year after the beginning of the transitional period, negotiations will take place to determine the final status of the West Bank and Gaza and its relationship with its neighbors, and to conclude a peace treaty between Israel and Jordan by the end of the transitional period. These negotiations will be conducted among Egypt, Israel, Jordan and the elected representatives of the inhabitants of the West Bank and Gaza. Two separate but related committees will be convened, one committee consisting of representatives of the four parties which will negotiate and agree on the final status of the West Bank and Gaza, and its relationship with its neighbors, and the second committee, consisting of representatives of Israel and representatives of Jordan to be joined by the elected representatives of the inhabitants of the West Bank and Gaza, to negotiate the peace treaty between Israel and Jordan, taking into account the agreement reached on the final status of the West Bank and Gaza. The negotiations shall be based on all provisions and principles of UN Security Council Resolution 242. The negotiations will resolve, among other matters, the location of the boundaries and the nature of the security arrangements. The resolution from the negotiations must also recognize the legitimate rights of the Palestinian people and their just requirements. In this way, the Palestinians will participate in the determination of their own future through:

1) The negotiations among Egypt, Israel, Jordan and the representatives of the inhabitants of the West Bank and Gaza to agree on the final status of the West Bank and Gaza and other outstanding issues by the end of the transitional period.

2) Submitting their agreement to a vote by the elected representatives of the inhabitants of the West Bank and Gaza.

3) Providing for the elected representatives of the inhabitants of the West Bank and Gaza to decide how they shall govern themselves consistent with the provisions of their agreement.

4) Participating as stated above in the work of the committee negotiating the peace treaty between Israel and Jordan.

2. All necessary measures will be taken and provisions made to assure the security of Israel and its neighbors during the transitional period and beyond. To assist in providing such security, a strong local police force will be constituted by the self-governing authority. It will be composed of the inhabitants of the West Bank and

Gaza. The police will maintain liaison on internal security matters with the designated Israeli, Jordanian, and Egyptian officers.

3. During the transitional period, representatives of Egypt, Israel, Jordan and the self-governing authority will constitute a continuing committee to decide by agreement on the modalities of admission of persons displaced from the West Bank and Gaza in 1967, together with necessary measures to prevent disruption and disorder. Other matters of common concern may also be dealt with by this committee.

4. Egypt and Israel will work with each other [and] with other interested parties to establish agreed procedures for a prompt, just and permanent implementation of the resolution of the refugee problem.

DECLARATION OF PRINCIPLES ON INTERIM SELF-GOVERNMENT ARRANGEMENTS AND TIMELINE FOR IMPLEMENTATION

The Government of the State of Israel and the P.L.O. team (in the Jordanian-Palestinian delegation to the Middle East Peace Conference) (the "Palestinian Delegation"), representing the Palestinian people, agree that it is time to put an end to decades of confrontation and conflict, recognize their mutual legitimate and political rights, and strive to live in peaceful coexistence and mutual dignity and security and achieve a just, lasting and comprehensive peace settlement and historic reconciliation through the agreed political process. Accordingly, the two sides agree to the following principles:

Article I—Aim of the Negotiations

The Aim of the Israeli-Palestinian negotiations within the current Middle East peace process is, among other things, to establish a Palestinian Interim Self-Government Authority, the elected Council (the "Council"), for the Palestinian people in the West Bank and the Gaza Strip, for a transitional period not exceeding five years, leading to a permanent settlement based on [United Nations] Security Council Resolutions 242 and 338.

It is understood that the interim arrangements are an integral part of the whole peace process and that the negotiations on the permanent status will lead to the implementation of Security Council Resolutions 242 and 338.

Article II—Framework for the Interim Period

The agreed framework for the interim period is set forth in this Declaration of Principles.

Article III—Elections

1) In order that the Palestinian people in the West Bank and Gaza Strip may govern themselves according to democratic principles, direct, free and general political elections will be held for the Council under agreed supervision and international observation, while the Palestinian police will ensure public order.

2) An agreement will be concluded on the exact mode and conditions of the elections in accordance with the protocol attached as Annex I, with the goal of holding the elections not later than nine months after the entry into force of this Declaration of Principles.

3) These elections will constitute a significant interim preparatory step toward the realization of the legitimate rights of the Palestinian people and their just requirements.

Article IV—Jurisdiction

Jurisdiction of the Council will cover West Bank and Gaza Strip territory, except for issues that will be negotiated in the permanent status negotiations. The two sides view the West Bank and the Gaza Strip as a single territorial unit, whose integrity will be preserved during the interim period.

Article V—Transitional Period and Permanent Status Negotiations

1) The five-year transitional period will begin upon the withdrawal from the Gaza Strip and Jericho area.

2) Permanent status negotiations will commence as soon as possible, but not later than the beginning of the third year of the interim period, between the Government of Israel and the Palestinian peoples' representatives.

3) It is understood that these negotiations shall cover remaining issues, including: Jerusalem, refugees, settlements, security arrangements, borders, relations and cooperation with other neighbors, and other issues of common interest.

4) The two parties agree that the outcome of the permanent status negotiations should not be prejudiced or preempted by agreements reached for the interim period.

Article VI—Preparatory Transfer of Powers and Responsibilities

1) Upon the entry into force of this Declaration of Principles and the withdrawal from the Gaza Strip and the Jericho area, a transfer of authority from the Israeli military government and its Civil Administration to the authorized Palestinians for this task, as detailed herein, will commence. This transfer of authority will be of a preparatory nature until the inauguration of the Council.

2) Immediately after the entry into force of this Declaration of Principles and the withdrawal in the West Bank and Gaza Strip, authority will be transferred to the Palestinians on the following spheres: education and culture, health, social welfare, direct taxation, and tourism. The Palestinian side will commence in building the Palestinian police force, as agreed upon. Pending the inauguration of the Council, the two parties may negotiate the transfer of additional powers and responsibilities as agreed upon.

Article VII—Interim Agreement

1) The Israeli and Palestinian delegations will negotiate an agreement on the interim period (the Interim Agreement).

2) The Interim Agreement shall specify, among other things, the structure of the Council, the number of its members, and the transfer of powers and responsibilities from the Israeli military government and its Civil Administration to the Council. The Interim Agreement shall also specify the Council's executive authority, legislative authority in accordance with Article IX below, and the independent Palestinian organs.

3) The Interim Agreement shall include arrangements, to be implemented upon the inauguration of the Council, for the assumption by the Council of all of the powers and responsibilities transferred previously in accordance with Article VI above.

4) In order to enable the Council to promote economic growth, upon its inauguration, the Council will establish, among other things, a Palestinian Electricity Authority, a Gaza Sea Port Authority, a Palestinian Development Bank, a Palestinian Export Promotion Board, a Palestinian Environmental Authority, a Palestinian Land Authority and a Palestinian Water Administration Authority, and any other Authorities agreed upon, in accordance with the Interim Agreement that will specify their powers and responsibilities.

5) After the inauguration of the Council, the Civil Administration will be dissolved, and the Israeli military government will be withdrawn.

Article VIII—Public Order and Security

In order to guarantee public order and internal security for the Palestinians of the West Bank and the Gaza Strip, the Council will establish a strong police force, while Israel will continue to carry the responsibility for defending against external threats, as well as the responsibility for overall security of Israelis for the purpose of safeguarding their internal security and public order.

Article IX—Laws and Military Orders

1) The Council will be empowered to legislate, in accordance with the Interim Agreement, within all authorities transferred to it.

2) Both parties will review jointly laws and military orders presently in force in remaining spheres.

Article X—Joint Israeli-Palestinian Liaison Committee

In order to provide for a smooth implementation of this Declaration of Principles and any subsequent agreements pertaining to the interim period, upon the entry into force of this Declaration of Principles, a Joint Israeli-Palestinian Liaison Committee will be established in order to deal with issues requiring coordination, other issues of common interest, and disputes.

Article XI—Israeli-Palestinian Cooperation in Economic Fields

Recognizing the mutual benefit of cooperation in promoting the development of the West Bank, the Gaza Strip and Israel, upon the entry into force of this Declaration of Principles, an Israeli-Palestinian Economic Cooperation Committee will be established in order to develop and implement in a cooperative manner the programs identified in the protocols attached as Annex III and Annex IV.

Article XII—Liaison and Cooperation with Jordon and Egypt

The two parties will invite the Governments of Jordan and Egypt to participate in establishing further liaison and cooperation arrangements between the Government of Israel and the Palestinian representatives, on the one hand, and the Governments of Jordan and Egypt on the other hand, to promote cooperation between them. These arrangements will include the constitution of a Continuing Committee that will decide by agreement of the modalities of admission of persons displaced from the West Bank and Gaza Strip in 1967, together with necessary measures to prevent disruption and disorder. Other matters of common concern will be dealt with by this Committee.

Article XIII—Redeployment of Israeli Forces

1. After the entry into force of this Declaration of Principles, and not later than the eve of elections for the Council, a redeployment of Israeli military forces in the West Bank and the Gaza Strip will take place, in addition to withdrawal of Israeli forces carried out in accordance with Article XIV.

2. In redeploying its military forces, Israel will be guided by the principle that its military forces should be redeployed outside populated areas.

3. Further redeployments to specified locations will be gradually implemented commensurate with the assumption of responsibility for the public order and internal security by the Palestinian police force pursuant to Article VIII above.

Article XIV—Israeli Withdrawal from the Gaza Strip and Jericho Area

Israel will withdraw from the Gaza Strip and Jericho area, as detailed in the protocol attached as Annex II.

Article XV—Resolution of Disputes

1) Disputes arising out of the application or interpretation of this Declaration of Principles, or any subsequent agreements pertaining to the interim period, shall be resolved by negotiations through the Joint Liaison Committee to be established pursuant to Article X above.

2) Disputes which cannot be settled by negotiations may be resolved by a mechanism of conciliation to be agreed upon by the parties.

3) The parties may agree to submit to arbitration disputes relating to the interim period, which cannot be settled through conciliation. To this end, upon the agreement of both parties, the parties will establish an Arbitration Committee.

Article XVI—Israeli-Palestinian Cooperation Concerning Regional Programs

Both parties view the multilateral working groups as an appropriate instrument for promoting a "Marshall Plan," the regional programs and other programs, including special programs for the West Bank and Gaza Strip, as indicated in the protocol attached as Annex IV.

Article XVII—Miscellaneous Provisions

1) This Declaration of Principles will enter into force one month after its signing.

2) All protocols annexed to this Declaration of Principles and Agreed Minutes pertaining thereto shall be regarded as an integral part hereof.

Done at Washington, D.C., this thirteenth day of September, 1993.

    For the Government of Israel—*Shimon Peres*
    For the P.L.O.—*Yasser Arafat*

TIMELINE OF EVENTS

October 13, 1993

- The Declaration of Principles on Palestinian self-rule takes force.
- Authority for education and culture, health, social welfare, direct taxation, and tourism is transferred from Israel to "authorized Palestinians" in the West Bank and Gaza, but it is not clear what authority they will have in East Jerusalem.
- Palestinians start building police force based on Palestine Liberation Organization fighters from outside West Bank and Gaza.
- Joint Israeli-Palestinian Liaison Committee is formed.
- Israeli-Palestinian Economic Cooperation Committee is established to work on water, electricity, energy, finance, transport, and communications including Gaza seaport, trade, industry, labor relations, training, environmental protection, and the news media, an internationally supported economic development program for the West Bank and Gaza and a regional economic development program.
- Jordan and Egypt invited to join Continuing Committee to decide on procedures for admission of Palestinians displaced from West Bank and Gaza in 1967 (estimated at about 800,000 people including dependents).

December 13, 1993

- Israel and Palestinians sign agreement on Israeli withdrawal from Gaza Strip and Jericho area and detailed arrangements for Palestinian control of the two areas.
- Israelis begin withdrawal from Gaza and Jericho.
- Five-year interim period of Palestinian self-rule officially begins.

April 13, 1994

- Latest date for Israel to complete withdrawal from Gaza and Jericho.

July 13, 1994

- Latest date for elections for Palestinian Council, which is to operate under an as yet undetermined interim agreement. Palestinians from East Jerusalem will be able to vote and perhaps run in the elections.
- Israeli military forces, already withdrawn from Gaza and Jericho, would redeploy outside populated areas in the rest of the West Bank by the eve of elections. Israeli forces would remain responsible for security of Israeli settlers.
- Israeli military government withdrawn and Civil Administration dissolved.

December 13, 1994

- Latest date for talks to start on permanent agreement.

December 13, 1998

- Permanent agreement takes effect.

A Palestinian man lifts his shirt to be checked by Israeli soldiers at the main entrance to the West Bank city of Nablus, July 14, 2004.

LESSON 3

THE ARAB-ISRAELI CONFLICT

Activity 5

What issues stand between Israel and the Palestinians?

ACTIVITY OBJECTIVE

The student will analyze and evaluate recent Middle East peace proposals.

MATERIALS AND RESOURCES

❑ SCIS Videotape, *The Middle East in Transition*, Lesson 3, "The Arab-Israeli Conflict"
❑ Handout 3.10, "Citizens-in-Waiting in Gaza and the West Bank"
❑ Worksheet 3.1, "Palestinian Self-Rule: Challenges and Opportunities"

STRATEGIES

After examining the history that led to the 1993 agreements between Israel and the PLO, show students the SCIS videotape, *The Middle East in Transition*, Lesson 3, "The Arab-Israeli Conflict," concentrating especially on the last part of the video segment in which the former Secretaries of State in their 1994 meeting discuss the reasons why the peace agreement was signed and the problems that it still must overcome.

Students should be provided an opportunity to discuss these problems and to examine in more depth the issues that still need to be resolved in order for the Palestinians to achieve true autonomy.

Distribute Handout 3.10, "Citizens-in-Waiting in Gaza and the West Bank," for students to examine. Students should use these data to identify issues and to answer questions and propose solutions related to those issues. Worksheet 3.1, "Palestinian Self-Rule: Challenges and Opportunities," provides a format for outlining and recording student responses.

Student responses might include such items as:

Issue	Questions	Proposed Solutions
Israeli settlements in Gaza and the West Bank	What is to become of these people if these areas become a Palestinian state?	Student answers will vary
Palestinians living outside the Occupied Territories	Will they be granted a right of return? Can the Occupied Territories accommodate them?	Student answers will vary
Economic independence	Can the Palestinian economy continue to be so heavily dependent on Israel?	Student answers will vary
Unemployment	What can be done about the high level of unemployment in the Occupied Territories?	Student answers will vary
Other topics to consider could include access to water, energy sources, transportation networks, communications systems, status of Jerusalem, etc.		

This activity can be expanded into a more sophisticated look at the peace process by assigning these topics to students for additional in-depth research and asking students to write position papers on the issues to be resolved.

CITIZENS-IN-WAITING IN GAZA AND THE WEST BANK

Palestinian Territories/ Israel Trade, 2002

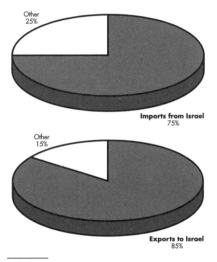

Other
25%

Imports from Israel
75%

Other
15%

Exports to Israel
85%

Source: Palestine Economic Policy
Research Institute (MAS), 2002.

Unemployment

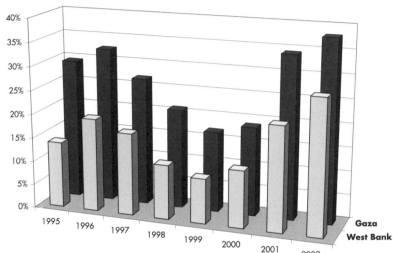

Gaza
West Bank

Source: Palestinian Central Bureau of Statistics, 2003.

Jobs in Israel

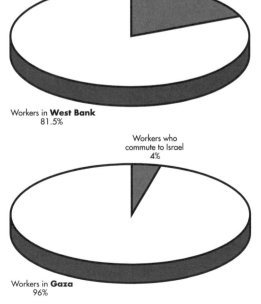

Workers who
commute to Israel
18.5%

Workers in **West Bank**
81.5%

Workers who
commute to Israel
4%

Workers in **Gaza**
96%

Source:
Palestinian Central Bureau of Statistics, 2003.

Location of Palestinians

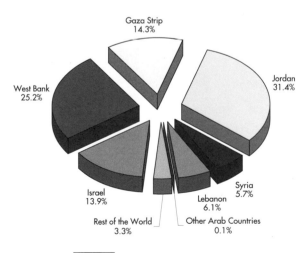

Gaza Strip
14.3%

Jordan
31.4%

West Bank
25.2%

Syria
5.7%

Israel
13.9%

Lebanon
6.1%

Rest of the World
3.3%

Other Arab Countries
0.1%

Source: Palestinian Central Bureau of
Statistics, 2000.

CITIZENS-IN-WAITING IN GAZA AND THE WEST BANK

Quality of Life in 2002

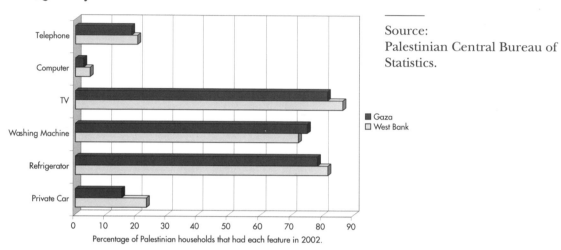

Source:
Palestinian Central Bureau of Statistics.

■ Gaza
□ West Bank

Percentage of Palestinian households that had each feature in 2002.

Palestinian and Israeli Per Capita Income (GNI)

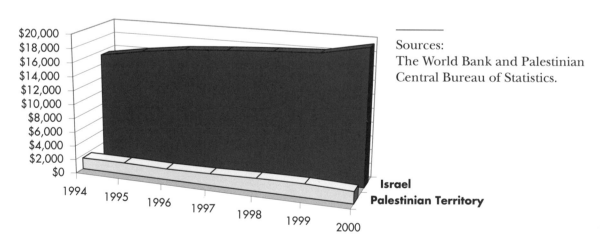

Sources:
The World Bank and Palestinian Central Bureau of Statistics.

Israel
Palestinian Territory

Education

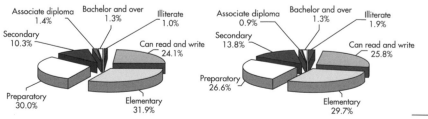

Educational attainment of Palestinians age 10-24 West Bank

Associate diploma 1.4%
Bachelor and over 1.3%
Illiterate 1.0%
Secondary 10.3%
Can read and write 24.1%
Preparatory 30.0%
Elementary 31.9%

Educational attainment of Palestinians age 10-24 in Gaza

Associate diploma 0.9%
Bachelor and over 1.3%
Illiterate 1.9%
Secondary 13.8%
Can read and write 25.8%
Preparatory 26.6%
Elementary 29.7%

Source:
Palestinian Central Bureau of Statistics, 2001.

166

CITIZENS-IN-WAITING IN GAZA AND THE WEST BANK

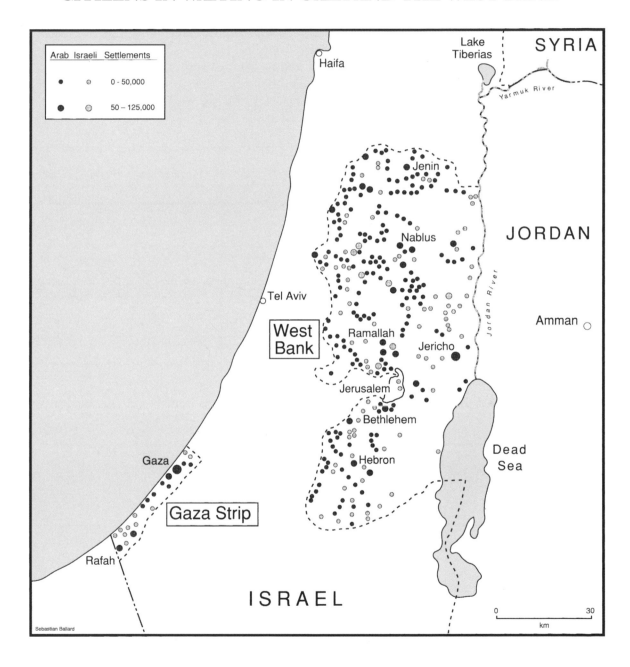

PALESTINIAN SELF-RULE:
CHALLENGES AND OPPORTUNITIES

Directions: Use the data in the charts, graphs, maps, and tables in Handout 3.10, "Citizens-in-Waiting in Gaza and the West Bank," to identify issues related to Palestinian self-rule, questions to be resolved related to those issues, and possible solutions to these problems.

Issue	Questions	Proposed Solutions

LESSON 3

THE ARAB-ISRAELI CONFLICT

Activity 6

What comes next?

ACTIVITY OBJECTIVE

The student will assess the Arab-Israeli peace process since the 1993 Oslo Accords.

MATERIALS AND RESOURCES

❑ SCIS Videotape, *The Middle East in Transition*, Lesson 3,
   "The Arab-Israeli Conflict"
❑ Handout 3.11, "Key Events in the Middle East Peace Process Since Oslo"
❑ Teacher Resource 3.1, "Major Points of Difference"
❑ Worksheet 3.2, "Evaluating a Peace Plan"
❑ Handout 3.12, "2001 Negotiations in Taba, Egypt: Summary"
❑ Handout 3.13, "2003 Geneva Accord: Key Points"
❑ Handout 3.14, "2003 Road Map for Peace: Summary"

STRATEGIES

More than a decade after the 1993 Oslo Accord, many of the issues at the heart of the Arab-Israeli conflict remain unresolved. There have been several agreements, initiatives, and proposals working to keep the peace process going—including the 1998 Wye River Memorandum, the 2000 Camp David negotiations, the 2001 talks in Taba, Egypt, the 2003 Geneva Accord, and the 2003 Road Map for Peace—but in 2004 peace remains elusive. This activity allows students to examine the Arab-Israeli peace process since Oslo, as well as to develop their own ideas as to how peace can be achieved.

Begin this activity by having students watch the SCIS videotape, *The Middle East in Transition*, Lesson 3, "The Arab-Israeli Conflict." They can watch just the introductory footage, or, if time allows, the introductory footage and the conversations with the Secretaries of State and Defense. Each of these segments sets the stage for discussion of ongoing issues. (Please note: the teacher should alert the students as to the dates of each clip.) As the students watch the video, they should write down key points with respect to the conflict.

As a quick review of events that have occurred since the 1993 Oslo Accord, have students examine Handout 3.11, "Key Events in the Middle East Peace Process Since Oslo." This handout can be reproduced and distributed, or made into a transparency for the class to examine together. Have the students highlight the events they feel are critical for understanding the conflict since 1993.

Next, using a transparency of Teacher Resource 3.1, "Major Points of Difference," lead a class discussion on the issues of contention between the Palestinians and the Israelis, as listed on the Teacher Resource. Fill in the transparency as the students discuss each point. Note that when discussing the issues of Jerusalem, permanent borders, and Israeli settlers, the teacher may want to project Teacher Resource 3.2, "Israel's Fence: Affected Populations" and Teacher Resource 3.3, "Jerusalem" from activity 3.7 as a visual aid. Next, use Teacher Resource 3.1, "Major Points of Difference: KEY" to fill in the gaps of student knowledge and help spark discussion. To conclude this portion of the activity, ask students:

- What are the conflicting positions taken by the Israelis and Palestinians on these key issues?
- What will have to be done in order to resolve them?

To continue, divide the class into three groups and assign each group one of the following: the 2001 Taba negotiations, the 2003 Geneva Accord, and the 2003 Road Map for Peace. Distribute to each group the summary of their assigned proposal as found in Handout 3.12, "2001 Negotiations in Taba, Egypt: Summary," Handout 3.13, "2003 Geneva Accord: Key Points," and Handout 3.14, "2003 Road Map for Peace: Summary." Alternatively, the teacher may assign primary documents related to these proposals, which can be found at www.southerncenter.org/material_updates.html.

Have each group use Worksheet 3.2, "Evaluating a Peace Plan," to outline the solutions offered in its proposal. Please note that each proposal does not necessarily address all the points. The groups should also discuss their assigned peace proposal and be prepared to present what they think are its strengths and weaknesses.

Next, have each group present the pros and cons of the proposal it examined and have the class decide which of the proposals shows the most promise.

Questions that can be raised include:

- How does your proposal deal with each of the issues on the worksheet?
- Is it best to come up with a final solution or take small steps?
- How would the various factions within the Israeli and Palestinian communities react to your plan?
- What other countries and organizations might have a stake in the final outcome of any Arab-Israeli peace plan? How much importance should their views be given as final decisions are made?

The teacher may also want to discuss with the class the current leaders, their positions, and how personalities of those involved affect the negotiations as well as the final decisions. This information can be found in the background essay as well as in the updates and Infolinks posted on www.southerncenter.org.

As a possible extension to this activity, have the groups come up with a peace proposal of their own, using what they feel are the best parts of the plans that have been offered. Ask how they think the Arab and Israeli communities would receive the solutions and whether the peace plans are possible given the current personalities and dynamics. An alternative extension would be to have the groups develop political cartoons depicting their thoughts on peace between Arabs and Israelis. Instructions for creating political cartoons can be found in *Africa in Transition*, Handout 4.7, "Creating Political Cartoons" and *Europe in Transition*, Teacher Resource 2.1, "Creating Political Cartoons."

KEY EVENTS IN THE MIDDLE EAST PEACE PROCESS SINCE OSLO

October 26, 1994—Israel and Jordan sign peace treaty.

November 4, 1995—Israeli Prime Minister Yitzhak Rabin is assassinated by a Jewish fundamentalist.

May 29, 1996—Benyamin Netanyahu is elected prime minister of Israel.

October 23, 1998—The Wye River Memorandum is signed, outlining a new timetable for implementing the Oslo Accords, as well as new intermediate steps.

May 17, 1999—Ehud Barak is elected prime minister of Israel.

May 24, 2000—Israel completes its withdrawal from Lebanon.

July 25, 2000—Peace talks at Camp David collapse.

September 28, 2000—Israeli opposition leader Ariel Sharon visits a controversial holy site, sparking a Palestinian Intifada, or uprising.

October 22, 2000—Israeli Prime Minister Ehud Barak suspends peace talks amidst warlike violence.

February 6, 2001—Ariel Sharon is elected prime minister of Israel as violence between Israelis and Palestinians continues.

September 11, 2001—Terrorist attacks in the United States destroy the World Trade Center complex and part of the Pentagon, sparking a global "war on terrorism."

March 2002—Sharon labels the Palestinian Authority a "terrorist-supporting organization." In response to a series of Palestinian suicide bombings, the Israeli army reoccupies much of the West Bank and Gaza Strip and attacks Palestinian Authority targets, trapping Yasser Arafat in his headquarters for more than a month.

June 2002—Israel begins construction of a highly controversial wall dividing Israeli- and Palestinian-held territory and cutting through portions of the Occupied Territories previously held by Palestinians.

April 29, 2003—Palestinian legislators confirm their first prime minister, Mahmoud Abbas, as part of a program of political reform.

April 30, 2003—The U.S., Russia, the EU, and the UN introduce the "road map for peace" plan.

September 2003—Mahmoud Abbas resigns as prime minister amid a protracted power struggle with Yasser Arafat, who then nominates Ahmed Qurei, also known as Abu Alaa, as the new prime minister.

October 13, 2003—A group of Israeli politicians and Palestinian representatives, acting in a private capacity, presents a peace plan known as the Geneva Accord.

MAJOR POINTS OF DIFFERENCE

Issue	Israeli Position	Palestinian Position
Final Status of Jerusalem		
Permanent Borders/Statehood		
Right of Return for Palestinian Refugees		
Access to Water		
Security Issues		

172

MAJOR POINTS OF DIFFERENCE

Issue	Israeli Position	Palestinian Position
Final Status of Jerusalem	• Jerusalem will be the capital of Israel. • Israel will have sovereignty over Jerusalem, including Jewish religious sites.	• Jerusalem will be the capital of Palestine. • Palestinians will have sovereignty over Arabic neighborhoods and Islamic religious sites.
Permanent Borders/Statehood	• Israel will annex parts of the Occupied Territories to provide for natural expansion of the Israeli population and security for Israeli citizens.	• Israel will withdraw to its 1967 borders and a Palestinian state will be created in 100% of the West Bank and Gaza Strip, which will be linked territorially.
Right of Return for Palestinian Refugees	• Only a small number of Palestinian refugees will be admitted to Israel. The remainder will be relocated to the Palestinian state or a third country.	• Each Palestinian refugee will have the right to return to Israel in accordance with UN Resolution 194 and will be compensated for confiscated and abandoned property.
Access to Water	• Israel will have access to water and not be dependent on the Palestinians or other Arab states for its water.	• Palestinians will have access to water and not be dependent on Israel for their water.
Security Issues	• Israel must be free from attack by Palestinians and other Arabs. • Palestine will be non-militarized.	• Palestinians must be free from attacks by the Israeli military and settlers. • Palestine will have limited arms.

Please note, these are not universally held positions. Differences exist among Palestinians and Israelis over these issues.

EVALUATING A PEACE PLAN

Name of Plan: _____

Issue	Israel Is Offered	Palestine Is Offered
Final Status of Jerusalem		
Permanent Borders/Statehood		
Right of Return for Palestinian Refugees		
Access to Water		
Security Issues		
Status of Israeli Settlements		
Compensation for Lost Property		
Role of the International Community		
Additional Points		

What is the plan's potential for success?

2001 NEGOTIATIONS IN TABA, EGYPT: *Summary*

In an attempt to salvage the peace effort before Israel's 2001 election, Israeli and Palestinian negotiators met in the Egyptian resort of Taba. The Barak government, in a departure from positions put forward at Camp David, modified long-standing, territorially based, security demands, allowing for a significant transformation of its settlement-related requirements. The Palestinians, in turn, for the first time presented a map acceding to Israel's annexation of some West Bank (and East Jerusalem) territory where settlements had created demographic realities that were hard to ignore, in return for land of equal value in Israel. Issues discussed at Taba included the following:

Territory

- The two sides agreed that in accordance with UN Security Council Resolution 242, the June 4, 1967 lines would be the basis for the borders between Israel and the state of Palestine.
- The Israeli maps were principally based on the concept of annexing Israeli settlement blocs that would involve annexing 6 percent of the West Bank, incorporating approximately 80 percent of the settlers into Israel, not counting those in annexed East Jerusalem. The Palestinian map presented 3.1 percent annexation in the context of a land swap. The Palestinian side did not accept proposals to annex blocs, saying they would cause significant harm to the interests and rights of Palestinians residing in areas Israel sought to annex.
- Both sides agreed that Israeli and Palestinian sovereign areas would have respective sovereign contiguity. Palestinian maps stressed the importance of the contiguity of the West Bank and Jerusalem.
- Although both sides agreed on the principle of a land swap, the proportionality of it remained under discussion. The Israeli side wished to count "assets" such as Israelis' "safe passage/corridor" proposal as being part of the land swap, even though the proposal would not give Palestine sovereignty over these "assets." The Palestinian side maintained that land not under Palestinian sovereignty should not be counted against them in the calculation of the swap.
- Both sides agreed that there was going to be a safe passage from the north of Gaza to the Hebron district, and that the West Bank and Gaza Strip would be territorially linked. The nature of control and sovereignty over the territorial link was not agreed upon.
- Neither side presented maps over the Gaza Strip, as it was implied that it would be under total Palestinian sovereignty. All settlements would be evacuated.

Jerusalem

- Both sides accepted that the city of Jerusalem would be the capital of the two states.
- Both sides accepted in principle the idea of Palestinians having sovereignty over Arab neighborhoods and Israel having sovereignty over Jewish neighborhoods.

175

- Both sides favored the idea of an Open City. The Israeli proposal encompassed only the Old City plus an area defined as the Holy Basin. The Palestinians maintained that the Open City should encompass the full municipal borders of both East and West Jerusalem.
- Both parties accepted the principle of respective control over each side's respective holy sites (religious control and management). However, the question of the Temple Mount/Haram al-Sharif, a place holy to both sides, had not been resolved.

Refugees

- The Palestinian side insisted that Palestinian refugees be compensated for confiscated and abandoned property and that each Palestinian refugee have the right to return to Israel in accordance with UN Resolution 194. The Israelis insisted on the admission of only a limited number of refugees, and suggested that the refugees be relocated to the Palestinian state or a third country.
- Both sides agreed to the establishment of an International Commission and an International Fund as a mechanism for dealing with all compensation requests, including those made by Palestinians and Israelis.

Security

- The Israeli side maintained that the state of Palestine would be non-militarized. The Palestinian side was prepared to accept limitations on its acquisition of arms, and be defined as a state with limited arms. The two sides had not agreed on the scope of arms limitations.
- Both sides recognized that Palestine would have sovereignty over its airspace.
- Israel agreed to a withdrawal from the West Bank over a 36-month period with an additional 36 months for the Jordan Valley. The Palestinians proposed an 18-month period for withdrawal with an additional 10-month period for the Jordan Valley, arguing that a lengthy process would exacerbate tensions.
- Both sides were prepared to commit themselves to promoting security cooperation and fighting terror.

Adapted from Ambassador Miguel Moratinos, EU Special Representative to the Middle East Process, "Taba Negotiations: The Moratinos Non-Paper," Mideastweb.org, January 2001, http://www.mideastweb.org/moratinos.htm.

2003 GENEVA INITIATIVE: *Key Points*

Preamble: This agreement marks the recognition of the right of the Jewish people to statehood and the recognition of the right of the Palestinian people to statehood, without prejudice to the equal rights of the Parties' respective citizens. The Parties recognize Palestine and Israel as the homelands of their respective peoples.

Article 1—Purpose: The implementation of this Agreement will settle all of the claims of the Parties arising from events occurring prior to its signature. No further claims related to events prior to this Agreement may be raised by either Party.

Article 4—Borders & Settlements: The border between the states of Palestine and Israel shall be based on the June 4th 1967 lines with reciprocal modifications on a 1:1 basis. Approximately 97.5% of the West Bank and 100% of Gaza will become part of Palestine, plus 2.5% of Israel from two areas: one area near Gaza to widen the Gaza Strip by 90 square kilometers, and another area adjacent to the southern West Bank. All of the 2.5% of West Bank territory that will become part of Israel comes from around Jerusalem. (See below for more on Jerusalem.)

- The state of Israel shall be responsible for resettling the Israelis residing in Palestinian sovereign territory outside this territory. Israel shall keep intact the immovable property, infrastructure, and facilities in Israeli settlements to be transferred to Palestinian sovereignty. The value of Israeli fixed assets that remain intact shall be deducted from Israel's contribution to the International Fund established to compensate Palestinian refugees (see below). In addition to evacuating settlers from most smaller settlements, a number of large settlements will also be left for the Palestinian state, including Ariel, Efrat, Kiryat Arba, Ofra, Elon Moreh, Bet El, Eli, and Har Homa. Israel will absorb settlement blocs that contain 110,000 settlers, in addition to the Jewish neighborhoods in East Jerusalem which include 200,000 Israelis. 110,000 Israelis living in 120 out of 140 West Bank settlements, and all settlements in the Gaza Strip, will be evacuated.

- The states of Palestine and Israel will establish a corridor linking the West Bank and Gaza Strip. The corridor, which will traverse Israeli territory, will be under Palestinian administration and under Israeli sovereignty, and it will be permanently open.

Articles 3 & 5—Implementation & Security: An International Implementation and Verification Group (IVG)—including the U.S., Russia, the EU, the UN and others—and a Multinational Force (MF) in Palestine will be established to provide security guarantees to both parties, act as a deterrent, and to help insure implementation and to monitor compliance by both parties to the terms of the agreement.

- Palestine shall be a non-militarized state, with a strong security force. The MF will protect the territorial integrity of the state of Palestine and oversee the Israeli withdrawal from Palestinian territory. The MF will help enforce anti-terrorism measures, monitor Palestinian security compliance, and train the Palestinian Security Service. The force cannot be withdrawn except by consent of both Israel and Palestine.

- Existing irregular forces and armed groups shall be disbanded and prevented from reforming at any future date. A Trilateral Security Committee—including Israel, Palestine, and the U.S.—shall develop comprehensive policies and guidelines to fight terrorism and violence. Israel and Palestine will promulgate laws to prevent incitement to irredentism, racism, terrorism, and violence and vigorously enforce them and the IVG shall monitor compliance.

- Israeli military forces and settlers will be removed from Palestinian territory within 30 months.

- Israel will maintain a small military presence in the Jordan Valley under the authority of the MF for an additional 36 months. Israel may maintain two Early Warning Stations (EWS) in the northern and central West Bank at locations specified in the Agreement. The EWS will be staffed by the minimal required number of Israeli personnel and will use the minimal amount of land necessary for their operation. The MF will monitor and verify that the EWS is being used for purposes recognized by the Accord.

- All border crossings in the State of Palestine will be monitored by joint teams composed of members of the Palestinian Security Force and the Multinational Force. There will be no Israeli forces at border crossings between the state of Palestine and the Arab world following the 30-month Israeli withdrawal process; during the 30-month withdrawal period, Israel will be able to maintain only an unseen presence at a designated facility in passenger and cargo terminals.

- The Palestinian state will enjoy sovereignty and security control over all roads in its territory.

- The state of Palestine will enjoy sovereignty over its own airspace. The Israeli Air Force will be entitled to use the Palestinian sovereign airspace for training purposes.

Article 6—Jerusalem: Israel and Palestine shall have their mutually recognized capitals in areas of Jerusalem under their respective sovereignty.

- Israel will receive sovereignty over the "Wailing" Wall, the Jewish Quarter of the Old City, and Jewish neighborhoods in East Jerusalem, including Givat Ze'ev, Ma'aleh Adumim, and the original historically Jewish area of Gush Etzion. Israel shall administer the Tower of David, the Western Wall tunnel, and the Jewish Cemetery on the Mount of Olives.

- Palestine will receive sovereignty over al-Haram al-Sharif/Temple Mount (the "Compound"), the Muslim, Christian, and Armenian Quarters of the Old City, and the Arab neighborhoods of East Jerusalem.

- An international group, including members of the Organization of the Islamic Conference, will be established to monitor, verify, and assist in the implementation of the terms of the agreement regarding the Compound. The Compound will be open to people of all faiths, with the Multinational Force ensuring freedom of access to the site. In view of the sanctity of the Compound, and in light of the unique religious and cultural significance of the site to the Jewish people, there shall be no digging, excavation, or construction on the Compound, unless approved by the two Parties.

Article 7—Palestinian Refugees: The Parties recognize that, in the context of two independent states, Palestine and Israel, living side by side in peace, an agreed resolution of the Palestinian refugee problem is necessary for achieving a just, comprehensive and lasting peace between them. The Parties recognize that UN General Assembly Resolution 194, UN Security Council Resolution 242, and the Arab Peace Initiative concerning the rights of the Palestinian refugees represent the basis for resolving the refugee issue, and agree that these rights are fulfilled under the Accord.

- All Palestinian refugees shall be entitled to compensation for their refugeehood and for loss of property.

- Refugees will be given the choice to (1) move to the new Palestinian state, including areas formerly in Israel [unlimited numbers], (2) remain in the countries where they currently reside or move to a third country [numbers based on sovereign decision of the host country], or (3) move to Israel [numbers based on the sovereign decision of Israel]. In determining its numbers, Israel will consider the average of the numbers submitted by other countries. Refugees who opt to remain in countries where they now reside will also receive prompt and extensive development and rehabilitation programs for their communities.

- An international commission and international fund will be established to deal with implementation of these residence options and compensation. Funds will be disbursed to refugee communities in the former areas of UNRWA operation, and will be at their disposal for communal development and commemoration of the refugee experience. Israel will contribute an agreed amount based on the value of the loss of property resulting from the refugees' displacement. Refugee status of individual Palestinians will be terminated once a permanent residence option has been realized.

Article 10—Sites of Religious Significance: Israel and Palestine shall establish special arrangements to guarantee access to agreed sites of religious significance, which will apply, inter alia, to the Tomb of the Patriarchs, Rachel's Tomb, and Nabi Samuel.

Article 11—Palestinian Prisoners & Detainees: All Palestinian and Arab prisoners detained in the framework of the Israeli-Palestinian conflict prior to the date of signature of the agreement shall be released according to a three-phase plan as outlined in the agreement—some immediately, some within 18 months, and "exceptional cases" in 30 months.

Article 17—End of Conflict: The Parties agree that the Geneva Accord will replace and supplant all UN resolutions, including those dealing with refugees, as well as other previous agreements. The Parties request that the UN Security Council and UN General Assembly endorse the Accord and declare that it supersedes all previous UN resolutions.

Adapted from "The Geneva Accord," Information Clearing House, October 19, 2003, http://informationclearinghouse.info/article5019.htm.

2003 ROAD MAP FOR PEACE: *Summary*

The Road Map for Peace is the U.S.-Proposed, Performance-Based Roadmap to a Permanent Two-State Solution to the Israeli-Palestinian Conflict.

Phase I: Ending Terror and Violence, Present to May 2003

In Phase I, the Palestinians immediately undertake an unconditional cessation of violence; such action should be accompanied by supportive measures undertaken by Israel. Palestinians and Israelis resume security cooperation through restructured Palestinian security services. Palestinians undertake comprehensive political reform in preparation for statehood, including drafting a Palestinian constitution, and holding free, fair, and open elections. Israel takes all necessary steps to help normalize Palestinian life. Israel withdraws from Palestinian areas occupied from September 28, 2000. Israel also freezes all settlement activity. A partial list of steps to be taken at the outset of Phase I includes:

- Palestinian leadership issues a statement reiterating Israel's right to exist in peace and security and calling for an immediate and unconditional ceasefire to end armed activity and all acts of violence against Israelis anywhere. All official Palestinian institutions end incitement against Israel.
- Israeli leadership issues a statement affirming its commitment to the creation of an independent, viable Palestinian state and calling for an immediate end to violence against Palestinians everywhere. All official Israeli institutions end incitement against Palestinians.
- Palestinians undertake visible efforts on the ground to arrest, disrupt, and restrain individuals and groups conducting and planning violent attacks on Israelis anywhere.
- Israel takes no actions undermining trust, including deportations, attacks on civilians, confiscation and/or demolition of Palestinian homes and property, and destruction of Palestinian institutions and infrastructure as a punitive measure or to facilitate Israeli construction.
- As comprehensive security performance moves forward, Israeli Defense Forces (IDF) withdraw progressively from areas occupied since September 28, 2000. Palestinian security forces redeploy to areas vacated by IDF.
- Palestinians take immediate action on a credible process to produce a draft constitution for Palestinian statehood. Palestinians appoint an interim prime minister or cabinet empowered with executive decision-making authority.
- Israel takes measures to improve the humanitarian situation, lifting curfews and easing restrictions on movement of persons and goods, and allowing full, safe, and unfettered access of international and humanitarian personnel.
- Israel immediately dismantles settlement outposts erected since March 2001. Israel also freezes all settlement activity (including natural growth of settlements).

Phase II: Transition, June 2003–December 2003

In the second phase, efforts are focused on the option of creating an independent Palestinian state with provisional borders and attributes of sovereignty, based on the new constitution, as a way station to a permanent status settlement. Phase II starts after Palestinian elections and ends with the possible creation of an independent Palestinian state with provisional borders. Its primary goals are continued comprehensive security performance, continued normalization of Palestinian life and institution-building, further building on the goals outlined in Phase I, ratification of a democratic Palestinian constitution, formal establishment of the office of prime minister, consolidation of political reform, and the creation of a Palestinian state with provisional borders. A partial list of steps to be taken during Phase II includes:

- An International Conference is convened by the Quartet, in consultation with the parties, immediately after the successful conclusion of Palestinian elections, to support Palestinian economic recovery and launch a process leading to the establishment of an independent Palestinian state with provisional borders.
- A new constitution for a democratic, independent Palestinian state is finalized and approved by appropriate Palestinian institutions.
- An empowered reform cabinet with the office of prime minister is formally established, consistent with the draft constitution.
- Israelis and Palestinians continue to cooperate effectively to maintain comprehensive security performance on the bases laid out in Phase I.
- An independent Palestinian state is created with provisional borders through a process of Israeli-Palestinian engagement, launched by the international conference. As part of this process, prior agreements are implemented to enhance maximum territorial contiguity of the Palestinian state, including further action on removal of Israeli settlements.

Phase III: Permanent Status Agreement, 2004–2005

Phase III objectives are consolidation of reform and stabilization of Palestinian institutions, sustained, effective Palestinian security performance, and Israeli-Palestinian negotiations aimed at a permanent status agreement in 2005. A partial list of steps to be taken during Phase III includes:

- A second International Conference is convened by the Quartet, in consultation with the parties, to endorse agreement on an independent Palestinian state with provisional borders and formally to launch a process with the active, sustained, and operational support of the Quartet, leading to a final, permanent status resolution in 2005, including on borders, Jerusalem, refugees, settlements; and, to support progress toward a comprehensive Middle East settlement between Israel and Lebanon and Israel and Syria, to be achieved as soon as possible.
- Continued sustained and effective security performance, and sustained, effective security cooperation on the bases laid out in Phase I.

- International efforts to facilitate reform and stabilize Palestinian institutions and the Palestinian economy, in preparation for a final status agreement.
- Parties reach a final and comprehensive permanent status agreement that ends the Israel-Palestinian conflict, through a settlement negotiated between the parties based on UN Resolutions 242, 338, and 1397, that ends the occupation that began in 1967, and includes an agreed, just, fair, and realistic solution to the refugee issue, and a negotiated resolution on the status of Jerusalem that takes into account the political and religious concerns of both sides, and protects the religious interests of Jews, Christians, and Muslims worldwide, and fulfills the vision of two states living side-by-side in peace and security.
- Arab states accept full normal relations with Israel and security for all the states of the region in the context of a comprehensive Arab-Israeli peace.

Excerpted from "A Performance-Based Roadmap to a Permanent Two-State Solution to the Israeli-Palestinian Conflict," U.S. Department of State, April 30, 2003, http://www.state.gov/r/pa/prs/ps/2003/20062.htm.

Israeli rescue workers search the wreckage of a destroyed bus following an explosion in Jerusalem, January 29, 2004. At least ten people were killed when a suicide bomber blew himself up on a bus near Israeli Prime Minister Ariel Sharon's official residence in Jerusalem, security forces said.

Reuters/Nili Bassan

LESSON 3

THE ARAB-ISRAELI CONFLICT

Activity 7

What are the implications of the Israeli Wall in the West Bank?

ACTIVITY OBJECTIVE

Students will examine the proposed path of the Israeli Wall, assess the impact of the wall on those who live on both sides, and determine the implications of the wall for the ongoing peace process.

MATERIALS AND RESOURCES

❑ Teacher Resource 3.2, "Israel's Fence: Affected Populations"
❑ Teacher Resource 3.3, "Jerusalem"
❑ Teacher Resource 3.4, "Photographs of the Wall"
❑ Handout 3.15, "Differing Views On the Wall"
❑ Handout 3.16, "Overnight, a Towering Divide Rises in Jerusalem"

STRATEGIES

In June 2002, the Israeli government began to construct a wall that will eventually surround much of the West Bank. Construction of the first section of the wall was completed in July 2003. The estimated final length of the barrier will be more than 400 miles. It will cost approximately $2.5 million per mile and is made of reinforced concrete, barbed wire, electrical fencing, electronic motion detectors, guard towers, and security roads. When completed it will be four times as long and twice as high as the Berlin Wall.

Rather than following the internationally recognized borders of Israel, the wall incorporates areas of the West Bank, occupied by Israel in 1967, and eventually will include around 80 percent of Israel's West Bank settlements. Many Palestinians have been cut off from their neighbors and businesses, farmers have been separated from their land, and children separated from their schools. Ariel Sharon, prime minister of Israel, has declared that the fence is necessary for Israel's protection from suicide bombers and others intent on carrying out terrorist acts against the country. Palestinians maintain that the wall is an illegal land grab and an obstacle to any lasting peace settlement.

To begin a discussion of the many issues surrounding Israel's wall, project Teacher Resource 3.2, "Israel's Fence: Affected Populations." On the map, point out the demarcation of the 1967 truce border, known as the "Green Line," and review the facts about the 1967 cease-fire (teachers can refer to SCIS Lesson 3, Activity 3 for more information). Also point out the path of the new wall. Next, project a transparency of Teacher Resource 3.3, "Jerusalem," and point out the ways in which this important city has been divided by the barrier. As a third step, project a transparency of Teacher Resource 3.4, "Photographs of the Wall," to give students a visual sense of the barrier.

Lead a class discussion of the possible impacts of such a barrier on those who live nearby, as well as the implications for the country as a whole. Questions for the class to consider include:

- What has determined the route of the wall?
- Does the wall take into account the location of existing Palestinian villages?
- What will the wall's impact be on a Palestinian who finds himself/herself separated from his fields?
- How might the wall impact traffic from one West Bank village to another? How will it impact traffic in and out of the West Bank, particularly for Palestinians who work inside Israel?
- What will be the impact on Israeli settlers who find themselves separated from Israel?
- What might be the political impact of this barrier?
- Do you agree or disagree with Ariel Sharon's statement: "Terror built the fence"?
- Will the wall stop Palestinian terrorists from conducting attacks against Israel?

After the initial discussion, divide the class into four groups. Each class group will represent a different group affected by the security wall:

- Israeli settlers living in the West Bank
- Palestinians living in the West Bank
- Israelis living in Israel proper
- Israeli Arabs living in Israel proper

Give each group a copy of Handout 3.15, "Differing Views on the Wall" and Handout 3.16, "Overnight, a Towering Divide Rises in Jerusalem." Have each group read the quotes and review the article. Also note that a copy of Teacher Resource 3.2, "Israel's Fence: Affected Populations" can be projected for students to reference throughout their group discussions. Ask each group to prepare three main arguments that represent the views of their assigned population.

At the teacher's discretion, students may also view video segments on the wall available from PBS's Online NewsHour, which can be accessed through www.southerncenter.org/info_links.html. Two segments in particular—from February 9 and February 10, 2004—present the differing viewpoints on the wall. Note that this option requires the ability to view streaming video from the Internet. Alternatively, transcripts of the segments can be printed for students to read.

Bring the class back together and let each group present its case, either in the form of a debate or in a town-hall meeting format. The discussion should touch on the implications of the wall for any future Arab-Israeli peace negotiations.

To conclude this activity, ask each student to present his or her own view on the wisdom and practicality of the wall in the form of a letter to the editor of a newspaper, a position paper to a diplomat who will be involved in the Arab-Israeli peace process, or a political cartoon to be published in either an Israeli or Palestinian newspaper.

As an activity extension, students can consider the feasibility of the Israeli wall in light of other barriers that have existed in the past, such as the Berlin Wall and the Great Wall of China. Students can find information on these barriers by using the school's media center or the Internet. Lead a class discussion centered around the following questions:

- What was the purpose and the eventual fate of barriers such as the Great Wall of China or the Berlin Wall?
- What have the issues been surrounding the different security fences?
- Do good fences indeed make good neighbors? Or is the reverse often true?

An alternate activity extension is to have students discuss the applicability of Robert Frost's poem "Mending Wall" to this situation. The poem can be found in a number of anthologies of Frost's poetry or on the Internet at such Web sites as www.poets.org. Have students read the poem and discuss how it might apply to the wall being built in the West Bank. Discussion questions can include:

- What point is Frost making about walls in general?
- When are walls a good thing?
- What are their drawbacks?
- Are walls permanent or do they decay over time? What might that say about the nature of walls?
- Does someone wall things in or wall them out? What is the case with the Israeli wall?

ISRAEL'S FENCE: AFFECTED POPULATIONS

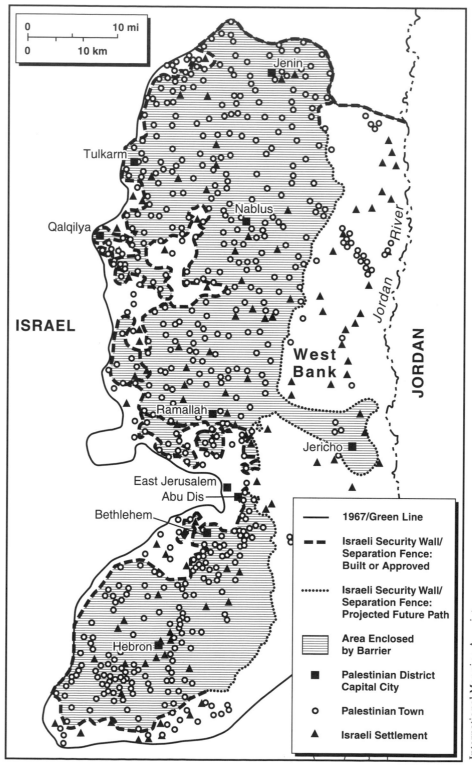

Legend:

— 1967/Green Line

- - - Israeli Security Wall/Separation Fence: Built or Approved

.... Israeli Security Wall/Separation Fence: Projected Future Path

▨ Area Enclosed by Barrier

■ Palestinian District Capital City

○ Palestinian Town

▲ Israeli Settlement

International Mapping Associates

JERUSALEM

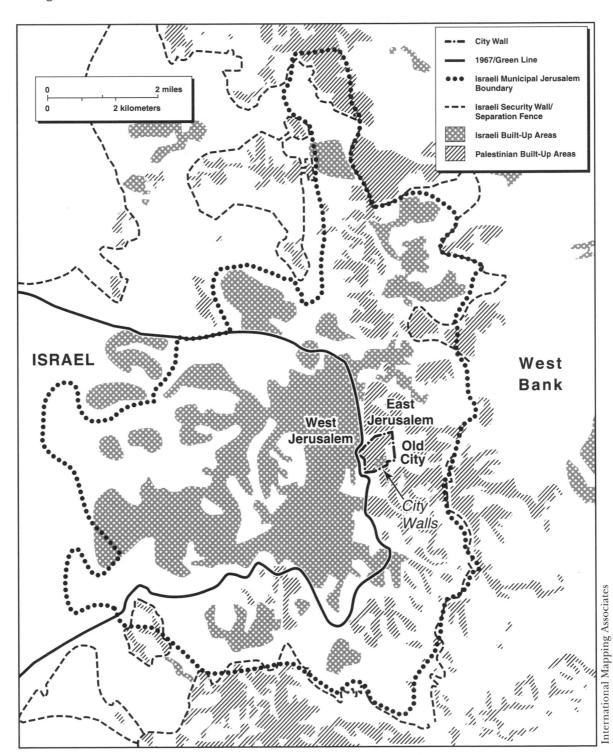

Legend:
- City Wall
- 1967/Green Line
- Israeli Municipal Jerusalem Boundary
- Israeli Security Wall/ Separation Fence
- Israeli Built-Up Areas
- Palestinian Built-Up Areas

ISRAEL

West Bank

East Jerusalem

West Jerusalem

Old City

City Walls

International Mapping Associates

PHOTOGRAPHS OF THE ISRAELI SECURITY WALL

February 17, 2004: An aerial view in Baqa El Gharbiya of Israel's controversial security barrier.

REUTERS/Nir Elias

February 21, 2004: Israel's security barrier in the city of Baqa El Gharbiya.

REUTERS/Reinhard Krause

REUTERS/Ammar Awad

December 12, 2003: Palestinian boys herd their animals in front of the Israeli wall on the outskirts of Jerusalem.

REUTERS/Mahfouz Abu Turk

January 5, 2004: A Palestinian woman squeezes through the Israeli barrier.

DIFFERING VIEWS ON THE WALL

Israelis living in Israel proper

SILVAN SHALOM,
Israeli foreign minister:
"We have the responsibility to protect our people, and that's why we are building this fence. We are doing it because it was the recommendation of the security forces. We adopted it, we are building it, and if we reach an agreement with the Palestinians . . . we will agree, one with each other, to move it."

— "The Barrier," Elizabeth Farnsworth,
Online NewsHour, February 9, 2004

MARY SCHWEITZER,
who moved to Israel from the U.S. 21 years ago:
"There's nothing about security in the wall. The wall represents humiliation. It represents degradation. There is no reason at all that Jews should be building ghettos. Jews should be the first people to stand against ghettos."

— "The Barrier" Elizabeth Farnsworth,
Online News Hour, February 9, 2004

ALEX YAKOBSON,
professor of classical history at the Hebrew University
of Jerusalem and a prominent Israeli public intellectual:
"The fence, it is true, is not nice. It is not aesthetic. It is not convenient. I do not underestimate the genuine hardship that it is causing. But it's also not nice when a bus full of passengers is blown up and their limbs and organs—hands and legs and heads—fly for tens of meters in all directions. From a purely moral point of view, nobody's freedom of movement is more precious than somebody else's life."

— "Good Fences Make Good Neighbors," Peter Berkowitz,
The Weekly Standard, March 1, 2004

Arabs living in Israel proper

RASHA,
an Arab-Israeli woman from a village near Kfar Sava, says Arabs want a normal life, not a war with Israel, but these barriers going up will only make peace less likely.
"It's good for the Israelis, but it's bad for the Arabs. In the end, they want work, they want money. It's not good for peace. It's not gonna bring peace. It's good for war, for continuing the situation of war."

— "How New Israeli Security Wall Is Seen by Israelis" Peter Kenyon,
All Things Considered, National Public Radio, September 2, 2003

KHALED ABU TOAMEH,
a prominent Arab-Israeli journalist:
"Of course Israelis are largely indifferent to Palestinian suffering. Of course Israelis do not really understand that the ordinary, average Palestinian is a normal person who wants to wake up in the morning, send his children to school, care for his family, go to work, and just lead a normal life. He doesn't care about other things. The Palestinian Authority. Israel. They are not that important. What is important is not to disrupt normal life. And this fence disrupts normal life. It turns the life of many Palestinians into hell."

> — "Good Fences Make Good Neighbors," Peter Berkowitz,
> *The Weekly Standard*, March 1, 2004

MOHAMMAD BAKRI,
the Arab-Israeli director of the controversial documentary *Jenin*:
"I feel deep sadness right now. Just looking at this wall, I feel the hope draining out of me."

> — "Two Sides of the 'Fence': I don't see it coming down," Mitch Potter,
> *The Toronto Star*, February 22, 2004

Israelis living in West Bank settlements

DIDI REMEZ,
a reserves captain in the Israel Defense Forces
who has served in the West Bank and Gaza Strip:
"I was born a Zionist, raised as a Zionist and taught that the Zionist reason we are in Israel was to create a Jewish and democratic state. Our continued occupation of the West Bank and Gaza is endangering our future as a Jewish and democratic state . . . I'm for a separate wall that runs along the 1967 border, one that does not add thousands of Palestinians to the Israeli state . . . Their excuse is security, but the wall being built is political. And its goal is to try to create a new boarder and boundary."

> — "Searching Jenin: Eyewitness Accounts of the Israeli Invasion 2002,"
> *Arab News*, March 23, 2003

ADI MINTZ,
secretary-general, Council of Jewish Settlements in Judea, Samaria, and the Gaza Strip:
"[We are on the] wrong side of the fence. . . . It is certainly a blow, but we have overcome terrorism and other problems, and will overcome this one too."

> — "Israeli Settlers Fear Separation Fence to End 'Dream of a Greater Israel,'"
> Matthew Gutman, *Global News Wire*, October 2, 2003

UNIDENTIFIED WOMAN,
an Israeli settler who declined to give her name:
"I feel secure. It makes me secure. That's all I have to say about it. My life is here."

> — "How New Israeli Security Wall Is Seen by Israelis" Peter Kenyon,
> *All Things Considered*, National Public Radio, September 2, 2003

Palestinians living in the West Bank

NASSER AL-KIDWA,
the Palestine Liberation Organization delegate to the United Nations:
"When you wall people into ghettos . . . you are creating a situation that will combust. This wall is not about security. It's about entrenching the occupation of West Bank land."

— "Israeli Barrier Challenged at World Court," Michael Matza,
Philadelphia Inquirer, February 24, 2004

TERRY BOULLATA,
school founder and headmistress:
"My family is in Jerusalem. My husband, his family, and his work is in West Bank, in Abu Dis. My children need both sides—need their grandfather in the West Bank and need their grandparents in the Jerusalem side. For us, we are one people and one land. My house was in a very luxury residential area. Overnight, we have become in the middle of a military base."

— "The Barrier," Elizabeth Farnsworth,
Online NewsHour, February 9, 2004

HANAN ASHRAWI,
Palestinian legislator:
"It's a wall that distorts any Palestinian reality that prevents any kind of emergence of a contiguous, viable Palestinian state. And at the same time it's an excuse for annexation of further land, annexation of water resources, and of course with the byproduct of displacement of Palestinians, of tremendous economic and daily living hardships. This is just incredible."

— "The Barrier," Elizabeth Farnsworth,
Online NewsHour, February 9, 2004

OVERNIGHT, A TOWERING DIVIDE RISES IN JERUSALEM

By James Bennet

With a towering concrete slab lowered almost tenderly into a ragged street, Israel began drawing a hard line around Jerusalem on Sunday, walling it off from Abu Dis, an Arab village joined to the city for generations.

The conflict between Israelis and Palestinians can look like the stalest of stalemates, a furious stand-off that defies measurement and maybe even change. But in this crowded neighborhood of east Jerusalem, the city's Arab section, there was something monumental, even defining, about the 30-foot slab descending from the twilight, just after a muezzin called the sunset prayer over the crane's roar.

Israel has begun work on other sections of the Jerusalem barrier, which it says is a necessary bulwark against suicide bombers. But it has not built in such a busy area or so close to Jerusalem's center and holy sites.

Bent with age, bundled in a shawl and white head scarf, Nadieh Shihabi, 90, picked her way past the growing barrier, crossing to her house on the Abu Dis side.

"I want to stay in my home," she said, wiping at tears.

Her daughter-in-law, Rada Shihabi, 53, replied, "You cannot." She would have to stay in Jerusalem with her family rather than risk separation, she said.

"Come and see your house for the last time," Rada Shihabi said gently.

Nadieh Shihabi said she had lost another house, in what is now a Jewish section of Jerusalem, in the Arab-Israeli war of 1948.

There were no camera crews and no demonstrators to witness as the mostly Arab construction crew showed up and began its task, under heavy military guard. The Israeli plans were announced some time ago, but no date was set publicly. The Palestinian leadership appeared caught flat-footed as construction began.

The prime minister, Ahmed Qurei, who lives in Abu Dis, a couple of blocks from the construction site, was in another West Bank village, Qalqiliya, which is enclosed by the West Bank barrier. There, he attacked the "racist separation wall."

Israel says the new barricade is not a permanent, political border but a reversible security measure.

"I know that people are talking about the fence," Prime Minister Ariel Sharon said Sunday. "You know who built the fence? Terror built the fence."

Speaking at a news conference in Jerusalem, he continued, "If not for the terror, maybe we wouldn't have done it."

Mr. Sharon was referring to the entire barrier of concrete, ditches, fencing, and barbed wire that Israel is building against West Bank Palestinians. Just Sunday, Mr. Sharon said, a Palestinian suicide bomber blew himself up in the West Bank after he spotted an Israeli patrol. No one but the bomber was killed or hurt. Mr. Sharon said the man had been headed for central Israel.

The longer West Bank barrier is to be joined to the one being built around Jerusalem, a roughly 21-mile stretch that will consume some West Bank land along the city's eastern outskirts. Planners have said only some segments will be solid concrete.

195

They also say they will include gates, but Palestinians say they fear that those gates will seldom be open, or that they will not be able to get the permits they will need to pass.

On the slope of the Mount of Olives, Abu Dis sits partly within Jerusalem's municipal boundaries, and negotiators once saw it as the possible capital of a Palestinian state.

The idea was that Abu Dis could do politically what it had already done socially and commercially: smudge the line between Jerusalem and the West Bank.

But distinctions are getting sharper here, not blurrier. As he often does, Mr. Sharon referred to Jerusalem on Sunday as "the eternal, united, and undivided capital of the Jewish people."

The new wall will actually divide Abu Dis, keeping part of it on the Jerusalem side, separating neighbors and relatives who live just blocks or even a street apart.

Months ago, Israel built another wall against Abu Dis. But it is only six or eight feet high, and every day thousands of Palestinians climb over it or squeeze between its slabs. Taxis idle on either side, as children with backpacks, men wearing suits or carrying tool boxes, and elderly people make their way from Abu Dis, which has counted on Jerusalem for basic services like health care.

Bassam Zagari, 38, said that after the first wall was built, he stopped sending his son, Ali, from his home in Abu Dis to a special school in Jerusalem. Mr. Zagari was no longer getting enough business at his vegetable stand to afford the fees, he said, and because Ali, now 14, cannot hear or speak, Mr. Zagari was afraid he would not stop if he were called by an Israeli patrol.

Mr. Zagari's business has limped along, thanks to commerce over the existing wall. "This will destroy us," he said of the new one. "Jerusalem gave life to the town."

With its base planted in a trench and its slabs slotted together, the wall going up on Sunday rose more than 25 feet above the ground and seemed certain to repel climbers.

"Look at the height of that thing," murmured one of the construction workers, a 42-year-old Israeli Arab, as the first slab went up. "What's the difference between a house here, and a house there?" he asked, indicating the facing sides of the street, the opposite sides of the barrier.

Much as Palestinian workers built many Israeli settlements in the West Bank and Gaza Strip, Arab citizens of Israel were building this section of wall even as they opposed its construction.

The 42-year-old man, who asked not to be identified, said that if he did not do the job, someone else would. "What we are doing is wrong," he said. "It's breaking my heart. But what can we do?"

As the construction workers unloaded a crane, it bowed a telephone wire strung in the path of the new wall, between what was being defined as strictly Jerusalem and strictly West Bank.

The Arab man climbed on top of a bulldozer. With a small pair of clippers, he cut the line.

Source: *The New York Times*, January 12, 2004. © 2004 The New York Times Company. Reprinted by permission.

LESSON 4

OTHER MIDDLE EASTERN ISSUES

Lesson 4 of 5 Lessons for the
Southern Center for International Studies'
Multimedia Educational Package
THE MIDDLE EAST IN TRANSITION

Reuters/Adrees Latif

Nearly one million pilgrims face the Kaaba in sunset prayers at the Grand Mosque in Mecca, Saudi Arabia, February 27, 2001. Over two million people were expected to perform the Hajj, the fifth pillar of Islam. The Grand Mosque is the holiest shrine in Islam.

Background Reading for

LESSON 4

of the SCIS Educational Package
THE MIDDLE EAST IN TRANSITION

OTHER MIDDLE EASTERN ISSUES

Many other issues, in addition to those examined in Lessons 1 through 3, divide the Middle East, its countries, its cultures, and its peoples. Here, we will examine four prominent regional concerns:

1) Islamic fundamentalism;
2) water resources;
3) the Kurds; and
4) Iran and regional stability.

ISLAMIC FUNDAMENTALISM

Often, the term "Islamic fundamentalism" is used to describe those Muslims who wish to follow a strict traditionalist interpretation of Islam. Although this term is widely used in relation to Islam, it is more often than not used incorrectly. "Fundamentalism" is actually a term borrowed from Christianity, where it connotes a belief in the literal meaning of the Bible. To apply the same terminology to distinguish between Muslims is misleading because all Muslims believe that the Koran represents the infallible word of God; indeed, this is a basic tenet of Islam.

With this in mind, a more accurate word to describe those Muslims who wish to follow a strict traditionalist interpretation of the Islamic faith is "Islamist." Beyond this, those who would use violence and terror to pursue their objective of creating a government that follows a strict traditionalist interpretation of Islam may be called "radical Islamists." The key point here is that the Islamic world is extremely divided on what it means to be Muslim and on what constitutes an Islamic government.

Nevertheless, many people in the Middle East, frustrated with the status quo and dissatisfied with traditional responses by their own country's government to their problems, have turned towards radical versions of Islam for solutions to the problems that they face. Throughout the Middle East, governments are confronted by a rise in support for Islamist and radical Islamist groups.

Conservative and moderate states throughout the Middle East have been concerned about Iran's radical Islamist government ever since Ayatollah Khomeini deposed the Shah in 1979. They fear Iran's efforts to export radical Islamic teachings and outlooks. This was a major reason that many Arab countries supported Iraq in its war against Iran from 1980 to 1988. This concern about Iran was further reinforced by Iran's efforts to influence Islamist movements in Afghanistan, Algeria, Lebanon, Sudan, and the newly independent Central Asian states that emerged after the Soviet Union's collapse.

In the West Bank and Gaza, Palestinian support for the radical Islamist movement Hamas has threatened the traditional secular leadership of the Palestine Liberation Organization (PLO). Hamas played a central role in the two *Intifadas*, or Palestinian uprisings, against Israeli control of the West Bank and Gaza. Hamas's growing influence was one of the major factors that led Israel and the PLO to reach an accord in September 1993.

Meanwhile, in southern Lebanon, another radical Islamist movement, Hezbollah, supported by both Syria and Iran, challenged Israel's continued presence. The Lebanese government in Beirut failed to control Hezbollah, and gradually much of the largely Shia population of southern Lebanon, disenfranchised from the traditional Christian and Sunni elites in the country, came to support Hezbollah.

During the 1980s and 1990s, Islamist and radical Islamist movements gained strength in other Middle Eastern states as well. In Tunisia, the government responded to the success of Islamist parties in elections by banning all Islamist parties. Similarly, in Algeria, the government refused to permit an Islamist party to take power despite its victory in an open election. Meanwhile, King Hussein in Jordan feared that elections might strengthen the political base of Jordan's Islamist movement. In Egypt, the government responded to violent attacks by radical Islamist groups against government officials and tourists with arrests, executions, and the imposition of severe restrictions on radical Islamist activities.

The September 11, 2001, terrorist attacks on the U.S. and the subsequent "war on terrorism" dramatically illustrated the impact that radical Islamist movements now have, not only in the Middle East, but in the world as a whole. It is important to restate, however, that Islamists range from moderates supporting democracy to radicals who would use violence to overthrow their government and establish a strict Islamist state. Only a few countries, such as Iran and Sudan, can be considered radical Islamist states, and more moderate regimes prevail in most of the Islamic world. The varied and complex nature of Islamist movements in the Middle East can be seen by examining three cases—Algeria, Egypt, and Saudi Arabia—as well as the actions of radical militants such as Osama bin Laden. The special case of Iran is discussed in the last section of this lesson.

Algeria

In Algeria, the Islamist opposition steadily strengthened during the 1980s. By the late 1980s and early 1990s, clashes between the government and the radical Islamic Salvation Front (FIS) were tense and often violent. However, in late 1991, after a short period of relative calm, elections for the National Assembly were held. The FIS dominated the first round of this vote and President Chadli Bendjedid initiated talks on power-sharing.

Unhappy with the power-sharing agreement, the military forced Bendjedid to resign in early 1992. A "High Security Council" dominated by the military nullified the election results, canceled the second round of the vote, and launched an "all-out war" against the Islamists. Since 1992, as many as 150,000 people have been brutally killed in what is best described as a vicious and gruesome civil war.[1]

In 1999, Abdel Aziz Bouteflika won the presidential election after all other candidates withdrew amid charges of electoral fraud. Bouteflika soon implemented a plan of national reconciliation that included amnesty for Islamic militants. In January 2000, the FIS's armed wing, the Islamic Salvation Army, disbanded itself and many armed militants surrendered under the amnesty program.

In April 2004, Bouteflika won a landslide victory in the country's presidential election, in large part because of his efforts to restore stability and promote national reconciliation. While the level of violence has declined markedly since the mid-1990s, residual fighting continued in 2004, fueled in part by the country's dire economic circumstances. Approximately 100 people continued to be killed each month by armed groups, security forces, and state-armed militias.[2] Exacerbating the situation were additional conflicts between the government and Algeria's Berber minority, who were demanding greater rights.

Egypt

In Egypt, violence between the country's long-standing radical Islamist opposition and the secular government of President Hosni Mubarak heated up considerably in the 1990s. The militants increasingly targeted government officials and foreign tourists in their attempt to destabilize the government. The government, for its part, engaged in torture and repression of its Islamist opponents.

The most horrific terrorist attack occurred in 1997, when 70 tourists were gunned down at the ancient Hatshepsut Temple near Luxor. However, after this attack, Islamist militancy noticeably declined. Some Egyptian analysts suggested that the Luxor massacre discredited radical Islamists. Many Islamist leaders themselves condemned the assault and renounced the use of violence. Mubarak's government began a harsh crackdown after the massacre.

By the turn of the century, violent opposition had subsided. Radical Islamist groups such as Gamaat Islamiya and al-Jihad announced cease-fires. More moderate Islamists, such as the outlawed Muslim Brotherhood, sought to work within the political system to create an Islamic state. In 2000, despite government efforts to discourage their participation, members of the Muslim Brotherhood won the second-largest bloc of seats in the country's parliament.

Nevertheless, in 2004, militant Islamic groups continued to garner support in parts of Egypt, particularly in slums where poverty and unemployment are widespread. While the government's tight, some would say repressive, grip on Egyptian politics had largely silenced attacks in the country, Egyptian militants were very active in international terrorist groups, such as al Qaeda. The question remains whether Islamists will be further integrated into the political process, or whether they will be shut out, spurring some to resort to violence in order to make their voices heard.

Saudi Arabia

Saudi Arabia is the birthplace of Islam and the location of Islam's holiest sites, Mecca and Medina. The Saudi government, ruled by the al-Saud family since the country's inception in 1932, officially practices a puritanical form of Islam known as Wahhabism. The country's laws are based on the *Sharia*, the sacred law of Islam, as derived from the holy book of Islam, the Koran, and interpreted by religious elders. Powerful Muslim clerics heavily influence Saudi social practices and daily life. The country has significant religious, political, and economic clout throughout the Muslim world and the royal family has long portrayed itself as the guardian of Islam's holy places.

Despite the Islamist nature of Saudi Arabia, for decades the country has been one of the most important U.S. allies in the Middle East. Saudi Arabia is the world's largest exporter of oil and is the third-largest exporter of oil to the U.S. after Mexico and Canada.[3] It also served as the primary staging ground for the 1991 Persian Gulf War against Saddam Hussein. Throughout the 1990s, the U.S. stationed thousands of troops at Saudi Arabia's Prince Sultan Air Base. By late 2003, however, the U.S. had pulled virtually all of its troops out of the country, in part to prevent Islamic extremists from using the American military presence as a rallying cry.

It is the contradictions of Saudi politics and society that make the country such an important case in understanding radical Islam. On the one hand, many of the country's schools are run by radical Muslim clerics who focus heavily on religious studies and often foster grass-roots anti-Americanism and support for individuals like Osama bin Laden. The government has also supported thousands of Islamic schools and charities around the world that promote radical Islam. The Saudi press, like the press in other corners of the Middle East, has often been strongly anti-American, with little attempt by the government to cultivate a more balanced view.

Standing in contrast is the government's strong political, military, and economic relationship with the United States, its suppression of political freedoms, and its inability to provide economic security for much of the country's burgeoning young population. As a result, many ordinary Saudis see the monarchy as corrupt and morally bankrupt, and turn to radical Islam, targeting the government and its U.S. backers. Although the Saudi government was well aware of the evolving anti-Americanism within its borders, it chose to ignore its potentially dangerous consequences. Even when it was discovered that 15 of the 19 hijackers involved in the September 11, 2001, terrorist attacks against the U.S. were Saudi, the government denied that its own conflicting practices had any role in the attacks.

Still, September 11 may have served as a wake-up call for the monarchy. Even more, a series of terrorist attacks in Saudi Arabia, including the bombings of several housing compounds in Riyadh in May and November 2003, underscored to the Saudi government that it too had become a target of Islamist terrorists. In response, the government stepped up its efforts to crack down on militant Islamists and made tentative steps toward political and economic reform. However, critics of the monarchy say reform efforts are far too timid. Moreover, Crown Prince Abdullah faces many obstacles, not least of which involve other members of the royal family intent on protecting their privileged positions.

Islamist Militants

It is also important to look at radical Islamists whose actions span across state borders, and indeed beyond the Middle East. Importantly, the relationships among such groups are less than clear; radical Islam is certainly not a monolithic entity. However, the September 11 terrorist attacks made clear the need to confront international terrorism sponsored by radical Islamists.

A main target in the "war on terrorism" has been the al Qaeda network led by the wealthy Saudi, Osama bin Laden. Bin Laden has sought to unify radical Islamists in pursuit of a *jihad*[4] against Western powers and their Middle Eastern allies. He was the mastermind, or at least the financial backer, of not just the September 11 attacks, but also the 1993 bombing of the World Trade Center in New York City, the 1996 bombing of an American military facility in Dhahran, Saudi Arabia, the 1998 bombings of the U.S. embassies in Kenya and Tanzania, and the October 2000 bombing of the USS Cole in Yemen. It was the September 11 attacks, however, that resulted in the U.S.-led "war on terrorism" which began in Afghanistan, where bin Laden had sanctuary. Despite this war and other efforts, at the beginning of 2004 bin Laden and other al Qaeda leaders remained at large. Importantly, Islamist groups like al Qaeda are not attacking Western targets for the purpose of defeating them militarily, or to occupy their countries, but rather to drive Western presence and influence out of the Middle East.

As the discussion so far in this lesson shows, Islamist militancy is a complex phenomenon that is driven not just by religious fervor, but also by a host of other factors, such as political disenfranchisement, corruption, repression, and poverty. To understand the root causes of terrorism in the Middle East, one also cannot look past the long-standing conflict between the U.S. and Iraq, the ongoing plight of the Palestinians, a perceived American bias toward Israel, U.S. support for corrupt and authoritarian governments in the region, and American unilateralism on the world scene. As long as economic, political, and social demands are not met by existing structures, it is probable that Islamist movements will continue to grow in strength. People will simply look for alternative solutions to their unmet needs. Thus, it should not be surprising that, throughout the Middle East, radical Islamist groups are able to find a sympathetic audience.

WATER RESOURCES

Competition over scarce water resources in the Middle East is another potential source of conflict. The Middle East is by far the world's driest region. While the region contains five percent of the world's population, it has less than one percent of the world's freshwater resources.[5] Limited water resources that cross national boundaries combine with political rivalries and increasing rates of consumption to add to existing tensions. Several leaders in the region have warned that if these issues are not resolved, the next major conflict in the Middle East will be over water, not oil. A few examples help show the enormity of this issue.

Israel and its Arab neighbors have a long history of competition over water resources. At the turn of the century, the original Zionist planners mapped out their intended homeland to include the major sources of water in areas that today include parts of each of Israel's neighbors. Over the years, Israel, the Palestinian Authority, Jordan, Syria, Lebanon, and several others have participated in complex multilateral negotiations regarding shared water resources. With growing populations, the existing ground and surface water resources are not sufficient to meet the combined demands of each country or group.

Israel currently obtains water from the Jordan and Yarmuk Rivers. It distributes this water to the entire country through an elaborate system of pipes, pumping stations, and conduits called the National Water Carrier. Other Israeli water sources include deep underground aquifers, many of which exist under the West Bank. Overuse of some of the aquifers has caused excessive depletion that has led to saltwater penetration from the Mediterranean Sea.

Since 1967, Palestinians in the West Bank and Gaza have faced severe restrictions by Israel on the pumping and use of water located under the Occupied Territories. Palestinians argue that Israel is exploiting these resources for its own needs and the needs of Israeli settlements in the Occupied Territories. For Palestinians, the problem is exacerbated by very old pipelines and irrigation systems, high population growth rates, and the development of new, deep wells in Israeli settlements. Israeli settlers consume about five times more water per capita than the Palestinians do, suggesting that any lasting peace plan would have to address a more balanced distribution of water resources.[6] However, Israelis worry that if they grant Palestinians the right to control water resources in their areas, Israel's own water security would be jeopardized.

Similarly, Jordan and Syria claim that Israel takes more water from the Jordan and Yarmuk Rivers than it should. Therefore, since they face severe water shortages, they demand changes in Israeli water use practices or compensation.

Turkey, Iraq, and Syria share the water resources of the Euphrates River. In addition, Turkey and Iraq benefit from the Tigris River. Turkey's $32 billion Southeastern Anatolia Project, an ambitious program to construct 22 dams along the Tigris-Euphrates river basin, has created serious tensions with Syria and Iraq because it regulates the flow of water into these downstream countries. Yet long-standing political divisions have kept the three countries from developing a regional plan regarding water usage in the Tigris-Euphrates river basin. Add to these political divisions high population growth rates, several years of drought, and growing irrigation needs and it becomes clear why some are worried about subregional stability.

A number of efforts have been taken to address water issues in the region. Tunisia, Jordan, and Yemen are attempting to reform their water sectors. The governments of Kuwait, Jordan, and Iran are utilizing electromagnetic flowmeters, devices used to more efficiently control the flow of water in their countries. Turkey has considered exporting surplus fresh water to its water-poor neighbors in the Middle East by pipeline or by tanker. Other countries, including Saudi Arabia, have explored creative options such as towing icebergs from Antarctica.

Another ray of hope comes from desalination technology, in which Israel is a world leader. While there are desalination plants located throughout the Persian Gulf, funded by the tremendous oil wealth in the region, the enormous cost of building and maintaining such plants has kept them from being built on the Mediterranean coast, where there are no other easily available sources of fresh water. Israeli Prime Minister Ariel Sharon is calling on the international community to build massive desalination plants on the Mediterranean coast, a move that would increase Israel's willingness to cede control of the West Bank, now an important source of water for Israel.

However, even the Persian Gulf countries that can now afford desalination plants face eventual water shortages. Desalination plants are purchased with oil revenues and fueled by oil. Even more, several Gulf countries are threatening to deplete their non-replenishable groundwater reserves because of over-pumping. In some areas, groundwater is being used for water-intensive agriculture production that cannot be maintained indefinitely. Since both oil and water are finite resources, these countries, with growing demand for water and increasing populations, may also eventually face water shortages unless new resources are found elsewhere.

THE KURDS

Another regional issue that the Persian Gulf War sharpened but left unanswered was the question of the future of the Kurds, an ethnic group that lives primarily in Iran (6 million Kurds out of a total population of 61 million), Iraq (3 million Kurds out of a total population of 18 million), and Turkey (10 million out of 60 million). The vast majority of Kurds are Sunni Muslims.

The Kurds have never had their own nation-state. However, for many years, many of them have struggled to create one. Kurdish separatist movements have operated in Iran, Iraq, and Turkey, sometimes resorting to propaganda and politics and other times resorting to violence and fighting. In all cases, Iran, Iraq, and Turkey have refused to consider Kurdish independence. Often, all three governments have brutally repressed the Kurds, sometimes killing thousands.

The combination of Iraq's defeat in the first Persian Gulf War and U.S. statements urging forces within Iraq to rise up against Saddam Hussein emboldened Iraqi Kurds to again attempt to achieve independence. In March 1991, the Kurdish Front, a grouping of most of the major Iraqi Kurdish parties and groups, seized all the major towns in the mountainous region in northern Iraq where most Iraqi Kurds lived.

Despite his military's weakened condition, Saddam counterattacked. By early April, Iraq's forces had recaptured many of the major towns in Kurdish areas of Iraq and were brutalizing the Kurds. Over one million Kurds fled the Iraqi counteroffensive, crossing the borders into Iran and Turkey.

The United States and other coalition countries warned Iraq to cease its assault on the Kurds, instituted a "no-fly zone" in Kurdish areas of northern Iraq, and threatened to shoot down any Iraqi aircraft that flew there. At the same time, the United States, this time acting under NATO auspices, began a major humanitarian relief operation called "Operation Provide Comfort" to the Kurds, but only after CNN and other international news outlets highlighted Saddam's forces' attacks against them.

Recognizing that he could not continue his assault on the Kurds without increasing the danger of confronting the United States and NATO, Saddam began to negotiate with the Kurdish Front about granting Kurds a limited degree of autonomy. However, it soon became evident that Saddam's real purpose was to divide and weaken the Kurdish Front and separate the rebellion in Iraq's north from the rebellion in the south. By the end of 1992, no progress had been made in the negotiations, and Iraq had instituted a de facto economic blockade around the Kurdish areas. On several occasions, Iraqi and Kurdish forces fought.

Unfortunately for Iran and Turkey, the resurgent Kurdish nationalist sentiment, political unrest, and military conflict could not be contained to Iraqi Kurds. As hopes for an autonomous Iraqi Kurdistan alternately rose and fell, Iranian Kurds and Turkish Kurds also began to hope for greater autonomy. A few even called for the establishment of a "Greater Kurdistan" made up of Kurdish people and territory from Iran, Iraq, and Turkey.

As hopes for autonomy and independence escalated among Iranian and Turkish Kurds, the Iranian and Turkish governments cracked down on Kurdish separatists within their own countries. Both governments also launched air attacks against Kurds living in northern Iraq who, the Iranian and Turkish governments claimed, were receiving military aid from the Iraqi government and using this aid to conduct terrorist attacks within both Iran and Turkey. On occasion, various Kurdish groups fought each other as well.

By 1994, then, the Kurdish question had become more complex than ever. Saddam Hussein's government in Iraq did not control the Kurdish territory in the north, but neither was the area independent. Nevertheless, it was relatively more independent than the parts of Iran and Turkey that were inhabited by Kurds. Iranian Kurds and Turkish Kurds, therefore, wanted greater autonomy, and some were willing to fight and die for it. The governments of Iran and Turkey, as always, opposed greater autonomy for the Kurds and in turn struck against Kurdish separatists, some of whom received aid from Iraq. Meanwhile, the U.S., even though it supported autonomy for Iraqi Kurds, promised Turkey, a close NATO ally, that it did not support the creation of an independent Kurdish state.

Despite the opposition that they faced, the Kurds continued their struggle, sometimes peacefully and sometimes violently. Indeed, in their most visible effort to publicize their cause and drive home the seriousness of their struggle, in June 1993 Turkish Kurds assaulted and took control of Turkish embassies, consulates, banks, and businesses in 19 cities throughout Europe. They also took over a UN office in Sydney, Australia.

Kurdish efforts to create an independent state have also been hindered by internal rivalries. In the mid-1990s, rivalry between competing Kurdish factions in northern Iraq led to open warfare, with one faction even turning to Saddam Hussein for military assistance. After a U.S. cruise missile attack compelled Saddam's forces to withdraw from the UN's northern no-fly zone, Washington brokered a cease-fire agreement essentially dividing control of northern Iraq between the two factions. Iraqi Kurds achieved a large degree of autonomy and relative economic prosperity under the protection of the no-fly zone. In many ways Iraqi Kurds enjoyed a higher standard of living than the rest of Iraq's population, due in large part to UN aid programs and revenue received from smuggling.

In Turkey, the Kurdish struggle gained international prominence in the mid-to-late 1990s, as the Turkish military repeatedly crossed into Iraq and Syria to attack Kurdish rebel forces. In 1998, under threat of military action, Syria expelled Abdullah Ocalan, leader of the Kurdish Workers Party (PKK) and Turkey's most-wanted fugitive. Ocalan was eventually apprehended by Turkish agents in Kenya, prompting violent demonstrations by Kurds in cities around the world.

In late 2002, the prospect of war in Iraq refocused international attention on the Kurdish issue. It was widely feared that the overthrow of Saddam Hussein would prompt Iraqi Kurds to fight for an independent state in northern Iraq. Turkey was extremely fearful that Turkish Kurds would then join the struggle in an attempt to create a larger, independent Kurdistan encompassing southeastern Turkey. As war became imminent, Turkish officials prepared to send large numbers of troops into northern Iraq to prevent a Kurdish uprising. They also made it clear they would not allow Kurdish control of the oil fields in Kirkuk and Mosul, fearing that these could become valuable sources of financing for a Kurdish rebellion.

As the war began, the U.S. sought to allay Turkish fears by assuring Turkey that the U.S. would protect Iraq's territorial integrity. At the same time, the U.S. recruited Kurdish forces to aid in the fight against Saddam's regime. Backed by U.S. Special Forces and air support, Kurdish fighters proved to be valuable allies, opening up a northern front and providing intelligence throughout the war.

With major combat operations now over, Kurds must negotiate their place in the world. As in the past, they are divided as to how they should proceed. Some Kurds continue to argue for an independent state, fearing that they will be worse off than before if reintegrated into Iraqi society. They worry that they will lose the unprecedented degree of autonomy and prosperity they enjoyed under the protection of the no-fly zone and that, as a minority, their rights may not be respected under a system of majority rule.

Other Kurds argue that political realities will not allow an independent Kurdistan in Iraq, and that their efforts are better spent expanding Kurdish influence in the emerging Iraqi government. Indeed, Kurds have already won some significant political victories, including representation on the Interim Iraqi Governing Council. The interim Iraqi constitution, signed in March 2004, provides for a federal system in which Kurds have a degree of autonomy, including the ability to retain a militia separate from the Iraqi national army. It also protects Kurdish as an official language and gives Kurds the power to veto a permanent constitution, a highly controversial measure.

IRAN AND REGIONAL STABILITY

In 1991, it appeared that Iraq's defeat in the Persian Gulf War eliminated one threat to stability in the Persian Gulf area. Nevertheless, in the eyes of many observers in the Middle East and beyond, another country in the region presented a sizeable and growing threat to regional stability. That country was Iran.

Iran created concerns for two different reasons. The first was Iran's continued adherence to radical Islam and its insistence that only governments and societies that strictly followed traditional Islamic beliefs were legitimate. Indeed, Islamic radicals throughout the Islamic world looked to Iran for guidance and direction. Many received financial and other support from the Iranian government as well.

As noted earlier, conservative and moderate states throughout the Middle East, such as Egypt, Kuwait, Morocco, Oman, Saudi Arabia, and the United Arab Emirates, had been concerned about Iran's Islamic radicalism ever since Ayatollah Khomeini led a revolution in Iran in 1979 that deposed the Shah. Their concern about Iran and its efforts to export its version of Islam was a major reason why they had supported Iraq in its war against Iran from 1980 to 1988. But there were other reasons as well. Iran was predominantly Shia and Persian rather than Arab, while the other states were Arab and controlled by Sunnis.

In the 1990s the potential threat posed by Iran diminished in the eyes of the Arab states, in part because Iran lost much of its military strength during the Iran-Iraq War. Nevertheless, Arab states in the region remained wary of Iran's large military expenditures. Iran used its oil wealth to expand its armed forces, purchasing conventional weapons from Russia, China, and North Korea. Iran also embarked on sizeable programs to develop chemical weapons and nuclear capabilities. Even though Iran insisted that its nuclear program was peaceful in nature, the Arab states and others were concerned about Iran's potential to emerge as a nuclear weapons power in the foreseeable future.

The May 1997 election of a liberal Muslim cleric, Muhammad Khatami, to the presidency was widely viewed as a groundbreaking event. In an election with almost 90 percent voter turnout, Khatami won a stunning 70 percent of the vote, trouncing the candidate backed by Iran's conservative religious establishment. Speaking to the parliament at his swearing-in ceremony, President Khatami called for a "dialogue of civilizations" and declared himself ready to improve relations with the West, and the United States in particular. Khatami's landslide victory raised hopes in the West that Iran was undergoing a political and social transformation that would result in a more moderate and friendly Iranian government and temper Islamist radicalism in the region.

However, there have been, and continue to be, sharp limits to what Khatami and his supporters can really accomplish. The pinnacle of power in Iranian politics is not the president, but the Supreme Religious Leader, a position held by the ultra-conservative Ali Khamenei. Khamenei and other conservative clerics in the parliament and judiciary have largely blocked Khatami's reform agenda, especially on the domestic front.

In many ways, the real struggle for reform is being waged by Iranian students. Two-thirds of Iranian society is under 30 years old, and most of these people are too young to remember or identify with the 1979 Islamic Revolution.[7] A turning point came in July 1999, when students demonstrated in Tehran against a law that reversed the press freedoms achieved by Khatami's government. A harsh crackdown by police and Islamist militias led to widespread, violent protests across the country.

Following the crackdown, students began to call for more fundamental reforms and even questioned the legitimacy of clerical control. Protests again flared in November 2002 when Tehran University professor Hashem Aghajari was sentenced to death for criticizing the ruling clerics. During 2003, students and other pro-reform activists became increasingly bold in holding protests and publishing open letters calling for an end to clerical rule. Importantly, the protesters became disillusioned by the slow pace of reforms and also began calling for Khatami to resign.

As parliamentary elections neared in early 2004, the Guardian Council responded to calls for reform by banning nearly one-third of the candidates running for office, almost all of them reformers, including many members of parliament standing for reelection. Angry at Khatami for not taking a stronger stand against the Guardian Council, many Iranians became apathetic toward Iranian politics, and voter turnout was low. As a result, Iran's conservatives easily won a majority of seats, taking control of the parliament away from reformers and making it highly unlikely that Khatami will be able to implement any more of his agenda before the end of his term in 2005.

Despite Khatami's failure to deliver on his promise to build a "religious democracy" based on the rule of law, he has presided over a number of smaller but important changes in Iranian society that suggest the reform movement will continue. For example, Iranian journalists now openly talk about the issue of political prisoners, and members of parliament send critical letters to the Ayatollah. Bans on alcohol, on watching satellite television, and on the mixing of men and women in public are increasingly ignored and resented. Even attempts by conservatives to demonize the United States as the "Great Satan" are dismissed by many Iranians, particularly in urban areas.

Khatami's greatest impact has been in the area of foreign policy. Iran has moved from confrontation to engagement with several European countries and local Arab states. Khatami has also held out an olive branch toward the United States, calling for a dialogue between Washington and Tehran. Under pressure from Europe, Russia, and the United States, Iran has even given international nuclear inspectors unrestricted access to its nuclear facilities.

Nevertheless, Iran continues to pursue a number of policies that the U.S. government fears may undermine regional stability. Chief among these are Iran's nuclear program and support for terrorist organizations such as Hezbollah and the Palestinian Islamic Jihad, policies that led the Bush administration to label Iran as part of an "axis of evil," along with Iraq and North Korea. Also of concern is Iran's influence with Shia groups seeking to establish an Islamic government in Iraq (for a more thorough discussion of all of these issues, see Lesson 1, "U.S. Interests in the Middle East").

Reuters/Shamil Zhumatov

A displaced Iraqi Kurdish family heads back home on a road to Kirkuk, Iraq, May 3, 2003. More than 120,000 Kurds, Turkmen, and Assyrians were expelled from the oil-rich city under a 1991 Arabization policy, according to a Human Rights Watch report. Many of these families have returned home since the fall of Saddam's regime.

LESSON 4

OTHER MIDDLE EASTERN ISSUES

Activity 1

Who are the Shia within Islam?

ACTIVITY OBJECTIVE

The student will describe the impact of religion on Middle Eastern affairs.

MATERIALS AND RESOURCES

❑ Worksheet 4.1, "The Shia Within Islam"

STRATEGIES

Islam, like all the world's major religions, is divided into various sects. The two most significant sects within Islam are the Sunni and Shia. An understanding of the beliefs and the demographics of the Shia is essential to any discussion of the trends and politics of the Middle East today.

This activity is designed to introduce students to the basic beliefs of the Shia sect and to allow them to evaluate the religious and political implications of the location of these groups. To illustrate this point, distribute Worksheet 4.1, "The Shia Within Islam," and have students complete the reading and analyze the chart in order to complete the map activity.

THE SHIA WITHIN ISLAM

Islam is divided into two major sects, the Sunni and Shia. Approximately eighty-five percent of the world's Muslims are Sunni; the other fifteen percent are Shia. The basic beliefs of the two sects are generally the same. Both accept the Koran and adhere to the Five Pillars, but there are some differences which are quite significant. The Shia have political control only in the country of Iran, although they constitute a majority in several other countries, particularly in the Gulf region. Because they have often been minorities in the countries in which they live, the Shia rarely have had great political power or economic advantage. Since the late 1970s, with the rise of interest in traditional Islamic values and the revolution in Iran, Shiism is attracting greater attention in both the Middle East and the Western world.

Shiism began in 632 A.D. following the death of the prophet Muhammad. A minority of the Muslims supported the claim of Muhammad's cousin and son-in-law Ali to be the rightful leader of the community. They became known as the "partisans of Ali," also called "Shi'at Ali" or "Shia." They continued to live in a society dominated by the Sunni, but they recognized the authority of a succession of leaders known as imams, whom they considered more legitimate because of their connection to the Prophet.

Because of their descent from the Prophet, Shia believe their imams to have the wisdom to offer interpretations of the Sunna, a practice which is not accepted by mainstream Sunni. In a Sunni congregation, an imam is designated to lead prayers in the mosque, but this individual is a layman rather than a member of the organized clergy. Shia imams hold a much more important position.

Iran, the only country where the Shia enjoy political control, converted to Shiism in the 1500s under the leadership of a ruler named Isma'il. In Iran, the clergy quickly began to assume an organization and independence that often had influence over the people equal to that of the state. As religious organization grew, many Iranian clergy gained independent sources of revenue which gave them additional political power. Local religious leaders known as mullahs worked under a central religious figure known as a mujtahed. As the number of mujtahed increased, a higher rank evolved, that of ayatollah. During the Iranian Revolution, this religious hierarchy became extremely influential. Although the Shia do not have political control in any other Middle Eastern country today, their large numbers in many countries give them political as well as religious significance outside as well as inside Iran.

The theme of martyrdom is an important one in Shia belief. Two of its annual religious observances commemorate the death of Ali and his son Hussein. The commemoration of Hussein's death at Kerbala is observed on Ashura, the 10th day of the Muslim month of Muharram. Because of the greater role played by its clergy, Shiism is also characterized by numerous local and regional saints whose tombs are the objects of lesser pilgrimages. Although not as important as the pilgrimage to Mecca, pilgrimages to Kerbala and An Najaf (the site of Ali's death) are important rituals performed by many Shia.

While the Shia have existed through the centuries as minorities in the countries in which they lived, they face the same pressures as their Sunni co-religionists in coming to terms with the contradictions between the modern world and traditional values. An understanding of the followers of this branch of Islam is essential to a broader understanding of the political, religious, and economic questions facing the Middle East today.

Adapted from: "The Shia Community Within Islam," Islamic Affairs Program, The Middle East Institute, Washington, DC, 1985.

THE SHIA WITHIN ISLAM

Country	Population	Ethnic	Religion
Bahrain	537,000	N/A	50% Shia 40% Sunni 7% Christian
Egypt	54,452,000	N/A	94% Sunni 6% Christian
Iran	59,051,000	9% Kurd	91% Shia 8% Sunni 1% Christian
Iraq	19,525,000	19% Kurd	62% Shia 35% Sunni 3% Christian
Israel	4,477,000	N/A	82% Jewish 13% Muslim 2% Christian
Jordan	3,413,000	70% Palestinian	93% Sunni 7% Christian
Kuwait	2,204,000	N/A	45% Sunni 30% Shia 10% Muslim
Lebanon	3,385,000	10% Palestinian	32% Shia 21% Sunni 45% Christian
Oman	1,534,000	N/A	75% Ibadhi (Muslim) 20% Muslim (Other)
Qatar	518,000	N/A	93% Sunni
Saudi Arabia	17,870,000	N/A	99% Sunni
Syria	12,966,000	6% Kurd	74% Sunni 16% Muslim (Other) 9% Christian
Turkey	58,581,000	11% Kurd	99% Sunni
United Arab Emirates	2,390,000	N/A	80% Sunni 16% Shia
Yemen	10,063,000	N/A	56% Sunni 44% Shia

THE SHIA WITHIN ISLAM

Directions: Use information in the reading and the demographic chart to complete the map activity and answer the questions.

Map

Use the following legend to create a demographic map of the Shia population distribution in the Middle East.

Over 50%   30–39%   10–29%   0–9%

Questions

1) In which countries do Shia constitute a majority of the population?
2) In which countries do the Shia constitute a significant plurality (30% or more) of the population?
3) In what part of the Middle East are the majority of the countries located? What is the economic significance of these countries? What is their strategic significance?
4) What events have taken place in the past two decades in which the tension between Shia and Sunni sects was a contributing factor?
5) Why might leaders of countries where the Shia are a significant minority or a majority be concerned about an increasingly large Shia population within their borders?

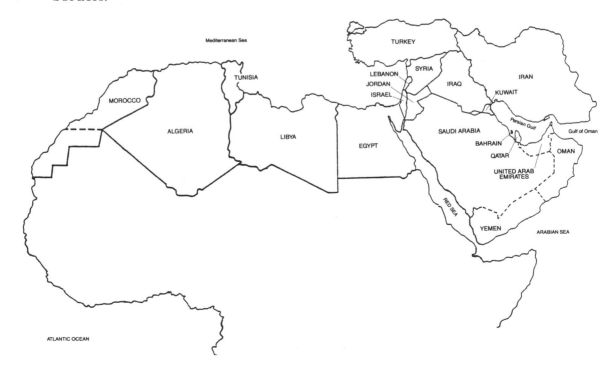

Smoke from the remains of New York City's World Trade Center shrouds lower Manhattan September 12, 2001, following the destruction of the towers by terrorists on September 11.

Reuters/Ray Stubblebine

LESSON 4

OTHER MIDDLE EASTERN ISSUES

Activity 2

What is Islamic fundamentalism, and what are its implications for the West?

ACTIVITY OBJECTIVE

The student will examine the diversity of modern Islamic movements and evaluate U.S. responses to Islamic revivalist politics.

MATERIALS AND RESOURCES

❑ SCIS Videotape, *The Middle East in Transition*, Lesson 4,
   "Other Middle Eastern Issues"
❑ Teacher Resource 4.1, "Islam and the Modern World"
❑ Worksheet 4.2, "Prominent Islamic Revivalist Groups"

STRATEGIES

Many Americans make the mistake of regarding "Islamic fundamentalism" as a unified movement that is counter to U.S. interests. The reality is that today's Islamic movements are characterized by considerable diversity, a point made by former Secretary Schlesinger in SCIS videotape, *The Middle East in Transition*, Lesson 4, "Other Middle Eastern Issues." Teacher Resource 4.1, "Islam and the Modern World," written in 1992, provides background information for the teacher on this topic.

Write the following statement made by former Secretary Schlesinger on the chalkboard:

> "We should not regard Islamic fundamentalism as a collectivity or as the enemy. Each situation is different. The fundamentalists in Algeria are quite different from those in Iran. And there is some tendency now to try to replace the Soviet threat with Islamic fundamentalism as the enemy of the United States. That would be a capital mistake."

Ask students to keep this quote in mind when completing the following activity which is designed to introduce students to the goals and strategies of several of these movements and to examine them within the context of different countries.

The teacher should divide the class into eight teams of students and assign each team one of the organizations to research. Students should center their research on the topics in the chart on Worksheet 4.2, "Islamic Revivalist Groups." The Infolinks at www.southerncenter.org are a good place for students to begin their research.

After each team has completed its research, reassemble the class and compile a master chart which will enable students to compare and contrast the different groups. A summary discussion should lead students to the conclusion that, although these groups share similar ideals, there are tremendous differences in their strategies, leadership, organization, and goals.

How does this complement former Secretary Schlesinger's point? Ask students to speculate as to what changes need to take place in the ways in which U.S. policymakers view these groups.

ISLAM AND THE MODERN WORLD

"Islamic fundamentalism" has often been regarded as a major threat to the regional stability of the Middle East and to Western interest in the broader Muslim world. The Iranian Revolution, attacks on embassies, hijackings and hostage taking, and other violent acts have reinforced images of an expansive and potentially explosive Islam in global politics. These events represent only one small facet of the efforts by many in the modern Middle East to reevaluate and redefine their society in ways that bring modernization into greater harmony with ideals inherited from Islamic tradition.

The term "fundamentalism" is largely a Western one, with understanding and perceptions of fundamentalism heavily influenced by American Protestantism. For many mainline or liberal Christians, "fundamentalism" is pejorative or derogatory, a term equated with extremism, even though the vast majority of Middle Eastern "fundamentalist" groups work within the established order. "Fundamentalism" is laden with Christian presuppositions and Western stereotypes and also implies a monolithic movement that in reality does not exist. More fitting terms are "Islamic revivalism" or "Islamic activism." Historically, Islam possesses a long tradition of revival (tajdid) and reform (islah).

In the nineteenth and twentieth centuries, the push for modernization in the Middle East equated development with progressive Westernization and the secularization of society. While a minority accepted and implemented a Western secular worldview, the majority of most Muslim populations did not internalize secular outlooks and values. Many found modern, secular nationalism wanting.

The modern world has brought great disillusionment to many in the Middle East. The disparity between rich and poor is striking in urban areas, and it is even more pronounced between Arab oil states and poor, densely populated countries like Egypt and Syria. Capitalism is regarded by many as the system of special interests. Many dismiss Marxism as a godless alternative. In many Middle Eastern countries today, idealism, study, and hard work are rewarded by unemployment or underemployment. Socially, culturally, and psychologically, modernization often seems to be a legacy of European colonialism perpetuated by Western-oriented elites who impose the twin processes of Westernization and secularization. Loss of village, family, and traditional values have accompanied the shock of modern life and its Westernized cultures and mores.

The 1970s saw the popularization of an idealized perception of early Islam, the Islamic paradigm found in the time of the Prophet Muhammad, the Golden Age of Islam. While Westernization and secularization of society are condemned, modernization as such is not. Science and technology are accepted, but the pace, direction, and extent of change are to be subordinated to Islamic belief and values in order to guard against the penetration of Western values and excessive dependence on them. Islamic movements may at times be anti-foreign, but they are seldom anti-modern. Many Muslims share a common call for the transformation of society not through a blind return to seventh-century Medina but through a response of Islamic reform in which the principles of Islam are applied to contemporary needs.

Just as the political economies and national experiences of Muslim countries vary in determining the different relations between governments and Islamic organizations, so too do differences in ideological orientation and strategy exist within Islamic movements. All major Islamic leaders and movements have emphasized and have been influenced by belief in the need to construct their own solutions to their specific contexts and local problems. Islamic politics must be viewed within specific country contexts; far from being a monolithic reality, it manifests a rich diversity of leaders and forms. Because of their diversity, it is difficult to speak of Islamic revivalists in terms of a single well-developed political agenda.

The 1990s will test the ability of political analysts and policymakers to distinguish between Islamic movements that are threats and those that represent indigenous attempts to reform and redirect Islamic societies. U.S. perception of a monolithic "Islamic threat" often contributes to support for repressive governments in the Muslim world and to the creation of a self-fulfilling prophecy. The many faces of contemporary Islamic revivalism tend to disappear under the monolith of "Islamic fundamentalism," which is equated with violence and fanaticism, with mullah-led theocracies, or small, radical guerrilla groups. The resurgence of Islam in Muslim politics has been far more indigenously rooted.

For many Muslims, Islamic revivalism is a social rather than a political movement whose goal is a more Islamically-minded and oriented society, not necessarily the creation of an Islamic state. In either case, Islam and most Islamic movements are not necessarily anti-Western, anti-U.S., or anti-democratic. While they are a challenge to the assumptions of the established order and to autocratic regimes, they do not necessarily threaten Western interests. The challenge for the West is to better understand the history and realities of the Muslim world. Recognizing the diversity and many faces of Islam counters the image of a unified Islamic threat. It lessens the risk of creating self-fulfilling prophecies about the "battle of the West against radical Islam." Guided by its stated ideals and goals of freedom and self-determination, the West has an ideal vantage point from which to appreciate the aspirations of many in the Muslim world as they seek to define new paths for their future.

PROMINENT ISLAMIC REVIVALIST GROUPS

Islamic Organization	Relationship To Government In Power	Leadership	Ideology	Organization	Strategy And Tactics
Al Qaeda (Afghanistan)					
Hamas (Palestinian territories)					
Islamic Jihad (Palestinian territories)					
Hezbollah (Lebanon)					
Jamaat al-Islamiyya (Egypt)					
Egyptian Islamic Jihad (Egypt)					
Armed Islamic Group (Algeria)					
Muslim Brotherhood (Egypt)					

Shia women in Basra gather water on July 13, 2003, from where the Tigris and Euphrates rivers converge on their way to the Persian Gulf. People along the river live in abject poverty and depend on the polluted water for cooking and cleaning.

LESSON 4

OTHER MIDDLE EASTERN ISSUES

Activity 3

Why has water become a political issue in the Middle East?

ACTIVITY OBJECTIVE

The student will evaluate access to water as a political issue in the modern Middle East.

MATERIALS AND RESOURCES

❑ Handout 4.1, "Map of the Jordan River Valley"
❑ Handout 4.2, "Map of Tigris and Euphrates River Valleys"

STRATEGIES

Many experts on the Middle East feel that the next regional conflict will be over access to rapidly dwindling water supplies. There are a number of water disputes in the region. This activity will provide students the opportunity to examine two of these disputes—the waters of the Jordan River and the waters of the Euphrates River.

Distribute Handout 4.1, "Map of the Jordan River Valley," and Handout 4.2, "Map of Tigris and Euphrates River Valleys," for students to examine. Explain to students that one of the overriding issues in the Arab-Israeli conflict has been the question of who has access to the limited waters of the Jordan River and its tributaries. Project a transparency of Handout 4.1 and lead a class discussion around the following questions:

- What country controls the headwaters of the Jordan River?
- What countries divert water from Lake Tiberias by pipeline or canal?
- What countries have built dams to limit the amount of water that flows into Lake Tiberias?
- What portions of this region are likely to suffer most by a reduction in water flow through the Jordan River?
- What makes the Litani River particularly valuable to the country of Lebanon?
- Given the political situation in this part of the Middle East, why will these water questions be particularly difficult to resolve?

Next, project a transparency of Handout 4.2. Continue the class discussion by asking such questions as:

- Trace the course of the Euphrates River. Through what countries does it flow? What do you know about the political relationship among these countries?
- Locate the Keban Dam and the Ataturk Dam. What will be the effect of these dams on water supply to Syria?
- Locate the Euphrates Dam. Why do you think Syria built this dam? What will be the impact of this dam on the water supply to Iraq?
- Trace the course of the Tigris River. Through what countries does it flow? Are the political implications of the dams along the Tigris different from those built along the Euphrates? Why or why not?

Armed with this information, conclude the activity by asking such questions as "Does a country have the right to build a dam that alters the availability of water to another country located downstream? What are the costs of such a decision in economic, ecological, and human terms? What sorts of regulations could be devised to ensure that water resources are allocated on an equitable basis?"

MAP OF THE JORDAN RIVER VALLEY

Sebastian Ballard

N

Beirut

SYRIA

LEBANON

A w a l i

Diversion
Tunnel

H a s b a n i

L i t a n i

"Jordan
Headwaters"

Dan

Banias

GOLAN

M e d i t e r r a n e a n

S e a

National Water Carrier

Lake
Tiberias

Yarmuk

Maqarin
Dam

Mukhaibah
Dam

Pipeline

King Abdullah
Canal

WEST
BANK

King Talal Dam

Tel Aviv

Jordan River

Amman

Jerusalem

Gaza

GAZA

Dead
Sea

EGYPT

ISRAEL

JORDAN

Sinai
Peninsula

	Major Dams
	Desalination Plants
	National Water Carrier
	Canals
	Occupied territories: status to be determined

0   30
km

Eilat   Aqaba

223

MAP OF TIGRIS AND EUPHRATES RIVER VALLEYS

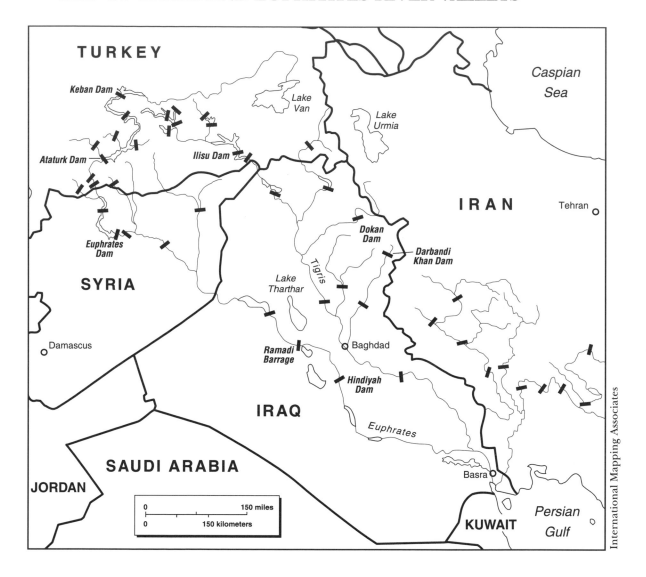

International Mapping Associates

LESSON 4

OTHER MIDDLE EASTERN ISSUES

Activity 4

What is the future of the Kurds?

ACTIVITY OBJECTIVE

The student will determine the impact of displaced populations on regional stability.

MATERIALS AND RESOURCES

❏ SCIS Videotape, *The Middle East in Transition*, Lesson 4, "Other Middle
   Eastern Issues"
❏ Handout 4.3, "Map of Kurdistan"
❏ Worksheet 4.3, "Nationalism"

STRATEGIES

The Kurds are an ethnic group which has figured prominently in a number of conflicts during the 20th century. In their discussions on the SCIS videotape, *The Middle
East in Transition*, Lesson 4, "Other Middle Eastern Issues," the former Secretaries of
Defense acknowledge that the Kurds were victims of the Persian Gulf War. The purpose of this activity is to introduce students to the Kurds as a people and to the political, economic, and strategic questions involved in Kurdish demands for recognition
and a homeland.

Students probably have little prior knowledge of the Kurds, their culture and history,
and their difficulties, particularly since World War II. The teacher will need to provide students background information needed to complete this activity.

The section of the SCIS background reading, Lesson 4, "Other Middle Eastern
Issues," related to the Kurds presents a good introductory essay. Additional resources
can be accessed on the Internet through the Infolinks on the SCIS Web site,
www.southerncenter.org.

After presenting the information found in these readings to students, have them
complete the following activity.

Distribute Handout 4.3, "Map of Kurdistan," and have students identify the countries
that would be involved in creating an independent Kurdistan. Ask such questions as:

  • Why was Saddam Hussein adamant about having complete control of the Kurds
     during the first Gulf War?
  • How did Kurdish loyalty become a factor during the Iran/Iraq War?

- What is the likelihood of Kurdistan becoming an independent country in the area indicated? Why or why not?
- Why did the United States implement the no-fly zone over Kurdish population centers north of the 36th parallel?
- Why did the United States decide to limit its support of the Kurds in the aftermath of the Gulf War?

Conclude this activity by distributing Worksheet 4.3, "Nationalism," and asking students to determine whether the Kurds meet the criteria to be considered a nation.

Kurds gather to celebrate Newroz *on the outskirts of Diyarbakir, Turkey, March 21, 2000 during the festivities marking the Kurdish new year. A banner carried by a young man reads in Turkish: "Abolish village guard systems and emergency rule," which asks for an end to the emergency rule in the area.*

MAP OF KURDISTAN

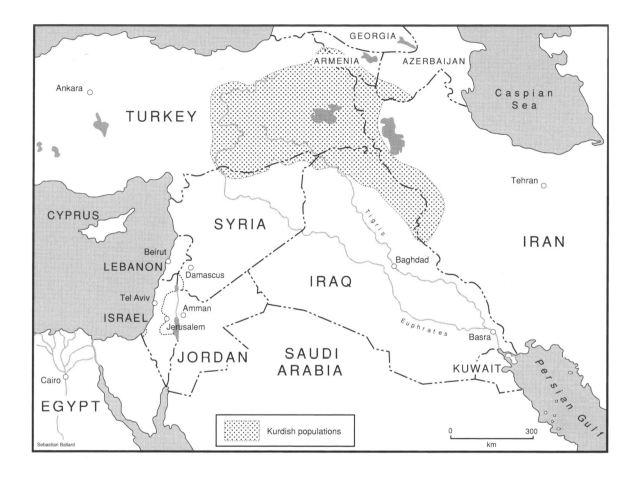

NATIONALISM

A nation is any group of people who believe they are linked together in some way, shape, or form. Often, a nation constitutes people who share common customs, origins, history, language, and/or religion. Often, members of a nation view their nation as an independent group within the world community. Nationalism is the devotion to one's nation and to its political, social, and cultural traditions.

Directions: Apply the criteria and definitions of nation and nationalism by using reference materials such as the Internet, almanacs, and atlases to answer the following question:

"Do the Kurds meet the criteria to be recognized as an independent nation?"

Examine the question in the following areas:

1) Common language?

2) Predominant religion?

3) Shared political and historical heritage?

4) Common geographic area?

5) Common symbols?

6) History of self-determination?

7) Body of art and/or literature?

Based on your findings, how legitimate is the claim of the Kurds to be recognized as an independent nation?

TRANSCRIPTS

BACKGROUND LESSON: An Overview of the Middle East
Since the videotape for this lesson consists primarily of newsreel footage, no transcript is included.

George Clark

Former Secretaries of Defense (left to right) Frank Carlucci, Donald Rumsfeld, Richard Cheney, James Schlesinger, and Harold Brown are led in a discussion on Middle Eastern issues by Moderator Marvin Kalb (4th from left) during the 1993 Secretaries of Defense conference in Washington, D.C.

U.S. Interests in the Middle East

The Sixth Annual Report of the Secretaries of Defense—1992

DAVID GERGEN I'd like to talk briefly about the Middle East. Where are we today in the Middle East? What are the prospects there for security—American security—particularly in the Persian Gulf area? Jim Schlesinger?

JAMES SCHLESINGER It's the tinderbox. It's volatile. We are always going to have to be wary. We've got some simple rules, it seems to me, for the Persian Gulf region, more generally in the Middle East, which are: keep the nuclear weapons out; protect access to the oil and support those regimes that have been friendly to us; and do not lecture them excessively on democracy—a lecture to which they won't respond well.

DAVID GERGEN But how can we push the Russians and the Chinese with regards to selling their weapons to Iran, for instance, when we ourselves are dramatically increasing the amount of arms we sell overseas?

HAROLD BROWN We will have modest success, if we don't sell any arms ourselves, in getting others not to sell. And we will have quite a bit less, none in fact, if we continue to sell ourselves.

DAVID GERGEN And you think we are? I mean you think we are reigning in the sales, then, of American arms?

JAMES SCHLESINGER You can't go to the Russians whose economy is collapsing in the way that we described in the outset of this discussion and say to them, "Don't sell for tactical or military reasons." They say, "We've got nothing else to sell," when we ourselves are deciding that we're going to ship arms to Kuwait, to Taiwan, elsewhere, for political reasons. For what are admitted to be political reasons.

FRANK CARLUCCI Which may be sound political reasons.

JAMES SCHLESINGER Well, it may be sound…

HAROLD BROWN …in some cases.

FRANK CARLUCCI I disagree with you, Harold. You say [we would] have modest success if we exercise restraint. I think we'll have no success. Success will have us turning over markets to our competitors. The only solution to this problem is a demand-side solution. Solve the political issues.

HAROLD BROWN Those are even harder.

JAMES SCHLESINGER We can only work on the nuclear aspect of the weapon-spread problem, and if we work on it we might have some success. If we try to do everything, we will achieve nothing.

HAROLD BROWN I want to put in a good word for democracy, which has not gotten a very good rep here so far.

DONALD RUMSFELD Oh Harold, now. No one was knocking democracy here.

HAROLD BROWN I recognize that a good…

MELVIN LAIRD This is some sort of a "strawman" here.

DONALD RUMSFELD Yes. I think you're pulling a "Laird." [LAUGHTER]

HAROLD BROWN The record exists. Everyone heard what you all said. I agree that a good many of the regimes friendly to us are not democratic, and that it is at least as important to us whether they're friendly to us as it is how they treat their own people—probably more important to first approximation. But there is going to be a move toward democratization. I think Jim is right, so-called Islamic fundamentalism is not monolithic; but we have to accept that greater participation on the part of the public in many Islamic countries is going to mean xenophobia, anti-Americanism, and more difficulty for us. But it's going to happen anyway. It's rather like television—you're stuck with it. And our long-run relations with many of these countries are going to depend upon how we are seen by the inheritors of power in those countries.

DONALD RUMSFELD Someone once told me a prime minister in the Middle East said that if a problem has no solution, it may well not be a problem but a fact—not to be solved but to be coped with over time. And it seems to me there are a number of problems in that part of [the] world that we ought not to assume that we are failing terribly if we can't go in and make everything fine. What we need to do is to cope with it, to work with it, to deal with it, and to hope that it doesn't deteriorate into something vastly worse. And if you're not working on it, it might. But the fact that it's not solved is not necessarily some great problem because they've gone on for a long time.

The Eighth Annual Report of the Secretaries of State—1990

EDWIN NEWMAN Is it possible that the United States could become independent, or relatively independent, of oil from that part of the world?

CYRUS VANCE We started along that road in the late '70s, and unfortunately we fell off of that and have been doing virtually nothing since that time. I think it behooves us to begin to deal very seriously with the problem of creating greater independence for ourselves in so far as oil is concerned.

GEORGE SHULTZ I agree that we should work to be more independent in our energy policy, and at least from my lights, the way to do it is to get gasoline priced somewhere near where it's priced in all the rest of the developed world. We pay a third of what they pay in Europe and Japan for gasoline.

The Seventh Annual Report of the Secretaries of Defense—1993

MARVIN KALB Is there any unfinished business with respect to Iraq that may face the U.S. military in 1994? Secretary Cheney?

RICHARD CHENEY Now clearly, given our interests in that part of the world which will run through at least the next century—energy requirements—the United States is going to have a continuing need to be able to work with our friends in the region to periodically deploy to the region, to help with training and equipping those forces, and when necessary, to be able to go back in a crisis to make certain we can protect our friends there. And of course, the major threats, I think, will continue to be Iraq and Iran, in that sense.

MARVIN KALB And the protection of our friends also involves the protection of the oil routes to make sure that they remain open because that's critically important?

RICHARD CHENEY No question but what that's a major interest for us in that part of the world.

The First Annual Report of the Secretaries of State—1984

EDWIN NEWMAN Has the United States become excessively committed to the cause of Israel?

WILLIAM ROGERS I think it is undisputed that we have a moral commitment to support Israel and we have to do that—we have to continue to do that.

DEAN RUSK We have to be a little careful about how we use the term "commitment" as between the United States and Israel. Every President, beginning with Harry Truman, has pledged us to the support of the independence and the security of the State of Israel, and those commitments have had strong support in our Congress. But I know of no commitment that we have made to assist Israel in retaining the territory seized in June 1967. And so there are potentially some very serious issues between us and the State of Israel.

And again, I would put my emphasis upon the necessity for those in the area to do something themselves about making peace. Now, the feelings on both sides are so strong and so deep that it may be—may well be—that the governments in the area, at the moment, cannot make the concessions necessary to get peace and remain in power.

On the Arab side, they will talk to you about assassinations and coup d'etats, and you can't tell them they are wrong. On the Israeli side, we know that the Knesset can throw out a government with a snap of the finger; so, its not going to be easy.

And, with diffidence, let me remind you of another factor: my experience with Northern Ireland, and Turkish and Greek Cypriots, and India and Pakistan, and Israel and its Arab neighbors, has been that where two sides come to the negotiating table and each side is convinced that it is speaking for God, you have a very difficult negotiation. I had an Arab foreign minister read to me from the Koran. I've had an Israeli foreign minister read to me from the Books of Moses. I couldn't sit there and say, "Now, come on, don't give me that stuff!"

So this is inherently the most stubborn, complex, unyielding problem that we have had in the post-war world, and I have great respect for its difficulty; but I hope, somehow, we can inch along toward a better situation than we have now.

WILLIAM ROGERS I can't imagine a total solution about the future of Jerusalem—most people don't even want to talk about that.

CYRUS VANCE When we sat down at Camp David, the first two days both sides presented their positions. They argued and it was absolutely clear there was no way that they were going to get together. So, the United States then tabled a document which tried to take the two positions, and both Israel and Egypt said: "Okay we agree, we can't do it, and we will take this as a basis." That was the document we worked with, and that finally led to the agreement.

So the United States can play an important middle role.

THE PERSIAN GULF WAR

The Fourth Annual Report of the Secretaries of Defense—1990

EDWIN NEWMAN The United Nations Security Council has called for Iraq to withdraw from Kuwait by the 15th of January. If Iraq refuses should the United States begin a military offensive to bring that about?

MELVIN LAIRD We have a very important period here in which negotiations can be carried forward. Is it a mistake for us to announce military plans [about] what we will do or will not do after January 15th? There are a lot of things that have to happen. First, there will be a big debate in the Congress and this President will take no action without congressional support.

EDWIN NEWMAN Secretary McNamara, you wanted to say something?

ROBERT MCNAMARA Yes, I think we should be very clear on what our objective is here. The objective is stated in the Security Council resolution 660 and it's been repeated in 8 or 10 subsequent resolutions. It's very simple. It is to obtain the unconditional withdrawal of Iraq from Kuwait. That is the stated objective. Subsequent resolutions have added: "and the release of hostages," but it's basically to obtain the unconditional withdrawal. To do that the Security Council authorized sanctions. On August 25th, it authorized the use of military force to enforce those sanctions. Those sanctions, supported by military force, are presently in place. We have not, by any means, proven they will not achieve our objective. Under no circumstances do I believe we should initiate action even with approval of the Security Council and U.S. Congress until we give those sanctions time to prove their effectiveness. That may require 12 or 18 months. I do not believe that the public, and I'm not sure all of us, really evaluate properly the effectiveness of those sanctions. To date, 150,000 expatriate laborers have been forced out of Iraq—the Yemenis, the Egyptians, etc. One out of three, or one out of four, able-bodied Iraqi males have been called up to service. Their imports and exports have been essentially foreclosed with the exception of importation of food and medicines. Their GNP has been cut 40 percent. This is after four months. I don't believe that any economy as large as Iraq, as integrated in the world economy as Iraq, can withstand sanctions of this type indefinitely. The pain will become so great, the political disorder will become so great that I believe Saddam will be forced to change through sanctions alone. However, I may be wrong. I wish to maintain the military option, but for God's sake let's give the sanctions a chance to work; let's not be forced into a war we could otherwise avoid.

EDWIN NEWMAN David Gergen.

DAVID GERGEN This debate seems to be boiling down in Washington to one between those who want to prepare for a military showdown after January 15th versus those who are counseling patience. Two of you here, so far, seem to be counseling patience. Melvin Laird has said, "Let's not tip our hand." Can we have the rest of you respond to this critical question?

ELLIOT RICHARDSON I think it should be strongly stressed that broad-based international concurrence in any use of force is an absolute precondition to the use of it, and that the single most extraordinary development that we are witnessing has been the degree of unanimity of the international response to Iraq's aggression. I think it ought to be very clear that securing that resolution is a necessary step. It's a base from which other actions could follow. I think an equally clear [and] necessary step will be to obtain a comparable degree of support within the Congress of the United States and from the American people.

FRANK CARLUCCI I would like to see the sanctions be given a chance to succeed. On the other hand, the military threat has to be credible in order for it to produce any kind of results.

EDWIN NEWMAN And to be credible there must be a date?

FRANK CARLUCCI You don't have to have a date. Mel is right, you don't foreshadow what you're going to do with the military. At the same time, Bob, you don't say [that] we're not going to use it for 18 months. What we are trying to do is work these two systems of pressure in tandem. Unfortunately, because of the high number of troops in Saudi Arabia, there's not a sufficient rotation base to keep the military going for the period that Bob advocates.

DAVID GERGEN I'm unclear. On January 16, if Saddam Hussein is still in Kuwait, would you launch a military offensive? Would you council the President to do that or would you council him to show patience?

FRANK CARLUCCI Like Mel, I wouldn't forecast it. I would see what the circumstances are at that time.

DAVID GERGEN Mr. Schlesinger. You've testified before Congress that you would counsel patience in the Middle East, and then a couple of days later the UN resolution was passed by the Security Council. Do you continue to believe we should show patience or does the UN resolution change your thinking at all?

JAMES SCHLESINGER I think that the UN resolution adds to the pressure on Saddam Hussein. From the first, Saddam Hussein has shown no inclination to respond to the pleas from the outside world—the declarations of the United Nations—until he is faced with the possibility of the use of military force against him. If the sanctions were to work it would be many more months before Saddam Hussein would show any sign of give. For that reason, there has been the buildup of the complementary military action … military capability. That puts us in a position in which we can use that, but there is no necessity to use it or to say now that we will use it.

DONALD RUMSFELD It seems to me that an important point is that our task ought to be to make Saddam Hussein's problem more difficult rather than simplifying [it]. I quite agree that we should not disabuse him of the thought that it is entirely possible that force could be used. I personally am not uncomfortable with our using force. I think that he's justified that. I have my own view as to what we ought to do, and I'm not terribly enamored of the idea of an effort on the ground going door to door in Kuwait City prying Iraqis out of buildings. I must say, on the other hand, I would be terribly disappointed if this thing ended and Saddam Hussein's unconventional weapon capabilities were left intact.

HAROLD BROWN I believe that there's always going to have to be negotiation even if there's military action, and so we need to pursue both of these tracts—being ready for military action and diplomatic activities. Whichever way we finally go, or whichever combination we finally decide on—and we don't have to decide on it by January 16th—I believe we'll be in a better position to judge what we ought to do if we allow the sanctions to continue to work for a time. I'm not saying how long because I don't know.

DONALD RUMSFELD Saddam Hussein is not going to be persuaded by diplomatic niceties. He understands force; he's used it all of his life. It will either be the threat of military power—which he understands very well—or it will be the fact that ultimately his economy is adversely affected sufficiently. Besides, it's in his interest to get out.

EDWIN NEWMAN You regarded him, you said, as persuadable.

DONALD RUMSFELD I do.

EDWIN NEWMAN You think he still is?

DONALD RUMSFELD I think the idea that Saddam Hussein is crazy is nonsense. He is a perfectly rational person, [but] has a couple of areas that are unusual. One is the fact that he's not well-traveled, and the second is that his advisors probably do not give him straight advice because he kills them from time to time. [LAUGHTER] I don't say that in any criticism of his advisors, because obviously they've learned their lessons well. I think a person who, over a sustained period of time, sees his photograph in every room he goes into and everyone kowtows to, probably begins to believe he's right on most things.

The Ninth Annual Report of the Secretaries of State—1991

EDWIN NEWMAN In the Gulf, what did we achieve apart from a military victory? Should anything have been done differently?

ALEXANDER HAIG Well, I don't want to be one to carp too much about the administration's handling of the Gulf War. I happen to think it was unique in post-World War II history. First, because the President went above that zoo we call our legislature in Washington [LAUGHTER] and went to the people to get support, and for that he deserves some credit. Secondly, he recognized the emerging interdependence between all of us—current isolationism not withstanding. He built a coalition of the United Nations and the Arab states. That took some very skilled diplomacy. Thirdly, and most importantly for an old soldier, this is the first war since World War II where an American President understood [that] if we were going to drop one ounce of American blood, we were going to put all of America's power behind it. And he did it, and God bless him. I'm only sorry that he quit in round ten.

GEORGE SHULTZ I'm a little sympathetic with what Al said—that it's too bad we didn't go on to the eleventh and twelfth rounds. I couldn't understand why we didn't have a cease-fire in place so that there was control over those forces. How this was negotiated, I have no idea; but General Schwartzkopf himself said about a day after he made that deal that he got snookered. I never could understand why he didn't go right back in and unsnooker himself while we had all of the power there. [LAUGHTER]

ALEXANDER HAIG A Middle Eastern leader told me that Saddam Hussein had an airplane lined up ready to take himself and his government to exile in Northern Africa, when suddenly the cease-fire was called. I think the timing was very bad, and it's a sad commentary on an otherwise brilliant piece of work.

THE ARAB-ISRAELI CONFLICT

The Ninth Annual Report of the Secretaries of State—1991

EDWIN NEWMAN Dr. Kissinger, do you hold out any hope for this Middle East peace process?

HENRY KISSINGER It depends how one visualizes peace. One visualizes peace as signing an agreement after which all tensions disappear and everybody lives together in harmony. This I don't believe is possible. On the other hand, if everybody sets more modest aims and moves for more rapid solutions rather than wait for an overall comprehensive settlement, I think we have a good chance; and I see nothing in the process that prevents this. They're starting with a big conference, but it's going into subgroups which are quite compatible with the approach I've described.

DEAN RUSK I see no prospect of peace through the conference method or negotiations of any sort because the attitude of the parties on fundamental issues is so far apart. For twenty years after the establishment of the State of Israel, the United States with the full agreement of a successive Israeli government, set out to convince the Arab governments that the notion of Israeli territorial expansion had no basis in fact. Well, the Prime Minister of Israel on the first day of the June 1967 War got on the radio and declared that Israel had no territorial objectives. Later that summer Eban even told me that we simply changed our minds. [LAUGHTER] He made a twenty-year liar out of the United States. Resolution 242 was very carefully negotiated by Arthur Goldberg for the United States. Resolution 242 did not contemplate the movement of substantial territory to Israel as resulted from the occupation. It was left a little vague because they wanted to rectify some anomalies in the western frontier of the West Bank. They wanted to leave the way open for demilitarization in the Sinai and in the Golan Heights. They wanted a chance to take a fresh look at Jerusalem. So the United States cannot back Israel's claim to territorial expansion, and the sooner we make that clear to Israel the better.

EDWIN NEWMAN Secretary Shultz, then Secretary Rogers.

GEORGE SHULTZ I think that when you are attacked as a small country from certain territorial areas in a coordinated way by other states as Israel was in 1967, then that can have a powerful effect on your thinking. So, it has always seemed to me that the security problems that Israel has have to be taken very seriously. I find myself a little more optimistic than Dean; not necessarily that things are suddenly going to happen in a positive way. But it seems to me there's an answer out there waiting to be found. And so, some answer that has a sort of mixed sovereignty basis, I think, basically holds a lot a promise.

EDWIN NEWMAN Are you talking there about…?

GEORGE SHULTZ Where you treat Palestinian things in one manner, and you treat economic things in another, you treat water rights in another, and you do it subject by subject. What you emerge with is something that looks mixed up by previous standards of sovereignty, but which just might work if there's any kind of will to make it work.

EDWIN NEWMAN Secretary Rogers.

WILLIAM ROGERS Israel has always doubted the willingness on the part of the United States to keep its commitment to come to the aid of Israel. I think what happened in the Gulf War shows that we are prepared to, and I think that does contribute somewhat to the prospects for a successful negotiated peace. I think it's in Israel's best interest. I realize they're reluctant to do it, but when you think of the size of that country and the surrounding neighbors, how many of them there are, and the hostilities that exist, if there isn't some adjustment it's going to continue forever. The young Arabs now are inheriting the same hostilities their fathers and grandfathers had. So, I think it's in the interest of the world community to make a serious effort, and I think there's a possibility that will work.

EDWIN NEWMAN Secretary Haig…

ALEXANDER HAIG I don't believe there will be a comprehensive settlement of any kind in any way. I do believe there will be a step-by-step confidence-building approach that may work, which is what worked at Camp David. Going for the Holy Grail is just too much to bear.

The Seventh Annual Report of the Secretaries of Defense—1993

MARVIN KALB And just shifting geographic focus for a minute, Israel and the Palestine Liberation Organization have signed an agreement which for the first time since the creation of the State of Israel, opens genuine prospects for an Arab-Israeli accommodation in that part of the world. And let me start with one question. Is there any specific way in which the U.S. military can function to facilitate, to ensure, to expand the possibilities of a peaceful accommodation in the Middle East?

RICHARD CHENEY I think to some extent we already have, Marvin. I would argue that one of the byproducts of the Gulf War was that we made Israel more secure from a military standpoint than she's been in decades—given what we did to the Iraqi military. That, combined with the end of the Cold War—the fact that the Soviets are no longer there to support Syria and so forth, the way they did in the past—creates a real possibility of peace between the Israelis and the Palestinians.

JAMES SCHLESINGER And there is the political aspect, too, which was that the way [in which] the Gulf War and the conflict in the Gulf unfolded, the PLO's funding from the Gulf Arab states ended and it was in a position in which its political future was deteriorating. This certainly enhanced its, uh, inclination to sign with the Israelis.

FRANK CARLUCCI But ironically, the biggest task now is to resuscitate the PLO. Since the peace agreement has been signed, Hamas has been gaining in popularity. Three PLO officials have been assassinated, and we now have to keep Arafat alive and going as a viable negotiator, otherwise the more radical elements will take over.

HAROLD BROWN Presumably that's what motivated Rabin to strike a deal with the

PLO. He saw them shrinking, and the Islamic fundamentalists gaining in strength.

FRANK CARLUCCI Absolutely.

MARVIN KALB Do you see the possibility as the U.S.—let's put it in the State Department's camp for a minute and in the White House—succeeds somehow in getting us much, much closer to a Palestine-Israel agreement and out of that involving Jordan perhaps?

FRANK CARLUCCI Well, the Norwegians played a role there too.

MARVIN KALB A very important role indeed. Do you see the United States as providing some kind of nuclear umbrella so that if Israel has to make further direct concessions she will be sufficiently reassured? Do you see a U.S. direct military [involvement]?

FRANK CARLUCCI No. We have a security commitment to Israel, and I see no reason to change that.

HAROLD BROWN I don't see a nuclear umbrella.

MARVIN KALB Right.

FRANK CARLUCCI That's an existing commitment, and it ought to continue.

JAMES SCHLESINGER Yes, we have said for many years that we will maintain Israel's technical edge, and we will continue to do that. That is a military function. It's largely in terms of the shipping of military equipment. Now if it means moving forces into the region, I think that you would have to have a much greater threat perceived by the American people to American interests before that is going to take place.

HAROLD BROWN It is conceivable that in a Golan Heights settlement one or the other of the sides—the Israelis or Syrians or both—might want a U.S. presence as a peacekeeping force?

MARVIN KALB The Secretary of State has already said that the United States considers sending in forces.

HAROLD BROWN He'd consider doing it, and of course we have such a force in Sinai which is a much easier case to manage.

The Eleventh Annual Report of the Secretaries of State—1994

CHARLAYNE HUNTER-GAULT Let's begin our discussion now with one of the most significant diplomatic successes of the past year, the landmark peace agreement between Israel and the Palestine Liberation Organization, the PLO. Mr. Haig, when you look at the situation now and you see the continued rejection of the accord by the more radical groups like Hamas and radical right-wing Israeli factions, how serious a threat do you think they pose to the peace process?

ALEXANDER HAIG Right now there are two dangers. One, of course, is the rejectionist front and the real question of whether Arafat himself, wounded as he was before the peace treaty, can manage his own constituency. And I'd say that's the greatest threat to whether or not there will be a successful outcome. But there's a second one, and that is the Israeli democratic government's ability to progress and take risks for peace, and it's there that I have some reservations about a premature dialogue with Syria. What I'm saying is, Israel can handle one dish at a time, one problem at a time, as they move forward, in my view. And we should let that peace process between the PLO and Israel progress a great deal farther before we throw another burden on Rabin's plate, or he may find himself out of office and a very strong conservative movement back in power in Israel.

CHARLAYNE HUNTER-GAULT What do you think about that, Mr. Baker?

JAMES BAKER Well, I think Al is absolutely right on the point that he makes about the weakness of the PLO. That's one of the main reasons that they came, I think, to the table on a Gaza-Jericho first deal. But remember that these two politicians and these two leaders now have a heck of a lot invested in this agreement. It is extraordinarily important to both of them that the agreement succeed. Also, I think when you start talking about Arab-Israeli peace you have to remember that there are two processes now going on here. This Israeli-PLO agreement is an interim self-governing agreement between Israelis on the one hand and Palestinians on the other, and it really is now limited to the Gaza-Jericho formula. The Israeli-Syrian front is an entirely different situation. I also agree with Al's point that the Israeli body politic is [going to] have a difficult time digesting two of these deals very close together. I'm not sure I agree that that means we should not be gently nudging and cajoling and trying to do what we can to push the parties toward peace.

WILLIAM ROGERS I agree with what my colleagues have said except for the fact that I don't think we have to be so intrusive. You referred, in your opening remarks, to quiet diplomacy. I think it's time for quiet diplomacy. We tend to say too much about the Middle East.

CHARLAYNE HUNTER-GAULT When have we done that? I mean, what examples?

WILLIAM ROGERS Well, I don't know if I can single out any individual, but the last time the President was there Mr. Rabin said we ought to stay out of it. He said "We have the will to do it, and please don't get involved so much in what we're doing, openly particularly," and I think he's right. And I think it's the time now [that] we should deal behind the scenes. And furthermore, I think we've sort of left the impression, maybe, that we think Arafat is the sole supporter of this peace agreement. Of course, that was not true. The Palestinian Organization took a very active role, and I don't see any place for them to go.

CHARLAYNE HUNTER-GAULT But what about U.S. interests? What are our interests now in Israel and how do we protect them? Mr. Muskie?

EDMUND MUSKIE Well, I think our foremost interest is to try to bring peace to the area.

CHARLAYNE HUNTER-GAULT Why? I mean, why is that in our interests? Why should we care?

EDMUND MUSKIE The fact [that] we got involved in the Persian Gulf War. We want to avoid the possibility of future wars. That's the main goal. But what I want to bring into this discussion [is], there is a commonality of interest in the development of the resources of that area which can help to bring them together—energy resources. For instance, the Gaza Strip has important gas resources. There are oil interests. I think that the investors are really flocking to develop those resources in the interests, not only of their own pocketbooks, but in the interests of serving the Israelis or the Palestinian interests long-range.

CHARLAYNE HUNTER-GAULT But what about U.S. interests?

JAMES BAKER You ask why though, and I think Ed gave you a very good answer. Why should we be so interested in peace in the Middle East? It's because of our special relationship with Israel, the only democracy in the Middle East. One final thing. What should the United States do besides trying to be a facilitator for peace? I think in this particular case we should look very carefully and closely at security guarantees by the United States with or without other countries. I mean, either as part of a multi-lateral situation or even unilaterally if it would mean peace between Arabs and Israelis. I think the American people would support that.

ALEXANDER HAIG Let me try to answer your question, which we haven't answered. We avoided, "What do we do about the rejectionists?"—and the answer to that is very much the same as it is in Bosnia. If the parties don't want peace and are not willing to sacrifice for it, there is no way that the United States can impose that peace without an undue loss of blood and vital interests for our own people.

OTHER MIDDLE EASTERN ISSUES

The Sixth Annual Report of the Secretaries of Defense—1992

DAVID GERGEN Is Iran the country we should be keeping an eye on now?

JAMES SCHLESINGER Oh, absolutely. When Mel and I were in the Nixon Administration, we said that we were going to make Iran the guardian of the Gulf. We finally have succeeded. [LAUGHTER] Not the way we originally intended, mind you.

HAROLD BROWN They're not the same people, anymore, either.

JAMES SCHLESINGER They are not the same people anymore, indeed. In the case of the eighties we recognized that we had to sustain Iraq as a counterweight to Iran. After the invasion of Kuwait essentially, we destroyed that counterweight. As a result we are in a position in which Iran's strength is growing, and the collapse of the Soviet Union has added to that. First by creating a fertile field in central Asia of the new Muslim republics and secondly because the Iranians can go out and buy Soviet tanks at a knock-down price of $60,000 or $70,000 per copy. They've rebuilt their military forces.

FRANK CARLUCCI They've been to the Soviet yard-sale.

DAVID GERGEN And they buy from the Chinese as well.

FRANK CARLUCCI And the Chinese as well. I was in the Middle East two weeks ago, and nobody's worrying about the Iraqi threat. They're worrying about the potential threat from Iran. There's another tension [over] there that's very real, and that's the tension between modernization and fundamentalism—weak internal security structures [and] regimes that are beginning haltingly to take some steps to broaden the participation; but they also are under great pressure from the fundamentalist elements in their societies. Those tensions will be exacerbated unless we are successful in keeping the peace process moving forward. That's the third element that is critically important as you look at this equation.

JAMES SCHLESINGER We should not regard Islamic fundamentalism as a collectivity or as the enemy. Each situation is different. The fundamentalists in Algeria are quite different from those in Iran. And there is some tendency now to try to replace the Soviet threat with Islamic fundamentalism as the enemy of the United States. That would be a capital mistake.

FRANK CARLUCCI And I certainly didn't mean to imply that. I agree with you a hundred percent on that issue.

The Ninth Annual Report of the Secretaries of State—1991

EDWIN NEWMAN There is a related point here. President Bush encouraged certain groups in Iraq to rise against Saddam Hussein. Did the United States government have the right to do that?

ALEXANDER HAIG Of course, you have the right to do anything if your lives are at risk and you're in a struggle with an enemy. The problem was they misread it. I think the administration tended to believe that the people around Saddam Hussein would rise up because he was brutalized, and [they] failed to look at the fact that it would be the Kurds and the Shiite Muslims.

EDWIN NEWMAN Well, does [that] suggest failure? There's been a lot of talk about that.

ALEXANDER HAIG Probably.

DEAN RUSK One of the shortcomings in the United Nations Security Council [was that] the Security Council did not authorize moving into Iraq to displace Saddam Hussein. That was one of the shortcomings of the whole enterprise. Had we tried to use American force to go in and occupy all of Iraq to get rid of this man, that would have been a very bloody affair. We missed a cue in the Security Council of the United Nations in not providing for Saddam Hussein.

EDWIN NEWMAN Secretary Shultz and then Secretary Muskie.

GEORGE SHULTZ One of the things that the Security Council did vote in a resolution was an undertaking to explore war crimes committed by Saddam Hussein and his government—complete brutality, torture and all kinds of things that could only be classified as war crimes which were committed by people under his control. Again, I don't understand why in the world we don't follow up or the Security Council doesn't follow up on that resolution and put Saddam Hussein in the dock. Now, maybe you can't go into Iraq and pull him out; but you can indict him. You can put all of that evidence forward and use the weight of the evidence to put as much pressure [on him] as possible and isolate him completely.

EDWIN NEWMAN Secretary Muskie.

EDMUND MUSKIE Well, I think there was what has proved to be an unfortunate ambiguity between our formal war aims and the hoped-for results that were not explicit war aims. It seemed to me the President kept encouraging others in order to get rid of Saddam Hussein. The American public confused that with the question of whether or not it was one of our war aims to get rid of Saddam Hussein. Certainly the President in discussing the oncoming war made it clear that he hoped the result would be to get rid of Saddam Hussein. Well, that's an ambiguous result, and we haven't got rid of him yet; and I don't see any early prospect that we will. His ambitions have not ended. His objectives for his country in the region, I don't think, have been ended. So, I think Saddam Hussein is there with the prospect of growing political support in his own country and perhaps elsewhere. I may be wrong.

BIOGRAPHICAL SKETCHES OF THE FORMER U.S. SECRETARIES OF STATE

BAKER, James. Secretary of State from 1989 to 1992 under President Bush. Directed Presidential Election Campaigns for Presidents Ford, Reagan, and Bush. White House Chief of Staff under President Reagan, 1981 to 1985. Secretary of the Treasury, 1985 to 1988. White House Chief of Staff under President Bush, 1992–1993.

Mr. Baker was Secretary of State during the Iraqi invasion of Kuwait and Operations Desert Shield and Desert Storm, the 1991–92 effort to provide humanitarian assistance to the Kurds, the beginning of the Arab-Israeli negotiations in the wake of the Persian Gulf War, and the post-Gulf War confrontation with Iraq over nuclear inspection.

EAGLEBURGER, Lawrence. Secretary of State from 1992 to 1993 under President Bush. Entered the U.S. Foreign Service in 1957. Ambassador to Yugoslavia, 1977–1981. Assistant Secretary of State for European Affairs, 1981–1982. Under Secretary of State for Political Affairs, 1982–1989. Deputy Secretary of State from 1989 to 1992.

Mr. Eagleburger was Secretary of State as the United States' post-Persian Gulf War confrontation with Iraq continued. He was also Secretary as Eastern European states struggled to construct post-communist societies, and as the U.S. reassessed its post-Cold War role in Europe.

HAIG, Alexander. Secretary of State from 1981 to 1982 under President Reagan. Deputy Assistant to the President for National Security Affairs, 1970 to 1973 under President Nixon, and White House Chief of Staff, 1973 to 1975 under President Ford. Served as Supreme Allied Commander in Europe from 1975 until 1979.

Mr. Haig was Secretary of State during the heightened U.S.-Soviet tensions of the first Reagan administration and the accompanying U.S. military buildup. He attempted to construct a "strategic consensus" in the Middle East linking Israel, Egypt, and Jordan in opposition to Soviet expansionism in the region.

KISSINGER, Henry. Secretary of State from 1973 to 1977 under Presidents Nixon and Ford. Assistant to the President for National Security Affairs from 1969 to 1975 under Presidents Nixon and Ford. Awarded the Nobel Peace Prize in 1973 for his efforts in arranging a cease-fire in Vietnam.

Mr. Kissinger was Secretary of State during the 1973 Arab-Israeli War and engaged in extensive "shuttle diplomacy" in an effort to resolve continuing Arab-Israeli tensions. He was also Secretary during the general improvement in East-West relations that took place in Europe during the Ford Administration.

MUSKIE, Edmund. Secretary of State from 1980 to 1981 under President Carter. Governor of Maine from 1954 to 1958, and U.S. Senator from Maine, 1958 to 1980. In 1968, he was the Democratic Party's nominee for Vice President.

Mr. Muskie was Secretary of State during the later stages of the Iranian hostage crisis when Iran held U.S. diplomats hostage in Tehran, the deterioration in U.S.-Soviet relations caused by the Soviet invasion of Afghanistan, and the growth of U.S. concern over Soviet activities elsewhere in the developing world, including the Middle East.

ROGERS, William. Secretary of State from 1969 to 1973 under President Nixon. Attorney General from 1957 to 1961 under President Eisenhower and U.S. Representative to the Twentieth Session of the UN General Assembly. In 1986, he was the

Chairperson on the Presidential Commission on the Challenger Disaster.

Mr. Rogers was Secretary of State during the Egyptian rapprochement with the U.S. in 1972, the implementation of the "Twin Pillar" strategy toward Iran and Saudi Arabia, and the development of the "Rogers Plan" for Middle Eastern peace, which included Israel returning land to the Arabs and the U.S. and the U.S.S.R. guaranteeing Israeli security.

RUSK, Dean. Secretary of State from 1961 to 1969 under Presidents Kennedy and Johnson. Assistant Secretary of State for United Nations Affairs and for Far Eastern Affairs, 1947 to 1952. From 1952 until 1960, he was President of the Rockefeller Foundation.

Mr. Rusk was Secretary of State during the 1967 Arab-Israeli War, the passage of UN Resolution 242, the Cuban Missile Crisis, and the Soviet invasion of Czechoslovakia. He was Secretary of State during the early years of the Vietnam War.

SHULTZ, George. Secretary of State from 1982 to 1989 under President Reagan. From 1946 to 1957, he was a faculty member at M.I.T., and from 1962 to 1968, he was a Dean at the University of Chicago. He was U.S. Secretary of Labor from 1969 to 1970, and Secretary of the Treasury and Assistant to President Nixon, 1972 to 1974.

Mr. Shultz was Secretary of State during the Iran-Iraq War, the civil war in Lebanon, the Iran-Contra affair, the improvement in East-West relations that accompanied Gorbachev's reforms in the U.S.S.R., and the many Reagan-Gorbachev summit meetings.

VANCE, Cyrus. Secretary of State from 1977 to 1980 under President Carter. In 1961, he was appointed General Counsel to the Department of Defense. He was appointed Secretary of the Army in 1962 and Deputy Secretary of Defense in 1964, and served as UN Special Envoy to Yugoslavia, 1991 to 1992.

Mr. Vance was Secretary of State during the Iranian revolution, when the Soviet Union invaded Afghanistan, during the beginning stages of the Iranian hostage crisis when Iran held U.S. diplomats hostage in Tehran, and as the remaining vestiges of the East-West detente of the 1970s ended.

BIOGRAPHICAL SKETCHES OF THE
FORMER U.S. SECRETARIES OF DEFENSE

BROWN, Harold. Secretary of Defense from 1977 to 1981 under President Carter. Other posts he has held include Director of the Lawrence Livermore Laboratory, Secretary of the Air Force, Under Secretary of Defense, President of the California Institute of Technology, and a member of the U.S. delegation to the Strategic Arms Limitation Talks.

Mr. Brown was Secretary of Defense during the Iranian revolution, when the Soviet Union invaded Afghanistan, during the hostage crisis when Iran held U.S. diplomats hostage in Tehran, and as the U.S. began its defense buildup under President Carter.

CARLUCCI, Frank. Secretary of Defense from 1987 to 1989 under President Reagan. Prior to that time he served as Assistant to the President for National Security Affairs. He has also been Deputy Director of Central Intelligence, President and Chief Operating Officer of Sears World Trade, and U.S. Ambassador to Portugal.

Mr. Carlucci was Secretary of Defense as the Iran-Iraq War ended and as more and more people in the West began to realize that the Gorbachev reforms were significantly reducing the Soviet threat in the Middle East and elsewhere as well.

CHENEY, Richard. Secretary of Defense from 1989 to 1993 under President George H. W. Bush. He served as Assistant to the President and White House Chief of Staff under the Ford administration. He also has been a six-term U.S. Congressman from Wyoming. In 2001, seven years after the original publication of this book, Cheney became Vice President of the United States.

Mr. Cheney was Secretary of Defense during Operation Desert Storm and Desert Shield, during the post-Persian Gulf War efforts to apply sanctions to Iraq because of its nuclear weapons programs, and during some of the defense change that followed the collapse of communism in Eastern Europe and the Soviet Union.

CLIFFORD, Clark. Secretary of Defense from 1968 to 1969 under President Johnson. He also was Special Counsel to President Truman and a member of the President's Foreign Intelligence Advisory Board.

Mr. Clifford was Secretary of Defense when the decision was made not to send more U.S. troops to Vietnam and when the Soviet Union invaded Czechoslovakia.

LAIRD, Melvin. Secretary of Defense from 1969 to 1973 under President Nixon. He was elected to the 83rd Congress in 1952 and served in that capacity for the next eight terms. In 1973, he was named Counselor to the President for Domestic Affairs.

Mr. Laird was Secretary of Defense when the "Twin Pillar" strategy was implemented, during the final U.S. withdrawal from Vietnam, and during the development of the Brezhnev-Nixon detente.

McNAMARA, Robert. Secretary of Defense from 1961 to 1968 under Presidents Kennedy and Johnson. He was named President of the Ford Motor Company in 1960 and was President of the World Bank from 1968 to 1981.

Mr. McNamara was Secretary of Defense during the 1967 Arab-Israeli War, the passage of UN Resolution 242, the Cuban Missile Crisis, the U.S. military buildup in Vietnam and the height of the Vietnam War, and the signing of the Nuclear Test Ban Treaty.

RICHARDSON, Elliot. Secretary of Defense in 1973 under President Nixon. Other posts he has held include U.S. Ambassador to Great Britain, Secretary of Commerce, Attorney General, Special U.S. Representative to the Law of the Seas Conference, and Under Secretary of State.

Mr. Richardson was Secretary of Defense during the last year of the Nixon presidency as the United States ended its involvement in the Vietnam War.

RUMSFELD, Donald. Secretary of Defense from 1975 to 1977 under President Ford. He also served as White House Chief of Staff under President Ford, U.S. Ambassador to NATO, President Reagan's Special Middle Eastern Envoy and Chief Executive Officer of Searle Pharmaceutical Company. In 2001, seven years after the original publication of this book, Rumsfeld once again took up public office, serving as the Secretary of Defense under President George W. Bush.

Under President Ford, Mr. Rumsfeld was Secretary of Defense during the period of cordial East-West relations in Europe that followed the Helsinki Conference on Security and Cooperation in Europe and during the Soviet-supported Cuban buildup in Angola.

SCHLESINGER, James. Secretary of Defense from 1973 to 1975 under Presidents Nixon and Ford. He has also been Acting Director of the Office of Management and Budget, Chairman of the Atomic Energy Agency, Director of the CIA, and Secretary of Energy.

Mr. Schlesinger was Secretary of Defense during the 1973 Arab-Israeli War, the development of OPEC as a major international actor, the Ford-Brezhnev Summit in Vladivostok, and the continued improvement in East-West relations that took place in the mid-1970s.

WEINBERGER, Caspar. Secretary of Defense from 1981 to 1987 under President Reagan. He has also been Chairman of the Federal Trade Commission, Director of the Office of Management and Budget, and Secretary of Health, Education and Welfare.

Mr. Weinberger was Secretary of Defense when the Reagan Administration instituted its large U.S. military buildup, during the period of heightened U.S.-Soviet tensions in the early and middle 1980s, as the U.S. began its active opposition to pro-Soviet states in the Third World, during the Iran-Iraq War, and during the Iran-Contra affair.

BIOGRAPHICAL SKETCHES OF MODERATORS

GERGEN, David. Mr. Gergen was appointed Counselor to the President by President Clinton in 1993. Earlier in his career, he served eight years in the White House under three other presidents, Nixon, Ford, and Reagan. He has also been an editor-at-large with *U.S. News & World Report*, during which time he also was a commentator on television and radio.

HUNTER-GAULT, Charlayne. Ms. Hunter-Gault is CNN Bureau Chief in Johannesberg, South Africa. In 1986, Ms. Hunter-Gault was named Journalist of the Year by the National Association of Black Journalists and received the prestigious George Foster Peabody Broadcast Award.

KALB, Marvin. Mr. Kalb is the Edward R. Murrow Professor of Press and Public Policy at Harvard University's John F. Kennedy School of Government and Director of the Joan Shorenstein Barone Center on the Press, Politics, and Public Policy. He has also served as diplomatic correspondent and anchorman at CBS and NBC and moderator of *Meet the Press*.

NEWMAN, Edwin. For 31 years before his retirement, Mr. Newman was a correspondent, anchorman, and essayist for NBC. He has received the Overseas Press Club Award, numerous Emmys, and other awards for journalism from the Universities of Wisconsin and Ohio. Mr. Newman is also the author of several books.

SMITH, Hedrick. Mr. Smith is the former *New York Times* Moscow Bureau Chief, and a frequent commentator on U.S. television on current domestic U.S. and international political, economic, and social affairs. He is the author of *The Russians* and *The New Russians*, as well as several other books.

APPENDIX—STATISTICAL INFORMATION

Algeria

Capital	Algiers
Type of Government	Republic
Area (sq. km.)	2,381,740
Arable Land	3% (1998 est.)
Population	32,818,500 (2003 est.)
Currency	Algerian dinar (DZD)
Life Expectancy at Birth (2001 est.)	Total population: 70.5 years; male: 69.1 years; female: 72.0 years
Ethnic Composition	Arab-Berber 99%, European <1%
Religions	Sunni Muslim (state religion) 99%, Christian and Jewish 1%
Languages	Arabic (official), French, Berber dialects
Literacy (age 15 and over can read and write) (2003 est.)	Total population: 70%; male: 78.8%; female: 61%
Natural Resources	petroleum, natural gas, iron ore, phosphates, uranium, lead, zinc
Agricultural Products	wheat, barley, oats, grapes, olives, citrus, fruits, sheep, cattle
Industries	petroleum, natural gas, light industries, mining, electrical, petrochemical, food processing
Labor Force	9.4 million (2001 est.)
Unemployment Rate	31% (2002 est.)
GDP per capita (PPP)	$5,400 (2002 est.)
External Debt	$21.6 billion (2002 est.)
Exports	$19.5 billion f.o.b., (2002 est.); petroleum, natural gas, and petroleum products 97%
Export Trading Partners	Italy 18.9%, Spain 13.1%, France 13%, U.S. 12.1%, Netherlands 6.9%, Brazil 5.9%, Canada 5.7%, Turkey 5.3%, Belgium 5.19% (2002)
Imports	$10.6 billion f.o.b. (2002 est.); capital goods, food and beverages, consumer goods
Import Trading Partners	France 37.3%, U.S. 11.3%, Italy 10.0%, Germany 7.6%, Spain (2001)

Bahrain

Capital	Manama
Type of Government	Constitutional hereditary monarchy
Area (sq. km.)	665
Arable Land	4% (1998 est.)
Population	667,238 (2003 est.)
Currency	Bahraini dinar (BHD)
Life Expectancy at Birth (2003 est.)	Total population: 73.72 years; male: 71.28 years; female: 76.24 years
Ethnic Composition	Bahraini 63%, Asian 19%, other Arab 10%, Iranian 8%
Religions	Shi'a Muslim 70%, Sunni Muslim 30%
Languages	Arabic, English, Farsi, Urdu
Literacy (age 15 and over can read and write) (2003 est.)	Total population: 89.1%; male: 91.9%; female: 85%
Natural Resources	oil, associated and nonassociated natural gas, fish, pearls
Agricultural Products	fruit, vegetables, poultry, dairy products, shrimp, fish
Industries	petroleum processing and refining, aluminum smelting, offshore banking, ship repairing, tourism
Labor Force	295,000 (1998 est.)
Unemployment Rate	15% (1998 est.)
GDP per capita (PPP)	$15,100 (2002 est.)
External Debt	$3.7 billion (2002 est.)
Exports	$5.8 billion (2002); petroleum and petroleum products, aluminum, textiles
Export Trading Partners	U.S. 4.5%, Saudi Arabia 3.4%, India 3.2%, Japan 2.8%, South Korea 2.1% (2000)
Imports	$4.2 billion f.o.b. (2002 est.); crude oil, machinery, chemicals
Import Trading Partners	Saudi Arabia 30.1%, U.S. 11.7%, Japan 7.1%, Germany 6.5%, U.K. 5.6% (2000)

Abbreviations: f.o.b.—free on board.
Source: *The WorldFactbook 2003* (Central Intelligence Agency)

Egypt

Capital	Cairo
Type of Government	Republic
Area (sq. km.)	1,001,450
Arable Land	3% (1998 est.)
Population	74,718,797 (2003 est.)
Currency	Egyptian pound (EGP)
Life Expectancy at Birth (2003 est.)	Total population: 70.41 years; male: 67.94 years; female: 73 years
Ethnic Composition	Eastern Hamitic stock (Egyptian, Bedouin, and Berber) 99%, Greek, Nubian, Armenian, other European (primarily Italian and French) 1%
Religions	Muslim (mostly Sunni) 94%, Coptic Christian and other 6%
Languages	Arabic (official), English and French widely understood by educated classes
Literacy (age 15 and over can read and write) (2003 est.)	Total population: 57.7%; male: 68.3%; female: 46.9%
Natural Resources	petroleum, natural gas, iron ore, phosphates, manganese, limestone, gypsum, talc, asbestos, lead, zinc
Agricultural Products	cotton, rice, corn, wheat, beans, fruits, vegetables, cattle, water buffalo, sheep, goats
Industries	textiles, food processing, tourism, chemicals, hydrocarbons, construction, cement, metals
Labor Force	20.6 million (2001 est.)
Unemployment Rate	12% (2001 est.)
GDP per capita (PPP)	$4,000 (2002 est.)
External Debt	$30.5 billion (2002 est.)
Exports	$7 billion f.o.b. (2002 est.); crude oil and petroleum products, cotton, textiles, metal products, chemicals
Export Trading Partners	U.S. 18.3%, Italy 13.7%, U.K. 8.4% (2002)
Imports	$15.2 billion f.o.b. (2002 est.); machinery and equipment, foodstuffs, chemicals, wood products, fuels
Import Trading Partners	U.S. 16.4%, Germany 7.9%, Italy 6.7%, France 6.5%, China 5%, U.K. 4.1% (2002)

Iran

Capital	Tehran
Type of Government	Theocratic republic
Area (sq. km.)	1,648,000
Arable Land	10% (1998 est.)
Population	68,278,826 (2003 est.)
Currency	Iranian rial (IRR)
Life Expectancy at Birth (2003 est.)	Total population: 69.35 years; male: 68.04 years; female: 70.73 years
Ethnic Composition	Persian 51%, Azeri 24%, Gilaki and Mazandarani 8%, Kurd 7%, Arab 3%, Lur 2%, Baloch 2%, Turkmen 2%, other 1%
Religions	Shi'a Muslim 89%, Sunni Muslim 10%, Zoroastrian, Jewish, Christian, and Baha'i 1%
Languages	Persian and Persian dialects 58%, Turkic and Turkic dialects 26%, Kurdish 9%, Luri 2%, Balochi 1%, Arabic 1%, Turkish 1%, other 2%
Literacy (age 15 and over can read and write) (2003 est.)	Total population: 79.4%; male: 85.6%; female: 73%
Natural Resources	petroleum, natural gas, coal, chromium, copper, iron ore, lead, manganese, zinc, sulfur
Agricultural Products	wheat, rice, other grains, sugar beets, fruits, nuts, cotton, dairy products, wool, caviar
Industries	petroleum, petrochemicals, textiles, cement and other construction materials, food processing (particularly sugar refining and vegetable oil production), metal fabricating, armaments
Labor Force	21 million (1998)
Unemployment Rate	16.3% (2003 est.)
GDP per capita (PPP)	$6,800 (2002 est.)
External Debt	$8.7 billion (2002 est.)
Exports	$24 billion f.o.b. (2002 est.); petroleum 85%, carpets, fruits and nuts, iron and steel, chemicals
Export Trading Partners	Japan 17.4%, Italy 10%, South Korea 10%, China 8.6%, Greece 5% (2001)
Imports	$21.8 billion f.o.b. (2002 est.); industrial raw materials and intermediate goods, capital goods, foodstuffs and other consumer goods, technical services, military supplies
Import Trading Partners	Germany 10.9%, Italy 9%, France 7.9%, China 7.4%, South Korea 6.5%, U.A.E. 4.4%, Japan 4.1%, Russia 4% (2002)

Iraq

Capital	Baghdad
Type of Government	in transition following April 2003 defeat of Saddam Hussein regime
Area (sq. km.)	437,072
Arable Land	12% (1998 est.)
Population	24,683,313 (2003 est.)
Currency	Iraqi dinar (IQD)
Life Expectancy at Birth (2003 est.)	Total population: 67.81 years; male: 66.7 years; female: 68.99 years
Ethnic Composition	Arab 75%-80%, Kurdish 15%-20%, Turkoman, Assyrian or other 5%
Religions	Muslim 97% (Shi'a 60%-65%, Sunni 32%-37%), Christian or other 3%
Languages	Arabic, Kurdish (official in Kurdish regions), Assyrian, Armenian
Literacy (age 15 and over can read and write) (2003 est.)	Total population: 40.4%; male: 55.9%; female: 24.4%
Natural Resources	petroleum, natural gas, phosphates, sulfur
Agricultural Products	wheat, barley, rice, vegetables, dates, cotton, cattle, sheep
Industries	petroleum, chemicals, textiles, construction materials, food processing
Labor Force	6.5 million (2002 est.)
Unemployment Rate	Not available
GDP per capita (PPP)	$2,400 (2002 est.)
External Debt	$120 billion (2002 est.)
Exports	$13 billion f.o.b. (2002 est.); crude oil
Export Trading Partners	U.S. 40.9%, Canada 8.2%, France 8.2%, Jordan 7.5%, Netherlands 6.4%, Italy 5.4%, Morocco 4.7%, Spain 4.4% (2002)
Imports	$7.8 billion f.o.b. (2002 est.); food, medicine, manufactures
Import Trading Partners	Jordan 11%, France 8.8%, China 8.4%, Germany 7.6%, Russia 7.3%, Australia 7.2%, Vietnam 6.6%, Italy 6.4%, Japan 5.6% (2002)

Israel

Capital	Jerusalem
Type of Government	Parliamentary democracy
Area (sq. km.)	20,770
Arable Land	17% (1998 est.)
Population	6,116,533 (2002 est.)
Currency	New Israeli shekel (ILS)
Life Expectancy at Birth (2001 est.)	Total population: 79.02 years; male: 76.95 years; female: 81.19 years
Ethnic Composition	Jewish 80.1% (Europe/America-born 32.1%, Israel-born 20.8%, Africa-born 14.6%, Asia-born 12.6%), non-Jewish 19.9% (mostly Arab) (1996 est.)
Religions	Jewish 80.1%, Muslim 14.6% (mostly Sunni Muslim), Christian 2.1%, other 3.2% (1996 est.)
Languages	Hebrew (official), Arabic used officially for Arab minority, English most commonly used foreign language
Literacy (age 15 and over can read and write) (2003 est.)	Total population: 95.4%; male: 97.3%; female: 93.6%
Natural Resources	timber, potash, copper ore, natural gas, phosphate rock, magnesium bromide, clays, sand
Agricultural Products	citrus, vegetables, cotton, beef, poultry, dairy products
Industries	high-technology projects (including aviation, communications, computer-aided design and manufactures, medical electronics), wood and paper products, potash and phosphates, food, beverages, tobacco, caustic soda, cement, diamond cutting
Labor Force	2.5 million (2002 est.)
Unemployment Rate	10% (2002 est.)
GDP per capita (PPP)	$19,500 (2002 est.)
External Debt	$42.8 billion (2001 est.)
Exports	$28.1 billion f.o.b. (2002 est.); machinery and equipment, software, cut diamonds, agricultural products, chemicals, textiles and apparel
Export Trading Partners	U.S. 39.2%, Belgium 6.5%, Germany 4.4%, U.K. 4.2% (2001)
Imports	$30.8 billion f.o.b. (2000 est.); raw materials, military equipment, investment goods, rough diamonds, fuels, consumer goods, grain
Import Trading Partners	U.S. 21.6%, Belgium 8.9%, Germany 6.7%, U.K. 6.6%, Switzerland 4.9%, Italy 4.5% (2002)

Jordan

Capital	Amman
Type of Government	Constitutional monarchy
Area (sq. km.)	92,300
Arable Land	3% (1998 est.)
Population	5,460,265 (2003 est.)
Currency	Jordanian dinar (JOD)
Life Expectancy at Birth (2003 est.)	Total population: 77.88 years; male: 75.42 years; female: 80.5 years
Ethnic Composition	Arab 98%, Circassian 1%, Armenian 1%
Religions	Sunni Muslim 92%, Christian 6% (majority Greek Orthodox, but some Greek Catholic, Roman Catholic, Syrian Orthodox, Coptic Orthodox, Armenian Orthodox, and Protestant denominations), other 2% (several small Shi'a Muslim and Druze populations) (2001 est.)
Languages	Arabic (official), English widely understood among upper and middle classes
Literacy (age 15 and over can read and write) (2003 est.)	Total population: 91.3%; male: 95.9%; female: 86.3%
Natural Resources	phosphates, potash, shale oil
Agricultural Products	wheat, barley, citrus, tomatoes, melons, olives, sheep, goats, poultry
Industries	phosphate mining, pharmaceuticals, petroleum refining, cement, potash, light manufacturing, tourism
Labor Force	1.36 million (2002 est.)
Unemployment Rate	16% official rate; actual rate is 25%-30% (2001 est.)
GDP per capita (PPP)	$4,300 (2002 est.)
External Debt	$8.2 billion (2002 est.)
Exports	$2.5 billion f.o.b. (2002 est.); phosphates, fertilizers, potash, agricultural products, manufactures, pharmaceuticals
Export Trading Partners	Iraq 20.1%, U.S. 14.5%, India 8.1%, Saudi Arabia 5.4%, Israel 4.4% (2002)
Imports	$4.4 billion f.o.b. (2002 est.); crude oil, machinery, transport equipment, food, live animals, manufactured goods
Import Trading Partners	Iraq 13.4%, Germany 8.8%, U.S. 8%, China 6%, France 4.2%, Italy 4.1%, U.K. 4.1% (2002)

Kuwait

Capital	Kuwait
Type of Government	Nominal constitutional monarchy
Area (sq. km.)	17,820
Arable Land	0% (1998 est.)
Population	2,183,161 (2003 est.)
Currency	Kuwaiti dinar (KWD)
Life Expectancy at Birth (2003 est.)	Total population: 76.65 years; male: 75.72 years; female: 77.62 years
Ethnic Composition	Kuwaiti 45%, other Arab 35%, South Asian 9%, Iranian 4%, other 7%
Religions	Muslim 85% (Sunni 70%, Shi'a 30%), Christian, Hindu, Parsi, and other 15%
Languages	Arabic (official), English widely spoken
Literacy (age 15 and over can read and write) (2003 est.)	Total population: 83.5%; male: 85.1%; female: 81.7%
Natural Resources	petroleum, fish, shrimp, natural gas
Agricultural Products	practically no crops; fish
Industries	petroleum, petrochemicals, desalination, food processing, construction materials
Labor Force	1.3 million (1998 est.)
Unemployment Rate	7% (2002 est.)
GDP per capita (PPP)	$17,500 (2002 est.)
External Debt	$10.4 billion (2000 est.)
Exports	$16 billion f.o.b. (2002 est.); oil and refined products, fertilizers
Export Trading Partners	Japan 24.4%, South Korea 12.9%, U.S. 11.9%, Singapore 10.1%, Taiwan 7%, Netherlands 4.5%, Pakistan 4.4% (2002)
Imports	$7.3 billion f.o.b. (2002 est.); food, construction materials, vehicles and parts, clothing
Import Trading Partners	U.S. 13.1%, Japan 11.1%, Germany 9.7%, Saudi Arabia 6.6%, U.K. 6%, Italy 5.4%, France 5.2% (2001)

Lebanon

Capital	Beirut
Type of Government	Republic
Area (sq. km.)	10,400
Arable Land	18% (1998 est.)
Population	3,727,703 (2003 est.)
Currency	Lebanese pound (LBP)
Life Expectancy at Birth (2003 est.)	Total population: 72.07 years; male: 69.64 years; female: 74.61 years
Ethnic Composition	Arab 95%, Armenian 4%, other 1%
Religions	Muslim 70% (including Shi'a, Sunni, Druze, Isma'ilite, Alawite or Nusayri), Christian 30% (including Orthodox Christian, Catholic, Protestant), Jewish (negligible number)
Languages	Arabic (official), French, English, Armenian
Literacy (age 15 and over can read and write) (2003 est.)	Total population: 87.4%; male: 93.1%; female: 82.2%
Natural Resources	limestone, iron ore, salt, water (surplus state in a water-deficit region), arable land
Agricultural Products	citrus, grapes, tomatoes, apples, vegetables, potatoes, olives, tobacco, sheep, goats
Industries	banking, food processing, jewelry, cement, textiles, mineral and chemical products, wood and furniture products, oil refining, metal fabricating
Labor Force	1.5 million. Note: There may be as many as 1 million foreign workers. (2001 est.)
Unemployment Rate	18% (1997 est.)
GDP per capita (PPP)	$4,800 (2002 est.)
External Debt	$9.3 billion (2002 est.)
Exports	$1 billion f.o.b. (2002 est.); foodstuffs and tobacco, textiles, chemicals, precious stones, metal products, electrical equipment, jewelry, paper products
Export Trading Partners	Switzerland 10.8%, Saudi Arabia 9%, U.A.E. 8.6%, U.S. 6.7%, Jordan 4.6%, Turkey 4.3% (2002)
Imports	$6 billion f.o.b. (2002 est.); foodstuffs, electrical products, vehicles, minerals, chemicals, textiles, fuels
Import Trading Partners	Italy 11.3%, France 10.7%, Germany 8.4%, U.S. 5.6%, Syria 5.4%, China 4.8%, Belgium 4.5%, U.K. 4.2% (2001)

Libya

Capital	Tripoli
Type of Government	Jamahiriya (a state of the masses) in theory, governed by the populace through local councils; in fact, a military dictatorship
Area (sq. km.)	1,759,540
Arable Land	1% (1998 est.)
Population	5,499,074 (2003 est.)
Currency	Libyan dinar (LYD)
Life Expectancy at Birth (2003 est.)	Total population: 76.07 years; male: 73.91 years; female: 78.34 years
Ethnic Composition	Berber and Arab 97%, Greek, Maltese, Italian, Egyptian, Pakistani, Turk, Indian, Tunisian
Religions	Sunni Muslim 97%
Languages	Arabic, Italian, and English are widely understood in major cities
Literacy (age 15 and over can read and write) (2003 est.)	Total population: 82.6%; male: 92.4%; female: 72%
Natural Resources	petroleum, natural gas, gypsum
Agricultural Products	wheat, barley, olives, dates, citrus, vegetables, peanuts, soybeans, cattle
Industries	petroleum, food processing, textiles, handicrafts, cement
Labor Force	1.5 million (2000 est.)
Unemployment Rate	30% (2001)
GDP per capita (PPP)	$6,200 (2002 est.)
External Debt	$4.4 billion (2001 est.)
Exports	$11.8 billion f.o.b. (2002 est.); crude oil, refined petroleum products
Export Trading Partners	Italy 42.6%, Germany 14.1%, Spain 13.6%, Turkey 6.9%, Switzerland 4.4% (2002)
Imports	$6.3 billion f.o.b. (2000 est.); machinery, transport equipment, food, manufactured goods
Import Trading Partners	Italy 25.6%, Germany 9.8%, South Korea 6.6%, U.K. 6.6%, Tunisia 6.5%, Japan 6.4%, France 5.7% (2001)

Morocco

Capital	Rabat
Type of Government	Constitutional monarchy
Area (sq. km.)	446,550
Arable Land	20% (1998 est.)
Population	31,689,265 (2003 est.)
Currency	Moroccan dirham (MAD)
Life Expectancy at Birth (2001 est.)	Total population: 70.04 years; male: 67.77 years; female: 72.41 years
Ethnic Composition	Arab-Berber 99.1%, Jewish 0.2%, other 0.7%
Religions	Muslim 98.7%, Christian 1.1%, Jewish 0.2%
Languages	Arabic (official), Berber dialects, French often the language of business, government, and diplomacy
Literacy (age 15 and over can read and write) (2003 est.)	Total population: 51.7%; male: 64.1%; female: 39.4%
Natural Resources	phosphates, iron ore, manganese, lead, zinc, fish, salt
Agricultural Products	barley, wheat, citrus, wine, vegetables, olives, livestock
Industries	phosphate rock mining and processing, food processing, leather goods, textiles, construction, tourism
Labor Force	11 million (1999 est.)
Unemployment Rate	19% (2002 est.)
GDP per capita (PPP)	$3,900 (2002 est.)
External Debt	$17.7 billion (2002 est.)
Exports	$7.5 billion f.o.b. (2002 est.); clothing, fish, inorganic chemicals, transistors, crude minerals, fertilizers (including phosphates), petroleum products, fruits, vegetables
Export Trading Partners	France 26.5%, Spain 14.3%, U.K. 7.9%, Germany 5.8%, Italy 5.6%, U.S. 4.8% (2002)
Imports	$10.4 billion f.o.b. (2002 est.); crude petroleum, textile fabric, telecommunications equipment, wheat, gas and electricity, transistors, plastics
Import Trading Partners	France 20.9%, Spain 12.6%, Italy 6.3%, Germany 5.5%, U.S. 4.6%, U.K. 4.1%, Saudi Arabia 4.1% (2001)

Oman

Capital	Muscat
Type of Government	Monarchy
Area (sq. km.)	212,460
Arable Land	0% (1993 est.)
Population	2,807,125 (2003 est.)
Currency	Omani rial (OMR)
Life Expectancy at Birth (2003 est.)	Total population: 72.58 years; male: 70.4 years; female: 74.86 years
Ethnic Composition	Arab, Baluchi, South Asian (Indian, Pakistani, Sri Lankan, Bangladeshi), African
Religions	Ibadhi Muslim 75%, Sunni Muslim, Shi'a Muslim, Hindu
Languages	Arabic (official), English, Baluchi, Urdu, Indian dialects
Literacy (2003 est.)	Total population: 75.8%; male: 83.1%, female: 67.2%
Natural Resources	petroleum, copper, asbestos, some marble, limestone, chromium, gypsum, natural gas
Agricultural Products	dates, limes, bananas, alfalfa, vegetables, camels, cattle, fish
Industries	crude oil production and refining, natural gas production, construction, cement, copper
Labor Force	920,000 (2002 est.)
Unemployment Rate	Not available
GDP per capita (PPP)	$8,300 (2002 est.)
External Debt	$5.7 billion (2002 est.)
Exports	$10.6 billion f.o.b. (2000 est.); petroleum, reexports, fish, metals, textiles
Export Trading Partners	Japan 20.5%, South Korea 18.5%, China 14.1%, Thailand 11.7%, U.A.E. 9.2%, Singapore 4.3%, U.S. 4.1% (2001)
Imports	$5.5 billion f.o.b. (2000 est.); machinery and transport equipment, manufactured goods, food, livestock, lubricants
Import Trading Partners	U.A.E. 27.5%, Japan 16.7%, U.K. 7.4%, U.S. 6.9%, Germany 5% (2002)

Qatar

Capital	Doha
Type of Government	Traditional monarchy
Area (sq. km.)	11,437
Arable Land	1% (1998 est.)
Population	817,052 (2003)
Currency	Qatari rial (QAR)
Life Expectancy at Birth (2003 est.)	Total population: 73.14 years; male: 70.65 years; female: 75.76 years
Ethnic Composition	Arab 40%, Pakistani 18%, Indian 18%, Iranian 10%, other 14%
Religions	Muslim 95%
Languages	Arabic (official), English commonly used as a second language
Literacy (age 15 and over can read and write) (2003 est.)	Total population: 82.5%; male: 81.4%; female: 85%
Natural Resources	petroleum, natural gas, fish
Agricultural Products	fruits, vegetables, poultry, dairy products, beef, fish
Industries	crude oil production and refining, fertilizers, petrochemicals, steel reinforcing bars, cement
Labor Force	280,122 (1997 est.)
Unemployment Rate	2.7% (2001)
GDP per capita (PPP)	$20,100 (2002 est.)
External Debt	$15.4 billion (2002 est.)
Exports	$10.9 billion f.o.b. (2002 est.); petroleum products, fertilizers, steel
Export Trading Partners	Japan 40.1%, South Korea 16.6%, Singapore 8.2%, U.S. 4.1% (2002)
Imports	$3.9 billion f.o.b. (2002 est.); machinery and transport equipment, food, chemicals
Import Trading Partners	France 17.8%, Japan 10.1%, U.S. 8.5%, U.K. 8.3%, Germany 8%, Italy 6.7%, U.A.E. 5.1%, Saudi Arabia 4.1%, South Korea 4% (2002)

Saudi Arabia

Capital	Riyadh
Type of Government	Monarchy
Area (sq. km.)	1,960,582
Arable Land	2% (1998 est.)
Population	24,293,844 (2003 est.)
Currency	Saudi riyal (SAR)
Life Expectancy at Birth (2001 est.)	Total population: 68.73 years; male: 66.99 years; female: 70.55 years
Ethnic Composition	Arab 90%, Afro-Asian 10%
Religion	Muslim 100%
Language	Arabic
Literacy (age 15 and over can read and write) (2003 est.)	Total population: 78.8%; male: 84.7%; female: 70.8%
Natural Resources	petroleum, natural gas, iron ore, gold, copper
Agricultural Products	wheat, barley, tomatoes, melons, dates, citrus, mutton, chickens, eggs, milk
Industries	crude oil production, petroleum refining, basic petrochemicals, cement, construction, fertilizer, plastics
Labor Force	7 million (1998 est.)
Unemployment Rate	25% (2002 est.)
GDP per capita (PPP)	$11,400 (2002 est.)
External Debt	$25.9 billion (2003 est.)
Exports	$71 billion f.o.b. (2001); petroleum and petroleum products 90%
Export Trading Partners	U.S. 18.6%, Japan 15.6%, South Korea 10.1%, Singapore 5.1%, China 4.6% (2002)
Imports	$39.5 billion f.o.b. (2001); machinery and equipment, foodstuffs, chemicals, motor vehicles, textiles
Import Trading Partners	U.S. 11.2%, Japan 8.8%, Germany 7.6%, U.K. 4.9%, Italy 4.1% (2002)

Syria

Capital	Damascus
Type of Government	Republic under military regime since March 1963
Area (sq. km.)	185,180
Arable Land	26% (1998 est.)
Population	17,585,540 (2002 est.)
Currency	Syrian pound (SYP)
Life Expectancy at Birth (2003 est.)	Total population: 69.39 years; male: 68.18 years; female: 70.67 years
Ethnic Composition	Arab 90.3%, Kurd, Armenian, and other 9.7%
Religions	Sunni Muslim 74%, Alawite, Druze, and other Muslim sects 16%, Christian (various sects) 10%, Jewish (tiny communities in Damascus, Al Qamishli, and Aleppo)
Languages	Arabic (official); Kurdish, Armenian, Aramaic, Circassian widely understood; French, English somewhat understood
Literacy (age 15 and over can read and write) (2003 est.)	Total population: 76.9%; male: 89.7%; female: 64%
Natural Resources	petroleum, phosphates, chrome and manganese ores, asphalt, iron ore, rock salt, marble, gypsum, hydropower
Agricultural Products	wheat, barley, cotton, lentils, chickpeas, olives, sugar beets, beef, mutton, eggs, poultry, milk
Industries	petroleum, textiles, food processing, beverages, tobacco, phosphate rock mining
Labor Force	5.2 million (2000 est.)
Unemployment Rate	20% (2002 est.)
GDP per capita (PPP)	$3,700 (2002 est.)
External Debt	$22 billion (2002 est.)
Exports	$6.2 billion f.o.b. (2002 est.); crude oil 70%, petroleum products 7%, fruits and vegetables 5%, cotton fiber 4%, clothing 3%, meat and live animals 2% (2000 est.)
Export Trading Partners	Germany 19.1%, Italy 17.5%, Turkey 7.8%, France 7.5%, Lebanon 5.2% (2002)
Imports	$4.9 billion f.o.b. (2000 est.); machinery and transport equipment 21%, food and livestock 18%, metal and metal products 15%, chemicals and chemical products 10%
Import Trading Partners	Italy 8.3%, Germany 7.4%, China 5.7%, South Korea 4.8%, France 4.6%, U.S. 4.4%, Turkey 4.1% (2002 est.)

Tunisia

Capital	Tunis
Type of Government	Republic
Area (sq. km.)	163,610
Arable Land	19% (1998 est.)
Population	9,924,742 (2003 est.)
Currency	Tunisian dinar (TND)
Life Expectancy at Birth (2003 est.)	Total population: 74.4 years; male: 72.77 years; female: 76.15 years
Ethnic Composition	Arab 98%, European 1%, Jewish and other 1%
Religions	Muslim 98%, Christian 1%, Jewish and other 1%
Languages	Arabic (official and one of the languages of commerce), French (commerce)
Literacy (age 15 and over can read and write) (2003 est.)	Total population: 74.2%; male: 84%; female: 64.4%
Natural Resources	petroleum, phosphates, iron ore, lead, zinc, salt
Agricultural Products	olives, olive oil, grain, dairy products, tomatoes, citrus fruit, beef, sugar beets, dates, almonds
Industries	petroleum, mining (particularly phosphates and iron ore), tourism, textiles, footwear, agribusiness, beverages
Labor Force	2.69 million (2001 est.)
Unemployment Rate	15.4% (2002 est.)
GDP per capita (PPP)	$6,800 (2002 est.)
External Debt	$13.6 billion (2003 est.)
Exports	$6.8 billion f.o.b. (2002 est.); textiles, mechanical goods, phosphates and chemicals, agricultural products, hydrocarbons
Export Trading Partners	France 31.3%, Italy 21.6%, Germany 11.5%, Spain 4.8%, Libya 4.7%, Belgium 4.3% (2002)
Imports	$8.7 billion f.o.b. (2002 est.); machinery and equipment, hydrocarbons, chemicals, food
Import Trading Partners	France 25.6%, Italy 19.5%, Germany 8.9%, Spain 5% (2002)

Turkey

Capital	Ankara
Type of Government	Republican parliamentary democracy
Area (sq. km.)	780,580
Arable Land	35% (1998 est.)
Population	68,109,469 (2003 est.)
Currency	Turkish lira (TRL)
Life Expectancy at Birth (2003 est.)	Total population: 71.8 years; male: 69.41 years; female: 74.3 years
Ethnic Composition	Turkish 80%, Kurdish 20% (est.)
Religions	Muslim 99.8% (mostly Sunni), other 0.2% (Christian and Jewish)
Languages	Turkish (official), Kurdish, Arabic, Armenian, Greek
Literacy (age 15 and over can read and write) (2003 est.)	Total population: 86.5%; male: 94.3%; female: 78.7%
Natural Resources	antimony, coal, chromium, mercury, copper, borate, sulfur, iron ore, arable land, hydropower
Agricultural Products	tobacco, cotton, grain, olives, sugar beets, pulse, citrus, livestock
Industries	textiles, food processing, autos, mining (coal, chromite, copper, boron), steel, petroleum, construction, lumber, paper
Labor Force	23.8 million (2003 est.)
Unemployment Rate	10.8% (plus underemployment of 6.1%) (2002 est.)
GDP per capita (PPP)	$7,300 (2002 est.)
External Debt	$118.3 billion (2001 est.)
Exports	$35.1 billion f.o.b. (2002); apparel, foodstuffs, textiles, metal manufactures, transport equipment
Export Trading Partners	Germany 16.6%, U.S. 9.2%, U.K. 8.5%, Italy 6.4%, France 6% (2002)
Imports	$50.8 billion (2002 est.); machinery, chemicals, semi-finished goods, fuels, transport equipment
Import Trading Partners	Germany 13.7%, Italy 8.1%, Russia 7.6%, U.S. 6%, France 5.9%, U.K. 4.8%, Switzerland 4.1% (2002 est.)

United Arab Emirates

Capital	Abu Dhabi
Type of Government	Federation with specified powers delegated to the U.A.E. federal government and other powers reserved to member emirates
Area (sq. km.)	82,880
Arable Land	0% (1998 est.)
Population	2,484,818 (2003 est.)
Currency	Emirati dirham (AED)
Life Expectancy at Birth (2001 est.)	Total population: 74.75 years; male: 72.28 years; female: 77.35 years
Ethnic Composition	Emirati 19%, other Arab and Iranian 23%, South Asian 50%, other expatriates (includes Westerners and East Asians) 8% (1982 est.)
Religions	Muslim 96% (Shi'a 16%), Christian, Hindu, and other 4%
Languages	Arabic (official), Persian, English, Hindi, Urdu
Literacy (age 15 and over can read and write) (2003 est.)	Total population: 77.9%; male: 76.1%; female: 81.7%
Natural Resources	petroleum, natural gas
Agricultural Products	dates, vegetables, watermelons, poultry, eggs, dairy products, fish
Industries	petroleum, fishing, petrochemicals, construction materials, some boat building, handicrafts, pearling
Labor Force	1.6 million (2000 est.)
Unemployment Rate	Not available
GDP per capita (PPP)	$22,100 (2002 est.)
External Debt	$18.5 billion (2002 est.)
Exports	$44.9 billion f.o.b. (2000 est.); crude oil 45%, natural gas, reexports, dried fish, dates
Export Trading Partners	Japan 27.8%, South Korea 10.1%, Singapore 3.8% (2002)
Imports	$30.8 billion f.o.b. (2002 est.); machinery and transport equipment, chemicals, food
Import Trading Partners	U.S. 8.1%, China 7.8%, Japan 6.6%, Germany 6.5%, India 5.7%, France 5.6%, U.K. 5.4%, South Korea 5.1%, Iran 4.2% (2002)

Yemen

Capital	Sanaa
Type of Government	Republic
Area (sq. km.)	527,970
Arable Land	3% (1998 est.)
Population	19,349,881 (2003 est.)
Currency	Yemeni rial (YER)
Life Expectancy at Birth (2003 est.)	Total population: 60.97 years; male: 59.16 years; female: 62.87 years
Ethnic Composition	Predominantly Arab; but also Afro-Arab, South Asian, European
Religions	Muslim including Shaf'i (Sunni) and Zaydi (Shi'a), small numbers of Jewish, Christian, and Hindu
Language	Arabic
Literacy (age 15 and over can read and write) (2003 est.)	Total population: 50.2%; male: 70.5%; female: 30%
Natural Resources	petroleum, fish, rock salt, marble, small deposits of coal, gold, lead, nickel, and copper, fertile soil in west
Agricultural Products	grain, fruits, vegetables, pulses, qat (mildly narcotic shrub), coffee, cotton; dairy products, livestock (sheep, goats, cattle, camels), poultry, fish
Industries	crude oil production and petroleum refining, small-scale production of cotton textiles and leather goods, food processing, handicrafts, small aluminum products factory, cement
Labor Force	Not available
Unemployment Rate	30% (1995 est.)
GDP per capita (PPP)	$800 (2002 est.)
External Debt	$6.2 billion (2002 est.)
Exports	$3.4 billion f.o.b. (2002 est.); crude oil, coffee, dried and salted fish
Export Trading Partners	India 21.1%, Thailand 16.9%, South Korea 11.2%, China 11.1%, Malaysia 7.7%, U.S. 6.7%, Singapore 4% (2002)
Imports	$2.9 billion f.o.b. (2002 est.); food and live animals, machinery and equipment
Import Trading Partners	U.S. 10.4%, Saudi Arabia 9.5%, China 8.7%, U.A.E. 6.9%, Russia 5.8%, France 4.7% (2002)

United States of America

Capital	Washington, D.C.
Type of Government	Constitution-based federal republic
Area (sq. km.)	9,629,091
Arable Land	19% (1993 est.)
Population	290,342,554 (2003 est.)
Currency	U.S. dollar (USD)
Life Expectancy at Birth (2003 est.)	Total population: 77.14 years; male: 74.37 years; female: 80.05 years
Ethnic Composition	white 77.1%, black 12.9%, Asian 4.2%, Amerindian and Alaska native 1.5% (2000)
Religions	Protestant 56%, Roman Catholic 28%, Jewish 2%, other 4%, none 10% (1989 est.)
Languages	English, Spanish (spoken by a sizable minority)
Literacy (age 15 and over can read and write) (1997 est.)	Total population: 97%; male: 97%; female: 97%
Natural Resources	coal, copper, lead, molybdenum, phosphates, uranium, bauxite, gold, iron, mercury, nickel, potash, silver, tungsten, zinc, petroleum, natural gas, timber
Agricultural Products	wheat, other grains, corn, fruits, vegetables, cotton, beef, pork, poultry, dairy products, forest products, fish
Industries	leading industrial power in the world, highly diversified and technologically advanced; petroleum, steel, motor vehicles, aerospace, telecommunications, chemicals, electronics, food processing, consumer goods, lumber, mining
Labor Force	141.8 million (includes unemployed) (2001)
Unemployment Rate	5.8% (2002)
GDP per capita (PPP)	$36,300 (2002 est.)
External Debt	$862 billion (1995 est.)
Exports	$687 billion f.o.b. (2002 est.); capital goods, automobiles, industrial supplies and raw materials, consumer goods, agricultural products
Export Trading Partners	Canada 23.2%, Mexico 14.1%, Japan 7.4%, U.K. 4.8% (2002)
Imports	$1.165 trillion f.o.b. (2002 est.); crude oil and refined petroleum products, machinery, automobiles, consumer goods, industrial raw materials, food and beverages
Import Trading Partners	Canada 17.8%, Mexico 11.3%, China 11.1%, Japan 10.4%, Germany 5.3% (2002)

NOTES

Background Lesson: An Overview of the Middle East

1. Energy Information Administration, "World Crude Oil and Natural Gas Reserves" (Washington, D.C.: U.S. Department of Energy, May 13, 2003).

2. Energy Information Administration, "World Crude Oil Production, 1992–2001" (Washington, D.C.: U.S. Department of Energy, March 14, 2003).

Lesson 1: U.S. Interests in the Middle East

1. "September 11 Death Toll Decreased by 40," United Press International, October 29, 2003.

2. See, for example, Urbina, Ian, "Military Buildup, by the Numbers," *Asia Times*, March 15, 2003; and Shanker, Thom, "Rumsfeld Doubles Estimate for Cost of Troops in Iraq," *The New York Times*, July 10, 2003.

3. Annan, Kofi A., "Fighting Terrorism on a Global Front," *The New York Times*, September 21, 2001.

4. See, for example, Dinmore, Guy, and Gillian Tett, "Bush Pressed to Pursue 'Regime Change' in Iran-U.S. Foreign Policy," *Financial Times*, June 18, 2003; and "Indian PM Arrives in Russia, Concerned over Rumsfeld's Remarks about Iran," *BBC Monitoring Reports*, May 30, 2003.

5. Energy Information Administration, "World Crude Oil Production, 1992–2001" (Washington, D.C.: U.S. Department of Energy, March 14, 2003).

6. *Ibid.* and Energy Information Agency, "World Crude Oil and Natural Gas Reserves," *op. cit.*

7. Energy Information Administration, "Crude Oil Imports from Persian Gulf 2002" (Washington, D.C.: U.S. Department of Energy, June 17, 2003).

8. European Commission, *Green Paper: Towards a European strategy for the security of energy supply* (Brussels: European Communities, 2001).

9. Energy Information Administration, "Persian Gulf Oil and Gas Exports Fact Sheet" (Washington, D.C.: U.S. Department of Energy, April 2003).

10. See, for example, Jackson, Derrick Z., "Bush's Deceptions on Iraq Intelligence," *The Boston Globe*, June 6, 2003; and Kristof, Nicholas, "Save Our Spooks," *The New York Times*, May 30, 2003.

11. Usborne, David, "WMD Just a Convenient Excuse For War, Admits Wolfowitz," *Financial Times*, May 30, 2003.

12. See, for example, the congressional testimony by U.S. Representative Elton Gallegly, House International Relations Committee, Subcommittee on International Terrorism, Nonproliferation, and Human Rights, *Federal Document Clearing House Congressional Testimony*, April 30, 2003.

Lesson 2: The Persian Gulf War and Its Continuing Aftermath

1. In the original publication of *The Middle East in Transition*, this section appeared in Lesson 4: Other Middle Eastern Issues.

2. Knights, Michael, "The Long View of No-Fly and No-Augmentation Zones," *PolicyWatch* (Washington, D.C.: The Washington Institute) Number 730, March 24, 2003.

3. "Rebuilding Iraq," *Online NewsHour*, November 27, 2003; and "Doomed, or Still Recoverable," *The Economist*, December 4, 2003.

4. *Ibid.*

5. "Defense Secretary Rumsfeld Says U.S. Officials Are in the Process of Accelerating the Training and Deployment of Iraqi Security Forces," transcript from *All Things Considered*, National Public Radio, October 30, 2003.

6. Burns, John F., "Once Skeptical, Briton Sees Iraqi Success," *The New York Times*, December 24, 2003.

7. McGeary, Johanna, "Al Qaeda's New Look," *Time Magazine*, March 29, 2004.

8. See, for example, Bowman, Tom, "Stubborn Insurgency Continues Despite the Capture of Hussein: Elements of uprising have no ties to ex-leader," *The Baltimore Sun*, January 14, 2004; Smith, Terrence, "View From Baghdad," *Online Newshour*, December 16, 2003; Ja'far, Musa, "Iraqis' Disillusion with U.S. Occupation Fuels Resistance," Xinhua News Agency, November 15, 2003; and Clover, Charles, "Clash of Cultures Fuels Low-level War of Increasing Animosity," *Financial Times*, June 2, 2003.

Lesson 3: The Arab-Israeli Conflict

1. By mid-2004, as this book went to print, nearly 3,000 Palestinians and 860 Israelis had been killed during the Intifada. Updated statistics on fatalities in the "al-Aqsa Intifada" can be found at http://www.btselem.org/.

2. "A Silent, Moderate Majority," *The Economist*, November 27, 2003.

3. STAT-USA, Israel Country Commercial Guide (Washington, D.C.: U.S. Department of Commerce, 2003); and "Budget Cuts to Impact on Israel's Poverty," Australian Broadcasting Corporation, March 25, 2003.

4. World Bank, "Two Years of Intifada, Closures and Palestinian Economic Crisis" (Washington, D.C.: International Bank for Reconstruction and Development, March 5, 2003); Hale, Ellen, "As Uprising Enters its 4th Year, Palestinians See Cycle of Misery," *USA Today*, September 15, 2003; and "A Safety Measure or a Land Grab?," *The Economist*, October 9, 2003.

Lesson 4: Other Middle Eastern Issues

1. Drummond, James, "Amnesty Condemns Algeria Rights Record," *Financial Times*, September 17, 2003.

2. *Ibid.*

3. Energy Information Administration, "Imports of Crude Oil and Petroleum Products into the United States by Country of Origin," *Petroleum Supply Monthly* (Washington, D.C.: U.S. Department of Energy, October 2003).

4. The term *jihad* means "striving or struggling in the way of God." Historically it refers to an inward spiritual struggle to know and do the will of God and resist vice, selfishness, and sinfulness. Over time, however, *jihad* has come to mean a variety of different things. It is the Wahhabi perspective on *jihad*, which emphasizes the struggle against "enemies of God," that has made the term a source of enormous controversy in the West and has led the term to be associated with radical Islamists. For a more in-depth description of *jihad*, see Wuthnow, Robert, ed., *Encyclopedia of Politics and Religion: Jihad* (Washington, D.C.: Congressional Quarterly, Inc., 1998).

5. The World Bank Group, "Water Resource Management" (Washington, D.C.: International Bank for Reconstruction and Development, April 2003).

6. Postal, Sandra, "Hydro Dynamics: Forget oil," American Museum of Natural History, No. 4, Vol. 112, May 1, 2003.

7. MacFarouhar, Neil, "Young Iranians Are Chafing Under Aging Clerics' Edicts," *The New York Times*, June 16, 2003.

SELECTED BIBLIOGRAPHIES

General Reference

Banks, Arthur S., and Thomas C. Muller, editors, *Political Handbook of the World 2000–2002* (Binghamton, NY: CSA Publications, 2004).

Country Background Notes, U.S. Department of State, 2004, http://www.state.gov/r/pa/ei/bgn/.

CultureGrams 2004 (Lindon, UT: Axiom Press, 2004).

Encyclopedia Britannica Online, Encyclopedia Britannica Premium Service, 2004, www.britannica.com.

Microsoft Encarta Online Encyclopedia, Microsoft Corporation, 2004, www.encarta.com.

The World Factbook 2003, Central Intelligence Agency, 2003, www.odci.gov/cia/publications/factbook/index.html.

Background Lesson: An Overview of the Middle East

Anderson, Roy, Robert F. Seibert, and Jon Wagner, *Politics and Change in the Middle East: Sources of Conflict and Accommodation*, sixth edition (Upper Saddle River, NJ: Prentice Hall, 2001).

Bill, James A. and Robert Springborg, *Politics in the Middle East*, fifth edition (Upper Saddle River, NJ: Pearson Longman, 1999).

Goldschmidt, Arthur, *A Concise History of the Middle East*, seventh edition (Boulder, CO: Westview Press, 2001).

Hourani, Albert Habib and Malise Ruthven, *A History of the Arab Peoples* (Cambridge, MA: Harvard University Press, 2003).

Lawrence, Bruce, *Defenders of God: The Fundamentalist Revolt Against the Modern Age* (Columbia, SC: University of South Carolina Press, 1995).

Lewis, Bernard, *The Middle East: A Brief History of the Last 2,000 Years* (New York, NY: Scribner Press, 1995).

Lewis, Bernard, *What Went Wrong: The Clash Between Islam and Modernity in the Middle East* (New York, NY: Oxford University Press, 2002).

Mackey, Sandra, *The Iranians: Persia, Islam, and the Soul of a Nation* (New York, NY: Dutton, 1996).

Lesson 1: U.S. Interests in the Middle East

Bahgat, Gawdat, *American Oil Diplomacy in the Persian Gulf and the Caspian Sea* (Gainesville, FL: University Press of Florida, 2003).

Falkenrath, Richard A., Newman, Robert D., and Thayer, Bradley A., *America's Achilles' Heel: Nuclear, Biological, and Chemical Terrorism and Covert Attack* (Cambridge, MA: MIT Press, 1998).

Kinzer, S., *All the Shah's Men: An American Coup and the Roots of Middle East Terror* (Hoboken, NJ: John Wiley & Sons, 2003).

Lippman, Thomas W., *Inside the Mirage: America's Fragile Partnership With Saudi Arabia* (Boulder, CO: Westview Press, 2004).

Makiya, Kanan, *Cruelty and Silence: War, Tyranny, Uprising, and the Arab World* (New York, NY: W. W. Norton, 1994).

Schram, Martin, *Avoiding Armageddon: The Companion Book to the PBS Series* (New York, NY: Basic Books, 2003).

Shannon, Vaughn P., *Balancing Act: U.S. Foreign Policy and the Arab-Israeli Conflict* (Hampshire, U.K.: Ashgate Publishing, 2003)

Spencer, William, *The United States and Iran* (Brookfield, CT: Twenty-first Century Books, 2000).

Telhami, Shibley, *The Stakes: America and the Middle East* (Boulder, CO: Westview Press, 2002).

Weiss, Thomas G., *Wars on Terrorism and Iraq: Human Rights, Unilateralism, and U.S. Foreign Policy* (New York, NY: Routledge, 2004).

Lesson 2: The Persian Gulf War and Its Continuing Aftermath

Ahrari, M.E. and James H. Noyes, editors, *The Persian Gulf After the Cold War* (Westport, CT: Praeger, 1993).

Dodge, Toby and Steven Simon, editors, *Iraq at the Crossroads: State and Society in the Shadow of Regime Change* (London: International Institute for Strategic Studies, 2003).

Head, William and Earl Tilford, *The Eagle in the Desert: Looking Back on U.S. Involvement in the Persian Gulf War* (Westport, CT: Greenwood Publishing Group, 1996).

Mackey, Sandra, *The Reckoning: Iraq and the Legacy of Saddam Hussein* (New York, NY: W.W. Norton, 2002).

Pickering, Thomas R., Eric P. Schwartz, and James R. Schlesinger, *Iraq: The Day After* (New York, NY: Council on Foreign Relations, August 2003).

Pollack, Kenneth M., *The Threatening Storm: The Case for Invading Iraq* (New York, NY: Random House, 2002).

Renshon, Stanley A., *The Political Psychology of the Gulf War: Leaders, Publics, and the Process of Conflict* (Pittsburgh, PA: University of Pittsburgh Press, 1993).

Tripp, Charles, *A History of Iraq,* second edition (Cambridge, U.K.: Cambridge University Press, 2000).

Yetiv, Steve A., *The Persian Gulf Crisis* (Westport, CT: Greenwood Publishing Group, August 1997).

Yetiv, Steve A., *Explaining Foreign Policy: How and Why the United States Went to War in the Persian Gulf* (Baltimore, MD: Johns Hopkins University Press, April 2004).

Lesson 3: The Arab-Israeli Conflict

Bickerton, Ian and Carla L. Klausner, *A Concise History of the Arab-Israeli Conflict,* fourth edition (Englewood Cliffs, NJ: Prentice-Hall, 2001).

Carter, Jimmy, *The Blood of Abraham: Insights into the Middle East* (Fayetteville, AR: University of Arkansas Press, 1993).

Gilbert, Martin, *Israel: A History* (New York, NY: Morrow, 1998).

Hunter, Robert H., *The Palestinian Uprising: A War by Other Means* (Berkeley, CA: University of California Press, 1993).

Khalidi, Rashid, *Palestinian Identity* (New York, NY: Columbia University Press, 1997).

Mishal, Shaul and Avraham Sela, *The Palestinian Hamas* (New York, NY: Columbia University Press, 1999).

Morris, Benny, *The Birth of the Palestinian Refugee Problem, 1947–49* (Cambridge, U.K.: Cambridge University Press, 1987).

Quandt, William B., *Peace Process: American Diplomacy and the Arab-Israeli Conflict Since 1967* (Washington, DC: The Brookings Institution, 2001).

Ross, Dennis, *The Missing Peace: The Inside Story of the Fight for Middle East Peace* (New York, NY: Farrar, Straus & Giroux, 2004).

Stein, Kenneth W., *Heroic Diplomacy: Sadat, Kissinger, Carter, Begin, and the Quest for Arab-Israeli Peace* (New York, NY: Routledge, 1999).

Lesson 4: Other Middle Eastern Issues

Allan, Tony, *The Middle East Water Question: Hydropolitics and the Global Economy* (New York, NY: I.B. Tauris, 2002).

Amery, Hussein and Aaron T. Wolf, *Water in the Middle East: A Geography of Peace* (Austin, TX: University of Texas Press, 2000).

Ansari, Ali, *A History of Modern Iran Since 1921: The Pahlavis and After* (Lebanon, IN: Longman, 2003).

El Fadl, Kahaled Abou, *The Place of Tolerance in Islam* (Boston, MA: Beacon, 2001).

Esposito, John L., editor, *The Iranian Revolution: Its Global Impact* (Gainesville, FL: University of Florida Press, 2001).

Izady, Mehrdad R., *The Kurds: A Concise Handbook* (New York, NY: Crane Russak & Co, 1992).

Keddie, Nikki R., *Modern Iran: Roots and Results of Revolution* (New Haven, CT: Yale University Press, 2003).

Kepel, Gilles, *Jihad: The Trial of Political Islam* (Cambridge, MA: Harvard University Press, 2002).

Lewis, Bernard, *The Crisis of Islam: Holy War and Unholy Terror* (New York, NY: Random House Trade, 2004).

McDowall, David, *A Modern History of the Kurds* (New York, NY: St. Martin's Press, 1996).

Reuters/Mona Sharaf

Egyptian Coptic Pope Shenouda III listens to Christmas hymns at the Cathedral in Cairo, January 7, 2000. Coptic Christians all over the world celebrate Christmas on January 7.

INDEX

Italic type indicates that the reference is a photograph, table, chart, or map.

September 11, 2001, attacks
    bin Laden behind, 201
    Muslim attitudes toward, 21
    radical Islamists in, 199
    Saudi Arabians in, 201
    war on terrorism as response to, 30, 38, 133,
        171, 202
settlements, Israeli
    Arab and Israeli settlements in Gaza and West
        Bank, *167*
    Begin on, 127
    in Camp David Accords, 126
    in Geneva Accord, 177, 178
    and Israeli-PLO Accords, 129, 132, 157, 161
    and Israeli Wall, 185, *188*
    as issue in Arab-Israeli conflict, 164
    in "road map" peace plan, 181, 182
    settlers on Israeli Wall, 193
    U.S. disagreeing with Israeli policy on, 33
    water consumption by, 203
Shahada, 8, 13
Shalom, Silvan, 192
Sharia, 114, 115, 200
Sharon, Ariel, 132–33, 135, 171, 195, 196, 203
Shia Muslims, 209–13
    defined, 22
    Hezbollah supported in Lebanon, 199
    imams, 210
    in Iran, 206, 210, *212*
    as Iraqi ethnoreligious group, 32, *112*, 114, *212*
    in Iraqi Governing Council, 86, 114, 116
    in Iraqi politics, 86, 87
    martyrdom in, 210
    population by country, *212*
    rebellion of Iraqi Shia, 82
    split from Sunnis, 4
Shultz, George
    on Arab-Israeli conflict, 238–39
    biographical sketch of, 246
    on Persian Gulf War (1990–1991), 236–37
    on UN not authorizing removal of Saddam
        Hussein, 244
    on U.S. independence from Middle Eastern oil,
        42, 46, 231
"shuttle diplomacy," 125
Sinai Peninsula, 125, 126–27, *150*, 238
sites of religious significance, 179–80
Six Day War (1967), 125, 238
Sixth Fleet (U.S.), 29
Smith, Hedrick, 249
Somalia, 3, 29
Southeastern Anatolia Project, 203
Soviet Union
    Arabs supported against Israel by, 33, 122
    and Camp David accords, 126
    in creation of modern Israel, 124
    diplomacy during Persian Gulf War (1990–1991),
        79
    invasion of Afghanistan, 29
    in Persian Gulf War (1990–1991), *101*
    in Suez crisis of 1956, 125
    U.S. counters pressure on Turkey in 1946, 28
    U.S. opposing influence in Persian Gulf, 30

See also Russia
Spain
    Arabs and Jews living peacefully in medieval, 123
    Islamic rule in, 4
    in Persian Gulf War (1990–1991), *101*
statistical information, 250–59
Strait of Gibraltar, 48
Strait of Hormuz, 48
Strait of Malacca, 48
Sudan, 6, 56, 198, 199
Suez Canal, 47, 48, 125
Sufism, 22
suicide bombings, 133, 134, 135, 171, 195
Sunni Muslims
    defined, 22
    as Iraqi ethnoreligious group, *112*, 114–15
    on Iraqi Governing Council, 86, 117
    Kurds, 204
    as percentage of all Muslims, 210
    population by country, *212*
    Shia split from, 4
Sweden, *101*
Syria
    in Arab-Israeli negotiations of 1990s, 127
    in Eastern Mediterranean area, 2
    Euphrates River water for, 203
    French mandate in, 5
    Golan Heights, 125, 127, 128, *150*, 238, 240
    Israeli-PLO Accords affecting, 129
    Kurds in, *212*, 227
    Lebanon as controlled by, 131
    Mongol invasion of, 4
    nationalist movement in, 4
    in 1948 war with Israel, 124
    in 1973 war with Israel, 125
    Palestinian population in, *165*
    Palestinian refugees in, 125
    in Persian Gulf War (1990–1991), 80–81
    on political map of Middle East, *9*
    poverty in, 3, 217
    remembering name and location of, 12
    revolutionary nationalism in, 6
    in "road map" peace plan, 182
    Shia population of, *212*
    in Six Day War of 1967, 125
    statistical information on, 257
    water negotiations with Israel, 202, 203
    weapons of mass destruction programs, *56*
Taba, Egypt, negotiations, 132, 175–76
Talabani, Jalal, 117
Taliban, 20, 21, 31, 32, 84
terrorism
    Iranian government supporting, 30, 32, 208
    Iraqi insurgency, 88
    by Islamists, 200
    Muslim attitudes toward, 21
    Palestinians turning to, 125
    in "road map" peace plan, 181
    root causes of Middle Eastern, 202
    in Saudi Arabia, 201
    suicide bombings, 133, 134, 135, 171, 195
    World Trade Center bombing of 1993, 201
    in Wye River Memorandum, 131